HENRY JAMES

THE FUTURE OF

THE NOVEL

HENRY JAMES

THE FUTURE OF THE NOVEL

ESSAYS ON THE ART OF FICTION

EDITED WITH AN INTRODUCTION

BY LEON EDEL

VINTAGE BOOKS

A Division of Random House

NEW YORK

VINTAGE BOOKS

are published by ALFRED A. KNOPF, INC.
and RANDOM HOUSE, INC.

INTRODUCTION

THIS VOLUME takes its title from a long-buried essay of
Henry James's which appeared in 1900 and which is reprinted now for the first time. He wrote it for one of
those "universal anthologies" which our fathers used to
purchase from itinerant salesmen as "educational sets,"
designed to make the entire family aware of the world's
literary heritage from Babylon to the Mississippi. The
particular anthology for which James wrote his essay was
a scholarly compendium; and yet his thoughtful pages
appear to have been inserted as an after-thought and,
incongruously enough, as preface to a volume containing
German drama: the text of the Oberammergau *Passion
Play*, Hauptmann's *The Weavers*, Freytag's *The Journal-
ists*. Thus isolated, it has gathered dust for five decades,
while the future of the novel of which he wrote was
acting itself out.

The American novelist obviously had nothing to do
with the strange position accorded his essay in this bulky
set of volumes; but the choice of subject was probably
his, or at least, if suggested to him, was one he found
highly congenial. Not that he was addicted to prophesy;
on the contrary, he was usually concerned with the immediate and the predictable. But now the century was
turning; a whole new block of time lay before the novel,
and James clearly could not forego this occasion to act as
oracle for the novel form—that form which had been the
high altar of his life, the center of his devotions. And so
he wrote his measured and vigorous essay, with all the
weight and authority of his thirty-five years of fiction-
writing.

We, who have lived more than half a century into the future of which James wrote, know some of the answers which the novelist could not have known in 1900. We know that the twentieth-century novel in England and America was to be—at its best—a thing of experiment and intelligence, as James hoped. And we, in turn, midway in the century, are now asking ourselves what future lies before the New Novel which has been forged in our time. To take but one example: within the past year Lionel Trilling has found occasion to ponder "The Novel Alive or Dead," and he has not been alone in asking the question and seeking an answer. Without abusing our easily possessed hindsight, it is therefore rewarding to reread a great theorist of fiction on the future he saw for the novel in this century, particularly as it was he who gave to modern criticism of fiction much of its basic terminology. And the essay fits quite properly into a volume which brings together, more completely than ever before, certain of Henry James's pronouncements about the art he practiced with such high professional devotion, from the days of the American Civil War to the eve of the First World War. It had been no accident that his first youthful essay, published anonymously in 1864, dealt with the state of the novel. It certainly was no accident that the last book he was able to see through the press in 1914 bore the title *Notes on Novelists*.

I

What strikes the reader today on going through James's essay is his essential optimism. We have listened so much to talk of the novel's death that it is illuminating to find James writing of a form that seemed to him indestructible. There is a highly contemporaneous ring in his complaints about the quantity of bad novels and the intense and constant production of mediocre books, as there is in his sense of the blindness of certain types of criticism and the laxities of the reading public. But he is convinced that so long as there will be people there will be novels; with a kind of prescience of a world capable of self-destruction he observes that "Till the world is an unpeopled void there will be the image in the mirror." The creation of mirror images by novelists, he says, provides the "great anodyne" so that man can turn from the realities of life to contemplate the enlarged realities of an artist's imagined world. So long as life has the power of "projecting itself upon man's imagination," says James, man will find that the novel can "work off the impression better than anything he knows."

One is not certain that this world be true today. James could not foresee certain powerful usurping mechanical anodynes, "audio-visual" in nature and quite hostile to the quiet practice of reading by one's fireside which the nineteenth century relished. His essay spoke for conditions he fully expected would remain unchanged. But if "mass media" crowd us today and represent a veritable revolution in the world of art, all of James's assumptions about the novel as an art form remain relevant; indeed, they acquire a certain urgency in the face of the soap opera and the hackneyed language of television. For the novel form still thrives among us—for how long we cannot say! —as the most characteristic literary form of our time. And critics today would be at one with James in wanting writers to create an image of life that remains "various and vivid." James himself had always sought to do this. He had experimented with "point of view" and the "central intelligence." He had sought to create the "well-made novel" as France had its "well-made play." He had talked about his art and practiced it so that it might serve as example to those who could come after him. Not many years were to elapse before Joyce would provide more experimentation than James dreamed of, but of which he was a distinct forerunner. And from the time of the First World War, which James did not survive, writers of fiction were to meet him more than halfway—indeed more than all the way—on the throbbing question raised by him in his Olympian search for the novel's future. I refer to James's recurrent complaint that the Anglo-American novel had not fully embraced adult life because it continued to look away—as James put it with a kind of elaborate Victorian reticence—from "the great relation between men and women, the constant world-renewal."

II

Today we would not struggle to find so global a euphemism for the word *sex*. That James should have protested so vigorously, as this essay shows, will not surprise those who have read his later work closely, or studied Edmund Wilson's much under-estimated essay on the American novelist's "ambiguity." There is a peculiar legend that Henry James was not interested in sex and that his novels are squeamish and emasculate. It has been customary to point out that there is only one kiss in *The Portrait of a Lady*—which the heroine does not enjoy— and it has been insisted, by a generation that often talks about James without reading him, that there is an absence of passion in his novels. If James were as prurient as he has been made out to be, how do we explain the deeply underlying sexuality of *The Ambassadors*, *The Wings of the Dove*, and *The Golden Bowl*, which are nothing if not novels about sex? His complaint—it is loud enough in "The Future of the Novel"—is that he was prevented from dealing with indiscretions and adulteries by the timidity of magazine editors for whom he wrote; that he was invariably reduced to writing on the level of the female adolescent into whose tender hands the current *Atlantic* or *Scribner's* might fall. Even as late as the planning of the final novel, *The Golden Bowl*, the American novelist could set down these words in his notebooks: "*Everything* about it qualifies it for *Harper* except the subject—or rather, I mean, except the adulterine element in the subject. But may it not be simply a question of handling that? For God's sake let me try." It had always been a problem for Henry James, this *handling* of sex for the Victorian audiences: a problem of trying to create adult characters in an adult world but always maintaining, as a backdrop, a kind of safety curtain against "the great relation . . . the constant world-renewal." James learned how to "handle" it: it is handled on every page of *What Maisie Knew* or *The Turn of the Screw*, with that verbal duplicity and mandarin politeness of which he became a master. James had discovered, early in his career, that he could say outrageous things behind an ornate façade of words. What, indeed, could be more outrageous than the bare story of *The Wings of the Dove:* a man making love to a dying girl so that he may inherit her money and thus marry the woman to whom he has been pledged and who becomes his mistress as part of the whole diabolical bargain?

In that future of the novel which James envisaged, he hoped that the English and American writer would be relieved of the burden of subterfuge and indirection and given the liberties of subject and treatment enjoyed by the French men of letters. In the early days, James pointed out, when the novel was young, it was robust and unafraid. Richardson, Fielding, Sterne, said things which Dickens, Scott, Stevenson did not even try to say. There had occurred, as a result, a "tremendous omission" in the English novel. The women novelists, he was to remark in another essay of this period, had done better than the men in reminding them "of man's relations with himself, that is with woman." And he added: "His relations with the pistol, the pirate, the police, the wild and the tame beast—are not these prevailingly what the gentlemen have given us?"

James's complaint, thus broadly stated, was valid enough, although certain novelists in Victorian England—not least George Moore during his Zola phase, and Thomas Hardy—had attempted to bring a more mature and less inhibited treatment of sex into the novel. Moore was to boast, indeed, in characteristic vein, "I invented adultery" —meaning that he liberated the English novel from pruriency. Whatever the historical merits of this pioneering claim, James's general description of the novelist's predicament at the turn of the century was accurate. Exceptions may be invoked, but as a whole the novelist in the English-speaking world did not enjoy the freedom of choice or treatment of his materials that prevailed across the Channel.

Henry James would have no cause for complaint today, or rather his complaint would inevitably be of another order. What it would be we can gather from his essay on Guy de Maupassant, in which he chides the French writer for his neglect of the reflective side of man's nature in favor of his sensual side. He puts the matter with some candor when he observes that "the impression of the human spectacle for him who takes it as it comes has less analogy with that of the monkey-cage" than Maupassant's account of it. In our time we can almost imagine him as saying (perhaps to Mr. Norman Mailer): *"Allons donc,* it's all very well to get into the bedroom, and even into bed, if you want to take the novel that distance—but aren't you, young man (and you are so outrageously young!), in going scarcely anywhere else, rather neglecting, shall we say, the daylight side of life?" In some such way he would still plead for variety as against monotony; and he would go farther, for he would argue that in taking the reader into endless bedrooms the modern novelist is being as immature as the Victorian who tried to pretend there were no such rooms at all.

III

I have spoken of James as the greatest of theorists in the art of novel. The first essay here reproduced, together with his letter to the Deerfield Summer School, has become, in the intervening half century, a kind of novelist's manifesto, one of those great pronouncements which seems to offer the last word on the subject. Concerning fictional theory James could talk—and did—without exhausting himself. And in this essay he has embodied the very core of his beliefs. The novel, the most elastic of literary forms, must be true to life; it must be imaginative and searching and written in absolute freedom. There are no rigid rules for rendering life; and who is to say where human experience begins and where it ends? It is precisely its limitless character that gives it variety from writer to writer—and James re-expressed this many years later with great subtlety in his preface to *The Portrait of a Lady*, in the notable passage on "the house of fiction." James wrote not only as an inhabitant of that many-windowed house, but as a discriminating critic as well, and when he spoke of the "individual vision" of each artist, seeing life through his particular window, he was at the same time telling criticism that it too could possess such an angle of vision. James the critic functions above all in the pages and passages selected here, and his code of criticism belonged to the tradition of Sainte-Beuve—that is, a tradition that the study of literature is an all-embracing thing, not a narrow function. Those who have sought to narrow down our perception of the literary art to the mere critical act would find small comfort in Henry James's felicitous description of the qualities that endeared Sainte-Beuve to him. "He was frankly and explicitly a critic; he attributed the highest importance to the critical function, and he understood it in so large a way that we can easily agree with him. The critic, in his conception, was not the narrow lawgiver or the rigid censor that he is often assumed to be; he was the student, the inquirer, the observer, the interpreter, the active, indefatigable commentator, whose constant aim was to arrive at justness of characterization." And again: "He valued life and literature equally for the light they threw upon each other; to his mind one implied the other; he was unable to conceive of them apart."

In James a critical faculty similar to Sainte-Beuve's flourished. He was one of the rare half-dozen imaginative writers of first rank in the whole range of American and English literature who embodied with creation at a high level a high critical faculty. And he was a writer wholly on the side of verisimilitude. Not only was he a confirmed realist who considered allegory an inferior form of writing, and who liked the fantastic only in the ghostly form, but also he devoted himself to devising methods by which the narrative technique itself could add further dimensions of reality to his story-telling. This is amply clear in the late critical prefaces to his own novels; and I have selected certain striking passages from them to illustrate the calculated art with which he worked.

In this volume will be found, therefore, two groups of James's critical writings: his generalizations about the art of fiction and his specific discussion of certain novelists, the majority of them French. There are no comparable essays on English novelists, perhaps because James was essentially an interpreter of Continental literature to his American and English readers and was less inclined to interpret their own novelists for them. Moreover, in a strictly practical sense, he found a better market for magazine articles on French literature than on English. About certain American literary figures, many of them personal friends, he wrote largely commemorative, reminiscential, or analytical papers which constitute a group apart among his non-fictional writings. His allusions to Dickens and Thackeray, Jane Austen and the Brontës are numerous, yet he never gave us evaluations of their work comparable to his writings on Balzac or Zola. It is true that he wrote much about George Eliot's novels, but save for an early paper on her in the *Atlantic*, written when he was twenty-two, he confined himself to reviewing her and never brought the totality of her work into a single focus as he did that of George Sand. The French novelists commanded his attention for other reasons than magazine interest in them: they were preoccupied with the very questions of "art, form, manner" which intrigued James himself; and while he could neither wholly participate in their compulsive literary habits (he found they had "the look of galley-slaves tied to a ball and chain, rather than of happy producers") nor accept their horizons, so much more limited than his own, which were more easy-going and cosmopolitan, his discussion of the craft of fiction could nevertheless be sharply focused through these writers. Each constituted the kind of "literary case" he enjoyed appraising—Balzac with his attempt to read the world into France, Zola with his large-scale plan to write the "natural history" of a family during the second Empire, Maupassant with his gift for throwing off in a few pages the sense of an entire life. James began by complaining of their subjects, the "Gallic lightness of soil in the moral region," yet he was among the first to argue that the creator must be allowed his subject and be held responsible only for what he does with it. It is curious to read his various writings on Zola. He begins with a rather strong antipathy, and yet in the end is filled with admiration for the total achievement. He was stating the truth when he wrote to his parents that he could see all round Flaubert "intellectually"—Flaubert whose *gueuler* was stronger than his logic. Yet for all of James's strictures, he recognized that the French novel had set out to record life and had indulged in a kind of candor and experiment that was unknown on the English side of the Channel—let alone the other side of the Atlantic.

What strikes us in going through James's essays on novelists is that his best papers are devoted to the very writers whom we still rank as the foremost practitioners of their craft. That he saw their importance before posterity had a chance to judge them, and singled out the very ones we have come to consider major writers, gives us some measure of James's critical acumen. His devotion to Turgenev stemmed not only from the personal friendship they formed, but also from the fact that even before they met, James found in Turgenev's work the very qualities he prized in the novel. The reservations he expressed about Dostoevsky and Tolstoy have been largely misunderstood because they have been read out of context. James at no time depreciated the work of the Russian

masters, although what he says seems at first glance to do
so; on the contrary, he esteemed them as among the
greatest of all novelists. What he was saying when he
talked of their novels as being "baggy monsters" or argued
that they were "fluid puddings" was that they were
beyond imitation, poor models for anyone who wanted
to write fiction. The novice in letters, he affirmed, could
learn much about life from reading them, but not how
to compose a novel: they failed completely as "subjects
of emulation." This was the burden of his complaint, and
in our time it has been recognized that imitation Tolstoy
or imitation Dostoevsky is doomed to be pretty poor
stuff. James's concern with the "lesson of Balzac" and his
complaint that Dostoevsky and Tolstoy offered only
themselves—but no lesson—must be understood as simply
meaning that certain artists are also teachers of their art,
like the Masters of painting who gathered schools around
them. And so a novelist like Balzac or James is filled with
precept and example, while others, Dickens or Tolstoy,
are relished for themselves, but do not create a "school."

In *Notes on Novelists* James included a long essay on
"The New Novel," an extended version of an article originally written for the *Times Literary Supplement* and in it
one finds, stated in the complex prose of the "later
manner," James's formula for fiction as opposed to that
of Tolstoy and the "saturation" school. It was this article
which led to the celebrated exchange with H. G. Wells
whose fictional methods came under James's criticism.
Wells and Arnold Bennett, James argued, worked up
much fictional detail, but failed as artists because they
found no form or mold into which to pour their saturated impression of life. James's image for this was sharp
enough: "They squeeze out to the utmost the plump
and more or less juicy orange of a particular acquainted
state and let this affirmation of energy, however directed
or undirected, constitute for them the 'treatment' of the
theme." With Henry James, form and matter were inseparable, and he turned away from Wells and Bennett to

praise the technique of Joseph Conrad—which was, to a degree, a case of the Master looking at his own image in a disciple's mirror. H. G. Wells was to take his revenge three years later in a cruel parody of James, very much as a small boy might reply to an elder's rebuke by leveling a pea-shooter. It is perhaps easier for us, almost fifty years afterwards, to say what Wells should have done; and few would disagree, I think, that a gentler course was open to him—that taken by Robert Louis Stevenson, for instance, during the James-Besant debate on the novel in the 1880's. Stevenson contributed his own views, in an article titled "A Humble Remonstrance," which remains a valued nineteenth-century statement by a writer on his art. That Wells preferred finally the way of parody is a matter for his biographer; we can be grateful to him at least for the fact that his bad manners elicited one of the most moving of James's letters, one of his finest statements about his view of the artist as the one individual who gives a permanent and enduring shape to a life that is evanescent and perishable.

IV

One final element, and it is an overriding one, exists in Henry James's writings about his own art. This is his humane approach to his material. No writer so authoritative was less doctrinaire. His plea is always for a kind of *laisser-faire* and *laisser-aller*, and it is this which, indeed, makes H. G. Wells's attack seem all the more crude and unmotivated. James's complaint to his French compeers was not that they seemed to want to write only about the seamy side of life to the exclusion of other aspects, but that the "human note" was missing. James wrote a long review of *Nana* in 1880 and he did not echo the refrain of Victorian London, that Nana was immoral and "dirty"; he complained that she was quite simply dull. And with a kind of airy wit, in the midst of the Victorians, James argued that the French writers proved themselves dull because they were conventional. "The figure of a brutal *fille*, without a conscience or a soul, with nothing but devouring appetites and impudence, has become the stalest of the stock-properties of French fiction," wrote James, "and M. Zola's treatment has here imparted to her no touch of superior verity." And he went on:

> He is welcome to draw as many figures of the same type as he finds necessary, if he will only make them human; this is as good a way of making a contribution to our knowledge of ourselves as another. It is not his choice of subject that has shocked us; it is the melancholy dryness of his execution, which gives us all the bad taste of a disagreeable dish and none of the nourishment.

This is an original approach to a novel read as a "shocker" in London. James allows Zola his subject, however much he may dislike it; as critic, it is the artistic failure that solely concerns him. And to this view James held with consistency through the years.

Because James was so loyal to his art and so eager a preceptor, his views of fiction continue to carry great weight in our time. It is something to conjure with that it was an American who came to the English and French novel at their moment of greatness (and when we ourselves had produced so little fiction upon the world's literary scene) and asked them to give an account of themselves; and who more searchingly than his predecessors or his followers examined the form and the techniques by which it was produced. If, in this, he was exhibiting that national trait which makes us pre-eminently a nation preoccupied with "know-how," we can say that Henry James had the "know-how" of fiction from the first. And he was never more eloquent, outside his own novels, than when he talked about the writing of them and about his fellow-writers—as may be judged from the pages here assembled.

LEON EDEL

New York University

CONTENTS

PART ONE: THE ART OF THE NOVEL

PART TWO: NOVELS AND NOVELISTS

CONTENTS

The Art of the Novel

*

another French word); and evidently if it be destined to suffer in any way for having lost its *naïveté* it has now an idea of making sure of the corresponding advantages. During the period I have alluded to there was a comfortable, good-humored feeling abroad that a novel is a novel, as a pudding is a pudding, and that our only business with it could be to swallow it. But within a year or two, for some reason or other, there have been signs of returning animation—the era of discussion would appear to have been to a certain extent opened. Art lives upon discussion, upon experiment, upon curiosity, upon variety of attempt, upon the exchange of views and the comparison of standpoints; and there is a presumption that those times when no one has anything particular to say about it, and has no reason to give for practice or preference, though they may be times of honor, are not times of development —are times, possibly even, a little of dullness. The successful application of any art is a delightful spectacle, but the theory too is interesting; and though there is a great deal of the latter without the former I suspect there has never been a genuine success that has not had a latent core of conviction. Discussion, suggestion, formulation, these things are fertilizing when they are frank and sincere. Mr. Besant has set an excellent example in saying what he thinks, for his part, about the way in which fiction should be written, as well as about the way in which it should be published; for his view of the "art," carried on into an appendix, covers that too. Other laborers in the same field will doubtless take up the argument, they will give it the light of their experience, and the effect will surely be to make our interest in the novel a little more what it had for some time threatened to fail to be—a serious, active, inquiring interest, under protection of which this delightful study may, in moments of confidence, venture to say a little more what it thinks of itself.

It must take itself seriously for the public to take it so. The old superstition about fiction being "wicked" has doubtless died out in England; but the spirit of it lingers

in a certain oblique regard directed toward any story
which does not more or less admit that it is only a joke.
Even the most jocular novel feels in some degree the
weight of the proscription that was formerly directed
against literary levity: the jocularity does not always
succeed in passing for orthodoxy. It is still expected, though
perhaps people are ashamed to say it, that a production
which is after all only a "make-believe" (for what else
is a "story"?) shall be in some degree apologetic—shall
renounce the pretension of attempting really to represent
life. This, of course, any sensible, wide-awake story declines to do, for it quickly perceives that the tolerance
granted to it on such a condition is only an attempt to
stifle it disguised in the form of generosity. The old
evangelical hostility to the novel, which was as explict as
it was narrow, and which regarded it as little less favorable to our immortal part than a stage play, was in
reality far less insulting. The only reason for the existence
of a novel is that it does attempt to represent life. When
it relinquishes this attempt, the same attempt that we
see on the canvas of the painter, it will have arrived at a
very strange pass. It is not expected of the picture that
it will make itself humble in order to be forgiven; and
the analogy between the art of the painter and the art
of the novelist is, so far as I am able to see, complete.
Their inspiration is the same, their process (allowing for
the different quality of the vehicle) is the same, their
success is the same. They may learn from each other,
they may explain and sustain each other. Their cause is
the same, and the honor of one is the honor of another.
The Mahometans think a picture an unholy thing, but it
is a long time since any Christian did, and it is therefore
the more odd that in the Christian mind the traces (dissimulated though they may be) of a suspicion of the
sister art should linger to this day. The only effectual way
to lay it to rest is to emphasize the analogy to which I just
alluded—to insist on the fact that as the picture is reality,
so the novel is history. That is the only general descrip-

tion (which does it justice) that we may give of the novel. But history also is allowed to represent life; it is not, any more than painting, expected to apologize. The subject-matter of fiction is stored up likewise in documents and records, and if it will not give itself away, as they say in California, it must speak with assurance, with the tone of the historian. Certain accomplished novelists have a habit of giving themselves away which must often bring tears to the eyes of people who take their fiction seriously. I was lately struck, in reading over many pages of Anthony Trollope, with his want of discretion in this particular. In a digression, a parenthesis or an aside, he concedes to the reader that he and this trusting friend are only "making believe." He admits that the events he narrates have not really happened, and that he can give his narrative any turn the reader may like best. Such a betrayal of a sacred office seems to me, I confess, a terrible crime; it is what I mean by the attitude of apology, and it shocks me every whit as much in Trollope as it would have shocked me in Gibbon or Macaulay. It implies that the novelist is less occupied in looking for the truth (the truth, of course I mean, that he assumes, the premises that we grant him, whatever they may be) than the historian, and in doing so it deprives him at a stroke of all his standing room. To represent and illustrate the past, the actions of men, is the task of either writer, and the only difference that I can see is, in proportion as he succeeds, to the honor of the novelist, consisting as it does in his having more difficulty in collecting his evidence, which is so far from being purely literary. It seems to me to give him a great character, the fact that he has at once so much in common with the philosopher and the painter; this double analogy is a magnificent heritage.

It is of all this evidently that Mr. Besant is full when he insists upon the fact that fiction is one of the *fine* arts, deserving in its turn of all the honors and emoluments that have hitherto been reserved for the successful profession of music, poetry, painting, architecture. It is impossible to

insist too much on so important a truth, and the place
that Mr. Besant demands for the work of the novelist
may be represented, a trifle less abstractly, by saying
that he demands not only that it shall be reputed artistic,
but that it shall be reputed very artistic indeed. It is
excellent that he should have struck this note, for his
doing so indicates that there was need of it, that his
proposition may be to many people a novelty. One rubs
one's eyes at the thought; but the rest of Mr. Besant's
essay confirms the revelation. I suspect in truth that it
would be possible to confirm it still further, and that one
would not be far wrong in saying that in addition to
the people to whom it has never occurred that a novel
ought to be artistic, there are a great many others who,
if this principle were urged upon them, would be filled
with an indefinable mistrust. They would find it difficult
to explain their repugnance, but it would operate strongly
to put them on their guard. "Art," in our Protestant communities, where so many things have got so strangely
twisted about, is supposed in certain circles to have some
vaguely injurious effect upon those who make it an important consideration, who let it weigh in the balance.
It is assumed to be opposed in some mysterious manner
to morality, to amusement, to instruction. When it is
embodied in the work of the painter (the sculptor is
another affair!) you know what it is: it stands there before
you, in the honesty of pink and green and a gilt frame;
you can see the worst of it at a glance, and you can be on
your guard. But when it is introduced into literature
it becomes more insidious—there is danger of its hurting
you before you know it. Literature should be either instructive or amusing, and there is in many minds an impression that these artistic preoccupations, the search for
form, contribute to neither end, interfere indeed with
both. They are too frivolous to be edifying, and too
serious to be diverting; and they are moreover priggish
and paradoxical and superfluous. That, I think, represents
the manner in which the latent thought of many people

who read novels as an exercise in skipping would explain
itself if it were to become articulate. They would argue,
of course, that a novel ought to be "good," but they would
interpret this term in a fashion of their own, which indeed
would vary considerably from one critic to another. One
would say that being good means representing virtuous
and aspiring characters, placed in prominent positions;
another would say that it depends on a "happy ending,"
on a distribution at the last of prizes, pensions, husbands,
wives, babies, millions, appended paragraphs, and cheerful
remarks. Another still would say that it means being full
of incident and movement, so that we shall wish to jump
ahead, to see who was the mysterious stranger, and if the
stolen will was ever found, and shall not be distracted
from this pleasure by any tiresome analysis or "description." But they would all agree that the "artistic" idea
would spoil some of their fun. One would hold it ac-
countable for all the description, another would see it
revealed in the absence of sympathy. Its hostility to a
happy ending would be evident, and it might even in some
cases render any ending at all impossible. The "ending"
of a novel is, for many persons, like that of a good dinner,
a course of dessert and ices, and the artist in fiction is
regarded as a sort of meddlesome doctor who forbids
agreeable aftertastes. It is therefore true that this conception of Mr. Besant's of the novel as a superior form
encounters not only a negative but a positive indifference.
It matters little that as a work of art it should really
be as little or as much of its essence to supply happy
endings, sympathetic characters, and an objective tone, as
if it were a work of mechanics: the association of ideas,
however incongruous, might easily be too much for it
if an eloquent voice were not sometimes raised to call
attention to the fact that it is at once as free and as
serious a branch of literature as any other.

Certainly this might sometimes be doubted in presence
of the enormous number of works of fiction that appeal
to the credulity of our generation, for it might easily

seem that there could be no great character in a com-
modity so quickly and easily produced. It must be
admitted that good novels are much compromised by bad
ones, and that the field at large suffers discredit from over-
crowding. I think, however, that this injury is only superficial, and that the superabundance of written fiction
proves nothing against the principle itself. It has been
vulgarized, like all other kinds of literature, like everything
else today, and it has proved more than some kinds accessible to vulgarization. But there is as much difference
as there ever was between a good novel and a bad one:
the bad is swept with all the daubed canvases and spoiled
marble into some unvisited limbo, or infinite rubbish-yard
beneath the back-windows of the world, and the good
subsists and emits its light and stimulates our desire for
perfection. As I shall take the liberty of making but a
single criticism of Mr. Besant, whose tone is so full of the
love of his art, I may as well have done with it at once.
He seems to me to mistake in attempting to say so
definitely beforehand what sort of an affair the good
novel will be. To indicate the danger of such an error as
that has been the purpose of these few pages; to suggest
that certain traditions on the subject, applied *a priori*, have
already had much to answer for, and that the good health
of an art which undertakes so immediately to reproduce
life must demand that it be perfectly free. It lives upon
exercise, and the very meaning of exercise is freedom.
The only obligation to which in advance we may hold
a novel, without incurring the accusation of being arbitrary, is that it be interesting. That general responsibility
rests upon it, but it is the only one I can think of. The
ways in which it is at liberty to accomplish this result
(of interesting us) strike me as innumerable, and such as
can only suffer from being marked out or fenced in by
prescription. They are as various as the temperament of
man, and they are successful in proportion as they reveal
a particular mind, different from others. A novel is in its
broadest definition a personal, a direct impression of life:

that, to begin with, constitutes its value, which is greater
or less according to the intensity of the impression. But
there will be no intensity at all, and therefore no value,
unless there is freedom to feel and say. The tracing of a
line to be followed, of a tone to be taken, of a form to
be filled out, is a limitation of that freedom and a suppression of the very thing that we are most curious about.
The form, it seems to me, is to be appreciated after the
fact: then the author's choice has been made, his standard
has been indicated; then we can follow lines and directions
and compare tones and resemblances. Then in a word we
can enjoy one of the most charming of pleasures, we can
estimate quality, we can apply the test of execution. The
execution belongs to the author alone; it is what is most
personal to him, and we measure him by that. The advantage, the luxury, as well as the torment and responsibility of the novelist, is that there is no limit to what he
may attempt as an executant—no limit to his possible
experiments, efforts, discoveries, successes. Here it is
especially that he works, step by step, like his brother of
the brush, of whom we may always say that he has
painted his picture in a manner best known to himself.
His manner is his secret, not necessarily a jealous one. He
cannot disclose it as a general thing if he would; he would
be at a loss to teach it to others. I say this with a due recollection of having insisted on the community of method
of the artist who paints a picture and the artist who
writes a novel. The painter *is* able to teach the rudiments
of his practice, and it is possible, from the study of good
work (granted the aptitude), both to learn how to paint
and to learn how to write. Yet it remains true, without
injury to the *rapprochement*, that the literary artist would
be obliged to say to his pupil much more than the other,
"Ah, well, you must do it as you can!" It is a question of
degree, a matter of delicacy. If there are exact sciences,
there are also exact arts, and the grammar of painting is
so much more definite that it makes the difference.

I ought to add, however, that if Mr. Besant says at the beginning of his essay that the "laws of fiction may be laid down and taught with as much precision and exactness as the laws of harmony, perspective, and proportion," he mitigates what might appear to be an extravagance by applying his remark to "general" laws, and by expressing most of these rules in a manner with which it would certainly be unaccommodating to disagree. That the novelist must write from his experience, that his "characters must be real and such as might be met with in actual life"; that "a young lady brought up in a quiet country village should avoid descriptions of garrison life," and "a writer whose friends and personal experiences belong to the lower middle-class should carefully avoid introducing his characters into society"; that one should enter one's notes in a common-place book; that one's figures should be clear in outline; that making them clear by some trick of speech or of carriage is a bad method, and "describing them at length" is a worse one; that English Fiction should have a "conscious moral purpose"; that "it is almost impossible to estimate too highly the value of careful workmanship—that is, of style"; that "the most important point of all is the story," that "the story is everything": these are principles with most of which it is surely impossible not to sympathize. That remark about the lower middle-class writer and his knowing his place is perhaps rather chilling; but for the rest I should find it difficult to dissent from any one of these recommendations. At the same time, I should find it difficult positively to assent to them, with the exception, perhaps, of the injunction as to entering one's notes in a common-place book. They scarcely seem to me to have the quality that Mr. Besant attributes to the rules of the novelist—the "precision and exactness" of "the laws of harmony, perspective, and proportion." They are suggestive, they are even inspiring, but they are not exact, though they are doubtless as much so as the case admits of: which is a proof of that liberty of interpretation for which I just contended. For the value of these different injunctions—so beautiful and so vague—is wholly in the meaning one attaches to them. The characters, the situation, which strike one as real will be those that touch and interest one most, but the measure of reality is very difficult to fix. The reality of Don Quixote or of Mr. Micawber is a very delicate shade; it is a reality so colored by the author's vision that, vivid as it may be, one would hesitate to propose it as a model: one would expose one's self to some very embarrassing questions on the part of a pupil. It goes without saying that you will not write a good novel unless you possess the sense of reality; but it will be difficult to give you a recipe for calling that sense into being. Humanity is immense, and reality has a myriad forms; the most one can affirm is that some of the flowers of fiction have the odor of it, and others have not; as for telling you in advance how your nosegay should be composed, that is another affair. It is equally excellent and inconclusive to say that one must write from experience; to our supposititious aspirant such a declaration might savor of mockery. What kind of experience is intended, and where does it begin and end? Experience is never limited, and it is never complete; it is an immense sensibility, a kind of huge spider-web of the finest silken threads suspended in the chamber of consciousness, and catching every air-borne particle in its tissue. It is the very atmosphere of the mind; and when the mind is imaginative —much more when it happens to be that of a man of genius—it takes to itself the faintest hints of life, it converts the very pulses of the air into revelations. The young lady living in a village has only to be a damsel upon whom nothing is lost to make it quite unfair (as it seems to me) to declare to her that she shall have nothing to say about the military. Greater miracles have been seen than that, imagination assisting, she should speak the truth about some of these gentlemen. I remember an English novelist, a woman of genius,[2] telling me that she

was much commended for the impression she had managed to give in one of her tales of the nature and way of
life of the French Protestant youth. She had been asked
where she learned so much about this recondite being, she
had been congratulated on her peculiar opportunities.
These opportunities consisted in her having once, in Paris,
as she ascended a staircase, passed an open door where,
in the household of a *pasteur*, some of the young Protes-
tants were seated at table round a finished meal. The
glimpse made a picture; it lasted only a moment, but that
moment was experience. She had got her direct personal
impression, and she turned out her type. She knew what
youth was, and what Protestantism; she also had the
advantage of having seen what it was to be French, so
that she converted these ideas into a concrete image and
produced a reality. Above all, however, she was blessed
with the faculty which when you give it an inch takes
an ell, and which for the artist is a much greater source of
strength than any accident of residence or of place in
the social scale. The power to guess the unseen from the
seen, to trace the implication of things, to judge the whole
piece by the pattern, the condition of feeling life in general so completely that you are well on your way to
knowing any particular corner of it—this cluster of gifts
may almost be said to constitute experience, and they
occur in country and in town, and in the most differing
stages of education. If experience consists of impressions,
it may be said that impressions *are* experience, just as
(have we not seen it?) they are the very air we breathe.
Therefore, if I should certainly say to a novice, "Write
from experience and experience only," I should feel that
this was rather a tantalizing monition if I were not careful
immediately to add, "Try to be one of the people on
whom nothing is lost!"

I am far from intending by this to minimize the im-

---

[2] Probably Anne Thackeray, Lady Ritchie, daughter of
Thackeray, whose first novel *The Story of Elizabeth* corresponds to James's description.

portance of exactness—of truth of detail. One can speak
best from one's own taste, and I may therefore venture to
say that the air of reality (solidity of specification) seems
to me to be the supreme virtue of a novel—the merit on
which all its other merits (including that conscious moral
purpose of which Mr. Besant speaks) helplessly and sub-
missively depend. If it be not there they are all as nothing,
and if these be there, they owe their effect to the success
with which the author has produced the illusion of life.
The cultivation of this success, the study of this exquisite
process, form, to my taste, the beginning and the end of
the art of the novelist. They are his inspiration, his despair,
his reward, his torment, his delight. It is here in very
truth that he competes with life; it is here that he competes with his brother the painter in *his* attempt to render
the look of things, the look that conveys their meaning,
to catch the color, the relief, the expression, the surface,
the substance of the human spectacle. It is in regard to
this that Mr. Besant is well inspired when he bids him
take notes. He cannot possibly take too many, he cannot
possibly take enough. All life solicits him, and to "render"
the simplest surface, to produce the most momentary illusion, is a very complicated business. His case would be
easier, and the rule would be more exact, if Mr. Besant
had been able to tell him what notes to take. But this,
I fear, he can never learn in any manual; it is the business
of his life. He has to take a great many in order to select
a few, he has to work them up as he can, and even the
guides and philosophers who might have most to say
to him must leave him alone when it comes to the application of precepts, as we leave the painter in communion
with his palette. That his characters "must be clear in
outline," as Mr. Besant says—he feels that down to his
boots; but how he shall make them so is a secret between
his good angel and himself. It would be absurdly simple if
he could be taught that a great deal of "description"
would make them so, or that on the contrary the absence
of description and the cultivation of dialogue, or the ab-

sence of dialogue and the multiplication of "incident," would rescue him from his difficulties. Nothing, for instance, is more possible than that he be of a turn of mind for which this odd, literal opposition of description and dialogue, incident and description, has little meaning and light. People often talk of these things as if they had a kind of internecine distinctness, instead of melting into each other at every breath, and being intimately associated parts of one general effort of expression. I cannot imagine composition existing in a series of blocks, nor conceive, in any novel worth discussing at all, of a passage of description that is not in its intention narrative, a passage of dialogue that is not in its intention descriptive, a touch of truth of any sort that does not partake of the nature of incident, or an incident that derives its interest from any other source than the general and only source of the success of a work of art—that of being illustrative. A novel is a living thing, all one and continuous, like any other organism, and in proportion as it lives will it be found, I think, that in each of the parts there is something of each of the other parts. The critic who over the close texture of a finished work shall pretend to trace a geography of items will mark some frontiers as artificial, I fear, as any that have been known to history. There is an old-fashioned distinction between the novel of character and the novel of incident which must have cost many a smile to the intending fabulist who was keen about his work. It appears to me as little to the point as the equally celebrated distinction between the novel and 'the romance—to answer as little to any reality. There are bad novels and good novels, as there are bad pictures and good pictures; but that is the only distinction in which I see any meaning, and I can as little imagine speaking of a novel of character as I can imagine speaking of a picture of character. When one says picture one says of character, when one says novel one says of incident, and the terms may be transposed at will. What is character but the determination of incident? What is incident but the illustration of character? What is either a picture or a novel that is *not* of character? What else do we seek in it and find in it? It is an incident for a woman to stand up with her hand resting on a table and look out at you in a certain way; or if it be not an incident I think it will be hard to say what it is. At the same time it is an expression of character. If you say you don't see it (character in *that—allons donc!*), this is exactly what the artist who has reasons of his own for thinking he *does* see it undertakes to show you. When a young man makes up his mind that he has not faith enough after all to enter the church as he intended, that is an incident, though you may not hurry to the end of the chapter to see whether perhaps he doesn't change once more. I do not say that these are extraordinary or startling incidents. I do not pretend to estimate the degree of interest proceeding from them, for this will depend upon the skill of the painter. It sounds almost puerile to say that some incidents are intrinsically much more important than others, and I need not take this precaution after having professed my sympathy for the major ones in remarking that the only classification of the novel that I can understand is into that which has life and that which has it not.

The novel and the romance, the novel of incident and that of character—these clumsy separations appear to me to have been made by critics and readers for their own convenience, and to help them out of some of their occasional queer predicaments, but to have little reality or interest for the producer, from whose point of view it is of course that we are attempting to consider the art of fiction. The case is the same with another shadowy category which Mr. Besant apparently is disposed to set up—that of the "modern English novel"; unless indeed it be that in this matter he has fallen into an accidental confusion of standpoints. It is not quite clear whether he intends the remarks in which he alludes to it to be didactic or historical. It is as difficult to suppose a person intending to write a modern English as to suppose him

writing an ancient English novel: that is a label which
begs the question. One writes the novel, one paints the
picture, of one's language and of one's time, and calling it
modern English will not, alas! make the difficult task any
easier. No more, unfortunately, will calling this or that
work of one's fellow-artist a romance—unless it be, of
course, simply for the pleasantness of the thing, as for
instance when Hawthorne gave this heading to his story
of *Blithedale*. The French, who have brought the theory
of fiction to remarkable completeness, have but one name
for the novel, and have not attempted smaller things in
it, that I can see, for that. I can think of no obligation to
which the "romancer" would not be held equally with the
novelist; the standard of execution is equally high for
each. Of course it is of execution that we are talking—
that being the only point of a novel that is open to contention. This is perhaps too often lost sight of, only to
produce interminable confusions and cross-purposes. We
must grant the artist his subject, his idea, his *donnée:*
our criticism is applied only to what he makes of it.
Naturally I do not mean that we are bound to like it or
find it interesting: in case we do not our course is perfectly simple—to let it alone. We may believe that of a
certain idea even the most sincere novelist can make
nothing at all, and the event may perfectly justify our
belief; but the failure will have been a failure to execute,
and it is in the execution that the fatal weakness is recorded. If we pretend to respect the artist at all, we must
allow him his freedom of choice, in the face, in particular
cases, of innumerable presumptions that the choice will
not fructify. Art derives a considerable part of its bene-
ficial exercise from flying in the face of presumptions, and
some of the most interesting experiments of which it is
capable are hidden in the bosom of common things.
Gustave Flaubert has written a story[3] about the devotion
of a servant-girl to a parrot, and the production, highly
finished as it is, cannot on the whole be called a success.

[3] *Un coeur simple.*

We are perfectly free to find it flat, but I think it might have been interesting; and I, for my part, am extremely glad he should have written it; it is a contribution to our knowledge of what can be done—or what cannot. Ivan Turgenev has written a tale about a deaf and dumb serf and a lap-dog,[4] and the thing is touching, loving, a little masterpiece. He struck the note of life where Gustave Flaubert missed it—he flew in the face of a presumption and achieved a victory.

Nothing, of course, will ever take the place of the good old fashion of "liking" a work of art or not liking it: the most improved criticism will not abolish that primitive, that ultimate test. I mention this to guard myself from the accusation of intimating that the idea, the subject, of a novel or a picture, does not matter. It matters, to my sense, in the highest degree, and if I might put up a prayer it would be that artists should select none but the richest. Some, as I have already hastened to admit, are much more remunerative than others, and it would be a world happily arranged in which persons intending to treat them should be exempt from confusions and mistakes. This fortunate condition will arrive only, I fear, on the same day that critics become purged from error. Meanwhile, I repeat, we do not judge the artist with fairness unless we say to him,

"Oh, I grant you your starting-point, because if I did not I should seem to prescribe to you, and heaven forbid I should take that responsibility. If I pretend to tell you what you must not take, you will call upon me to tell you then what you must take; in which case I shall be prettily caught. Moreover, it isn't till I have accepted your data that I can begin to measure you. I have the standard, the pitch; I have no right to tamper with your flute and then criticize your music. Of course I may not care for your idea at all; I may think it silly, or stale, or unclean; in which case I wash my hands of you altogether. I may

⁴ *Mumu.*

content myself with believing that you will not have succeeded in being interesting, but I shall, of course, not
attempt to demonstrate it, and you will be as indifferent
to me as I am to you. I needn't remind you that there
are all sorts of tastes: who can know it better? Some
people, for excellent reasons, don't like to read about
carpenters; others, for reasons even better, don't like to
read about courtesans. Many object to Americans. Others
(I believe they are mainly editors and publishers) won't
look at Italians. Some readers don't like quiet subjects;
others don't like bustling ones. Some enjoy a complete
illusion, others the consciousness of large concessions.
They choose their novels accordingly, and if they don't
care about your idea they won't, *a fortiori*, care about
your treatment."

So that it comes back very quickly, as I have said, to
the liking: in spite of M. Zola, who reasons less powerfully than he represents, and who will not reconcile himself to this absoluteness of taste, thinking that there
are certain things that people ought to like, and that they
can be made to like. I am quite at a loss to imagine anything (at any rate in this matter of fiction) that people
ought to like or to dislike. Selection will be sure to take
care of itself, for it has a constant motive behind it. That
motive is simply experience. As people feel life, so they
will feel the art that is most closely related to it. This
closeness of relation is what we should never forget in
talking of the effort of the novel. Many people speak of it
as a factitious, artificial form, a product of ingenuity, the
business of which is to alter and arrange the things that
surround us, to translate them into conventional, traditional moulds. This, however, is a view of the matter
which carries us but a very short way, condemns the art
to an eternal repetition of a few familiar *clichés*, cuts
short its development, and leads us straight up to a dead
wall. Catching the very note and trick, the strange ir-

regular rhythm of life, that is the attempt whose strenuous force keeps Fiction upon her feet. In proportion as in what she offers us we see life *without* rearrangement do we feel that we are touching the truth; in proportion as we see it *with* rearrangement do we feel that we are being put off with a substitute, a compromise and convention. It is not uncommon to hear an extraordinary assurance of remark in regard to this matter of rearranging, which is often spoken of as if it were the last word of art. Mr. Besant seems to me in danger of falling into the great error with his rather unguarded talk about "selection." Art is essentially selection, but it is a selection whose main care is to be typical, to be inclusive. For many people art means rose-colored window-panes, and selection means picking a bouquet for Mrs. Grundy. They will tell you glibly that artistic considerations have nothing to do with the disagreeable, with the ugly; they will rattle off shallow commonplaces about the province of art and the limits of art till you are moved to some wonder in return as to the province and the limits of ignorance. It appears to me that no one can ever have made a seriously artistic attempt without becoming conscious of an immense increase—a kind of revelation—of freedom. One perceives in that case —by the light of a heavenly ray—that the province of art is all life, all feeling, all observation, all vision. As Mr. Besant so justly intimates, it is all experience. That is a sufficient answer to those who maintain that it must not touch the sad things of life, who stick into its divine unconscious bosom little prohibitory inscriptions on the end of sticks, such as we see in public gardens—"It is forbidden to walk on the grass; it is forbidden to touch the flowers; it is not allowed to introduce dogs or to remain after dark; it is requested to keep to the right." The young aspirant in the line of fiction whom we continue to imagine will do nothing without taste, for in that case his freedom would be of little use to him; but the first advantage of his taste will be to reveal to him the absurdity of the little sticks and tickets. If he have taste, I

must add, of course he will have ingenuity, and my dis-
respectful reference to that quality just now was not
meant to imply that it is useless in fiction. But it is only
a secondary aid; the first is a capacity for receiving
straight impressions.

Mr. Besant has some remarks on the question of "the
story" which I shall not attempt to criticize, though they
seem to me to contain a singular ambiguity, because I do
not think I understand them. I cannot see what is meant
by talking as if there were a part of a novel which is the
story and part of it which for mystical reasons is not—
unless indeed the distinction be made in a sense in which
it is difficult to suppose that any one should attempt to
convey anything. "The story," if it represents anything,
represents the subject, the idea, the *donnée* of the novel;
and there is surely no "school"—Mr. Besant speaks of a
school—which urges that a novel should be all treatment
and no subject. There must assuredly be something to
treat; every school is intimately conscious of that. This
sense of the story being the idea, the starting-point, of
the novel, is the only one that I see in which it can be
spoken of as something different from its organic whole;
and since in proportion as the work is successful the idea
permeates and penetrates it, informs and animates it, so
that every word and every punctuation-point contribute
directly to the expression, in that proportion do we lose
our sense of the story being a blade which may be drawn
more or less out of its sheath. The story and the novel,
the idea and the form, are the needle and thread, and I
never heard of a guild of tailors who recommended the
use of the thread without the needle, or the needle without the thread. Mr. Besant is not the only critic who may
be observed to have spoken as if there were certain things
in life which constitute stories, and certain others which
do not. I find the same odd implication in an entertaining
article in the *Pall Mall Gazette*, devoted, as it happens,
to Mr. Besant's lecture. "The story is the thing!" says
this graceful writer, as if with a tone of opposition to

some other idea. I should think it was, as every painter who, as the time for "sending in" his picture looms in the distance, finds himself still in quest of a subject—as every belated artist not fixed about his theme will heartily agree. There are some subjects which speak to us and others which do not, but he would be a clever man who should undertake to give a rule—an *index expurgatorius*—by which the story and the no-story should be known apart. It is impossible (to me at least) to imagine any such rule which shall not be altogether arbitrary. The writer in the *Pall Mall* opposes the delightful (as I suppose) novel of *Margot la Balafrée* to certain tales in which "Bostonian nymphs" appear to have "rejected English dukes for psychological reasons." I am not acquainted with the romance just designated, and can scarcely forgive the *Pall Mall* critic for not mentioning the name of the author,[5] but the title appears to refer to a lady who may have received a scar in some heroic adventure. I am inconsolable at not being acquainted with this episode, but am uterly at a loss to see why it is a story when the rejection (or acceptance) of a duke is not, and why a reason, psychological or other, is not a subject when a cicatrix is. They are all particles of the multitudinous life with which the novel deals, and surely no dogma which pretends to make it lawful to touch the one and unlawful to touch the other will stand for a moment on its feet. It is the special picture that must stand or fall, according as it seem to possess truth or to lack it. Mr. Besant does not, to my sense, light up the subject by intimating that a story must, under penalty of not being a story, consist of "adventures." Why of adventures more than of green spectacles? He mentions a category of impossible things, and among them he places "fiction without adventure." Why without adventure, more than without matrimony, or celibacy, or parturition, or cholera, or hydropathy, or Jansenism? This seems to me to bring the novel back to

---

[5] The author, fairly obviously, is James himself, and the story alluded to clearly *An International Episode* (1879).

the hapless little *rôle* of being an artificial, ingenious
thing—bring it down from its large, free character of an
immense and exquisite correspondence with life. And
what *is* adventure, when it comes to that, and by what
sign is the listening pupil to recognize it? It is an adventure
—an immense one—for me to write this little article; and
for a Bostonian nymph to reject an English duke is an
adventure only less stirring, I should say, than for an
English duke to be rejected by a Bostonian nymph. I
see dramas within dramas in that, and innumerable points
of view. A psychological reason is, to my imagination, an
object adorably pictorial; to catch the tint of its complexion—I feel as if that idea might inspire one to Titian-
esque efforts. There are few things more exciting to me,
in short, than a psychological reason, and yet, I protest,
the novel seems to me the most magnificent form of art.
I have just been reading, at the same time, the delightful
story of *Treasure Island*, by Mr. Robert Louis Stevenson
and, in a manner less consecutive, the last tale from
M. Edmond de Goncourt, which is entitled *Chérie*. One
of these works treats of murders, mysteries, islands of
dreadful renown, hairbreadth escapes, miraculous coinci-
dences and buried doubloons. The other treats of a little
French girl who lived in a fine house in Paris, and died
of wounded sensibility because no one would marry her.
I call *Treasure Island* delightful, because it appears to
me to have succeeded wonderfully in what it attempts;
and I venture to bestow no epithet upon *Chérie*, which
strikes me as having failed deplorably in what it attempts
—that is in tracing the development of the moral consciousness of a child. But one of these productions strikes
me as exactly as much of a novel as the other, and as
having a "story" quite as much. The moral consciousness
of a child is as much a part of life as the islands of the
Spanish Main, and the one sort of geography seems to
me to have those "surprises" of which Mr. Besant speaks
quite as much as the other. For myself (since it comes
back in the last resort, as I say, to the preference of the

individual), the picture of the child's experience has the advantage that I can at successive steps (an immense luxury, near to the "sensual pleasure" of which Mr. Besant's critic in the *Pall Mall* speaks) say Yes or No, as it may be, to what the artist puts before me. I have been a child in fact, but I have been on a quest for a buried treasure only in supposition, and it is a simple accident that with M. de Goncourt I should have for the most part to say No. With George Eliot, when she painted that country with a far other intelligence, I always said Yes.

The most interesting part of Mr. Besant's lecture is unfortunately the briefest passage—his very cursory allusion to the "conscious moral purpose" of the novel. Here again it is not very clear whether he be recording a fact or laying down a principle; it is a great pity that in the latter case he should not have developed his idea. This branch of the subject is of immense importance, and Mr. Besant's few words point to considerations of the widest reach, not to be lightly disposed of. He will have treated the art of fiction but superficially who is not prepared to go every inch of the way that these considerations will carry him. It is for this reason that at the beginning of these remarks I was careful to notify the reader that my reflections on so large a theme have no pretension to be exhaustive. Like Mr. Besant, I have left the question of the morality of the novel till the last, and at the last I find I have used up my space. It is a question surrounded with difficulties, as witness the very first that meets us, in the form of a definite question, on the threshold. Vagueness, in such a discussion, is fatal, and what is the meaning of your morality and your conscious moral purpose? Will you not define your terms and explain how (a novel being a picture) a picture can be either moral or immoral? You wish to paint a moral picture or carve a moral statue: will you not tell us how you would set about it? We are discussing the Art of Fiction; questions of art are questions (in the widest

sense) of execution; questions of morality are quite another affair, and will you not let us see how it is that
you find it so easy to mix them up? These things are so
clear to Mr. Besant that he has deduced from them a
law which he sees embodied in English Fiction, and which
is "a truly admirable thing and a great cause for congratulation." It is a great cause for congratulation indeed
when such thorny problems become as smooth as silk. I
may add that in so far as Mr. Besant perceives that in
point of fact English Fiction has addressed itself preponderantly to these delicate questions he will appear to
many people to have made a vain discovery. They will
have been positively struck, on the contrary, with the
moral timidity of the usual English novelist; with his (or
with her) aversion to face the difficulties with which on
every side the treatment of reality bristles. He is apt to
be extremely shy (whereas the picture that Mr. Besant
draws is a picture of boldness), and the sign of his work,
for the most part, is a cautious silence on certain subjects. In the English novel (by which of coure I mean
the American as well), more than in any other, there is a
traditional difference between that which people know
and that which they agree to admit that they know, that
which they see and that which they speak of, that which
they feel to be a part of life and that which they allow to
enter into literature. There is the great difference, in short,
between what they talk of in conversation and what they
talk of in print. The essence of moral energy is to survey
the whole field, and I should directly reverse Mr. Besant's
remark and say not that the English novel has a purpose,
but that it has a diffidence. To what degree a purpose in
a work of art is a source of corruption I shall not attempt to inquire; the one that seems to me least dangerous is the purpose of making a perfect work. As for our
novel, I may say lastly on this score that as we find it in
England today it strikes me as addressed in a large degree
to "young people," and that this in itself constitutes a
presumption that it will be rather shy. There are certain

things which it is generally agreed not to discuss, not even to mention, before young people. That is very well, but the absence of discussion is not a symptom of the moral passion. The purpose of the English novel—"a truly admirable thing, and a great cause for congratulation"—strikes me therefore as rather negative.

There is one point at which the moral sense and the artistic sense lie very near together; that is in the light of the very obvious truth that the deepest quality of a work of art will always be the quality of the mind of the producer. In proportion as that intelligence is fine will the novel, the picture, the statue partake of the substance of beauty and truth. To be constituted of such elements is, to my vision, to have purpose enough. No good novel will ever proceed from a superficial mind; that seems to me an axiom which, for the artist in fiction, will cover all needful moral ground: If the youthful aspirant take it to heart it will illuminate for him many of the mysteries of "purpose." There are many other useful things that might be said to him, but I have come to the end of my article, and can only touch them as I pass. The critic in the *Pall Mall Gazette*, whom I have already quoted, draws attention to the danger, in speaking of the art of fiction, of generalizing. The danger that he has in mind is rather, I imagine, that of particularizing, for there are some comprehensive remarks which, in addition to those embodied in Mr. Besant's suggestive lecture, might without fear of misleading him be addressed to the ingenuous student. I should remind him first of the magnificence of the form that is open to him, which offers to sight so few restrictions and such innumerable opportunities. The other arts, in comparison, appear confined and hampered; the various conditions under which they are exercised are so rigid and definite. But the only condition that I can think of attaching to the composition of the novel is, as I have already said, that it be sincere. This freedom is a splendid privilege, and the first lesson of the young novelist is to learn to be worthy of it.

. . .

"Enjoy it as it deserves [I should say to him]; take possession of it, explore it to its utmost extent, publish it, rejoice in it. All life belongs to you, and do not listen either to those who would shut you up into corners of it and tell you that it is only here and there that art inhabits, or to those who would persuade you that this heavenly messenger wings her way outside of life altogether, breathing a superfine air, and turning away her head from the truth of things. There is no impression of life, no manner of seeing it and feeling it, to which the plan of the novelist may not offer a place; you have only to remember that talents so dissimilar as those of Alexandre Dumas and Jane Austen, Charles Dickens and Gustave Flaubert have worked in this field with equal glory. Do not think too much about optimism and pessimism; try and catch the color of life itself. In France today we see a prodigious effort (that of Émile Zola, to whose solid and serious work no explorer of the capacity of the novel can allude without respect), we see an extraordinary effort vitiated by a spirit of pessimism on a narrow basis. M. Zola is magnificent, but he strikes an English reader as ignorant; he has an air of working in the dark; if he had as much light as energy, his results would be of the highest value. As for the aberrations of a shallow optimism, the ground (of English fiction especially) is strewn with their brittle particles as with broken glass. If you must indulge in conclusions, let them have the taste of a wide knowledge. Remember that your first duty is to be as complete as possible—to make as perfect a work. Be generous and delicate and pursue the prize."

*

THE GREAT FORM

A LETTER TO THE DEERFIELD
SUMMER SCHOOL

[*Summer 1889*]

I AM afraid I can do little more than thank you for your courteous invitation to be present at the sittings of your delightfully sounding school of romance,[1] which ought to inherit happiness and honor from such a name. I am so very far away from you that I am afraid I can't participate very intelligently in your discussions, but I can only give them the furtherance of a dimly discriminating sympathy. I am not sure that I apprehend very well your apparent premise, "the materialism of our present tendencies," and I suspect that this would require some clearing up before I should be able (if even then) to contribute any suggestive or helpful word. To tell the truth, I can't help thinking that we already talk too much about the novel, about and around it, in proportion to the quantity of it having any importance that

[1] During the summer of 1889 James was invited to attend the Summer School at Deerfield, Massachusetts for a discussion of the art of the novel. He sent, instead, the letter here given, which was read during the proceedings and later published in the New York *Tribune* (August 4, 1889).

we produce. What I should say to the nymphs and swains who propose to converse about it under the great trees at Deerfield is: "Oh, do something from your point of view; an ounce of example is worth a ton of generalities; do something with the great art and the great form; do something with life. Any point of view is interesting that is a direct impression of life. You each have an impression colored by your individual conditions; make that into a picture, a picture framed by your own personal wisdom, your glimpse of the American world. The field is vast for freedom, for study, for observation, for satire, for truth." I don't think I really do know what you mean by "materializing tendencies" any more than I should by "spiritualizing" or "etherealizing." There are no tendencies worth anything but to see the actual or the imaginative, which is just as visible, and to paint it. I have only two little words for the matter remotely approaching to rule or doctrine; one is life and the other freedom. Tell the ladies and gentlemen, the ingenious inquirers, to consider life directly and closely, and not to be put off with mean and puerile falsities, and be conscientious about it. It is infinitely large, various and comprehensive. Every sort of mind will find what it looks for in it, whereby the novel becomes truly multifarious and illustrative. That is what I mean by liberty; give it its head and let it range. If it is in a bad way, and the English novel is, I think, nothing but absolute freedom can refresh it and restore its self-respect. Excuse these raw brevities and please convey to your companions, my dear sir, the cordial good wishes of yours and theirs,

                                                    Henry James.

THE FUTURE OF THE NOVEL

BEGINNINGS, as we all know, are usually small things, but continuations are not always strikingly great ones, and the place occupied in the world by the prolonged prose fable has become, in our time, among the incidents of literature, the most surprising example to be named of swift and extravagant growth, a development beyond the measure of every early appearance. It is a form that has had a fortune so little to have been foretold at its cradle. The germ of the comprehensive epic was more recognizable in the first barbaric chant than that of the novel as we know it today in the first anecdote retailed to amuse. It arrived, in truth, the novel, late at self-consciousness; but it has done its utmost ever since to make up for lost opportunities. The flood at present swells and swells, threatening the whole field of letters, as would often seem, with submersion. It plays, in what may be called the passive consciousness of many persons, a part that directly marches with the rapid increase of the multitude able to possess itself in one way and another of the *book*. The book, in the Anglo-Saxon world, is almost everywhere, and it is in the form of the voluminous prose fable that we see it penetrate easiest and farthest. Penetration appears really to be directly aided by mere mass and bulk. There is an immense public, if public be the name, inarticulate, but abysmally absorbent, for which, at its hours of ease, the printed volume has no other association. This public—the public that subscribes, borrows, lends, that picks up in one way and another, sometimes even by purchase—grows and grows each year, and nothing is thus more apparent than that of all the recruits it brings to the book the most numerous by far are those that it brings to the "story."

This number has gained, in our time, an augmentation from three sources in particular, the first of which, indeed, is perhaps but a comprehensive name for the two others. The diffusion of the rudiments, the multiplication of common schools, has had more and more the effect of making readers of women and of the very young. Nothing is so striking in a survey of this field, and nothing to be so much borne in mind, as that the larger part of the great multitude that sustains the teller and the publisher of tales is constituted by boys and girls; by girls in especial, if we apply the term to the later stages of the life of the innumerable women who, under modern arrangements, increasingly fail to marry—fail, apparently, even, largely, to desire to. It is not too much to say of many of these that they live in a great measure by the immediate aid of the novel—confining the question, for the moment, to the fact of consumption alone. The literature, as it may be called for convenience, of children is an industry that occupies by itself a very considerable quarter of the scene. Great fortunes, if not great reputations, are made, we learn, by writing for schoolboys, and the period during which they consume the compound artfully prepared for them appears—as they begin earlier and continue later—to add to itself at both ends. This helps to account for the fact that public libraries, especially those that are private and money-making enterprises, put into circulation more volumes of "stories" than of all other things together of which volumes can be made. The published statistics are extraordinary, and of a sort to engender many kinds of uneasiness. The sort of taste that used to be called "good" has nothing to do with the matter: we are so demonstrably in presence of millions for whom taste is but an obscure, confused, immediate instinct. In the flare of railway bookstalls, in the shop-fronts of most booksellers, especially the provincial, in the advertisements of the weekly newspapers, and in fifty places besides, this testimony to the general preference triumphs, yielding a good-natured corner at most to a bunch of treatises on athletics or sport, or a patch of theology old and new.

The case is so marked, however, that illustrations easily overflow, and there is no need of forcing doors that stand wide open. What remains is the interesting oddity or mystery—the anomaly that fairly dignifies the whole circumstance with its strangeness: the wonder, in short, that men, women, and children *should* have so much attention to spare for improvisations mainly so arbitrary and frequently so loose. That, at the first blush, fairly leaves us gaping. This great fortune then, since fortune it seems, has been reserved for mere unsupported and unguaranteed history, the *inexpensive* thing, written in the air, the record of what, in any particular case, has *not* been, the account that remains responsible, at best, to "documents" with which we are practically unable to collate it. This is the side of the whole business of fiction on which it can always be challenged, and to that degree that if the general venture had not become in such a manner the admiration of the world it might but too easily have become the derision. It has in truth, I think, never philosophically met the challenge, never found a formula to inscribe on its shield, never defended its position by any better argument than the frank, straight blow: "Why am I not so unprofitable as to be preposterous? Because I can do *that*. There!" And it throws up from time to time some purely practical masterpiece. There is nevertheless an admirable minority of intelligent persons who care not even for the masterpieces, nor see any pressing point in them, for whom the very form itself has, equally at its best and at its worst, been ever a vanity and a mockery. This class, it should be added, is beginning to be visibly augmented by a different circle altogether, the group of the formerly subject, but now estranged, the deceived and bored, those for whom the whole movement too decidedly fails to live up to its possibilities. There are people who have loved the novel, but who actually find themselves drowned in its verbiage, and for whom, even in some of its approved manifestations, it has become a terror they exert every ingenuity, every hypocrisy, to evade. The indifferent and the alienated testify, at any rate, almost as much as the omnivorous, to the reign of the great ambiguity, the enjoyment of which rests, evidently, on a primary need of the mind. The novelist can only fall back on that—on his recognition that man's constant demand for what he has to offer is simply man's general appetite for a *picture*. The novel is of all pictures the most comprehensive and the most elastic. It will stretch anywhere—it will take in absolutely anything. All it needs is a subject and a painter. But for its subject, magnificently, it has the whole human consciousness. And if we are pushed a step farther backward, and asked why the representation should be required when the object represented is itself mostly so accessible, the answer to that appears to be that man combines with his eternal desire for more experience an infinite cunning as to getting his experience as cheaply as possible. He will steal it whenever he can. He likes to live the life of others, yet is well aware of the points at which it may too intolerably resemble his own. The vivid fable, more than anything else, gives him this satisfaction on easy terms, gives him knowledge abundant yet vicarious. It enables him to select, to take and to leave; so that to feel he can afford to neglect it he must have a rare faculty, or great opportunities, for the extension of experience—by thought, by emotion, by energy—at first hand.

Yet it is doubtless not this cause alone that contributes to the contemporary deluge; other circumstances operate, and one of them is probably, in truth, if looked into, something of an abatement of the great fortune we have been called upon to admire. The high prosperity of fiction has marched, very directly, with another "sign of the times," the demoralization, the vulgarization of literature in general, the increasing familiarity of all such methods of communication, the making itself supremely felt, as it were, of the presence of the ladies and children— by whom I mean, in other words, the reader irreflective and uncritical. If the novel, in fine, has found itself, socially speaking, at such a rate, the book *par excellence*, so on the other hand the book has in the same degree found itself a thing of small ceremony. So many ways of producing it easily have been discovered that it is by no means the occasional prodigy, for good or for evil, that it was taken for in simpler days, and has therefore suffered a proportionate discredit. Almost any variety is thrown off and taken up, handled, admired, ignored by too many people, and this, precisely, is the point at which the question of its future becomes one with that of the future of the total swarm. How are the generations to face, at all, the monstrous multiplications? Any speculation on the further development of a particular variety is subject to the reserve that the generations may at no distant day be obliged formally to decree, and to execute, great clearings of the deck, great periodical effacements and destructions. It fills, in fact, at moments the expectant ear, as we watch the progress of the ship of civilization—the huge splash that must mark the response to many an imperative, unanimous "Overboard!" What at least is already very plain is that practically the great majority of volumes printed within a year cease to exist as the hour passes, and give up by that circumstance all claim to a career, to being accounted or provided for. In speaking of the future of the novel we must of course, therefore, be taken as limiting the inquiry to those types that have,

for criticism, a present and a past. And it is only superficially that confusion seems here to reign. The fact that
in England and in the United States every specimen that
sees the light may look for a "review" testifies merely to
the point to which, in these countries, literary criticism
has sunk. The review is in nine cases out of ten an effort
of intelligence as undeveloped as the ineptitude over which
it fumbles, and the critical spirit, which knows where it
is concerned and where not, is not touched, is still less
compromised, by the incident. There are too many reasons why newspapers must live.

So, as regards the tangible type, the end is that in its
undefended, its positively exposed state, we continue to
accept it, conscious even of a peculiar beauty in an appeal
made from a footing so precarious. It throws itself wholly
on our generosity, and very often indeed gives us, by
the reception it meets, a useful measure of the quality, of
the delicacy, of many minds. There is to my sense no
work of literary, or of any other, art, that any human
being is under the smallest positive obligation to "like."
There is no woman—no matter of what loveliness—in
the presence of whom it is anything but a man's unchal-
lengeably *own* affair that he is "in love" or out of it. It
is not a question of manners; vast is the margin left to
individual freedom; and the trap set by the artist occupies
no different ground—Robert Louis Stevenson has admirably expressed the analogy—from the offer of her charms
by the lady. There only remain infatuations that we
envy and emulate. When we do respond to the appeal,
when we *are* caught in the trap, we are held and played
upon; so that how in the world can there *not* still be a
future, however late in the day, for a contrivance possessed of this precious secret? The more we consider it
the more we feel that the prose picture can never be at
the end of its tether until it loses the sense of what it
can do. It can do simply everything, and that is its
strength and its life. Its plasticity, its elasticity are infinite; there is no color, no extension it may not take from

the nature of its subject or the temper of its craftsman. It has the extraordinary advantage—a piece of luck scarcely credible—that, while capable of giving an impression of the highest perfection and the rarest finish, it moves in a luxurious independence of rules and restrictions. Think as we may, there is nothing we can mention as a consideration outside itself with which it must square, nothing we can name as one of its peculiar obligations or interdictions. It must, of course, hold our attention and reward it, it must not appeal on false pretenses; but these necessities, with which, obviously, disgust and displeasure interfere, are not peculiar to it—all works of art have them in common. For the rest it has so clear a field that if it perishes this will surely be by its fault— by its superficiality, in other words, or its timidity. One almost, for the very love of it, likes to think of its appearing threatened with some such fate, in order to figure the dramatic stroke of its revival under the touch of a life-giving master. The temperament of the artist can do so much for it that our desire for some exemplary felicity fairly demands even the vision of that supreme proof. If we were to linger on this vision long enough, we should doubtless, in fact, be brought to wondering—and still for very loyalty to the form itself—whether our own prospective conditions may not before too long appear to many critics to call for some such happy *coup* on the part of a great artist yet to come.

There would at least be this excuse for such a reverie: that speculation is vain unless we confine it, and that for ourselves the most convenient branch of the question is the state of the industry that makes its appeal to readers of English. From any attempt to measure the career still open to the novel in France I may be excused, in so narrow a compass, for shrinking. The French, as a result of having ridden their horse much harder than we, are at a different stage of the journey, and we have doubtless many of their stretches and baiting-places yet to traverse. But if the range grows shorter from the moment we drop

to inductions drawn only from English and American
material, I am not sure that the answer comes sooner. I
should have at all events—a formidably large order—to
plunge into the particulars of the question of the present.
If the day *is* approaching when the respite of execution
for almost any book is but a matter of mercy, does the
English novel of commerce tend to strike us as a production more and more equipped by its high qualities for
braving the danger? It would be impossible, I think, to
make one's attempt at an answer to that riddle really
interesting without bringing into the field many illustrations drawn from individuals—without pointing the moral
with names both conspicuous and obscure. Such a freedom
would carry us, here, quite too far, and would moreover
only encumber the path. There is nothing to prevent our
taking for granted all sorts of happy symptoms and
splendid promises—so long, of course, I mean, as we keep
before us the general truth that the future of fiction is
intimately bound up with the future of the society that
produces and consumes it. In a society with a great and
diffused literary sense the talent at play can only be a
less neglible thing than in a society with a literary sense
barely discernible. In a world in which criticism is acute
and mature such talent will find itself trained, in order
successfully to assert itself, to many more kinds of precautionary expertness than in a society in which the art
I have named holds an inferior place or makes a sorry
figure. A community addicted to reflection and fond of
ideas will try experiments with the "story" that will be
left untried in a community mainly devoted to traveling
and shooting, to pushing trade and playing football. There
are many judges, doubtless, who hold that experiments—
queer and uncanny things at best—are not necessary to
it, that its face has been, once for all, turned in one way,
and that it has only to go straight before it. If that is
what it is actually doing in England and America the
main thing to say about its future would appear to be
that this future will in very truth more and more define

itself as negligible. For all the while the immense variety of life will stretch away to right and to left, and all the while there may be, on such lines, perpetuation of its great mistake of failing of intelligence. That mistake will be, ever, for the admirable art, the only one really en-excusable, because of being a mistake about, as we may say, its own soul. The form of novel that is stupid on the general question of its freedom is the single form that may, *a priori*, be unhesitatingly pronounced wrong.

The most interesting thing today, therefore, among ourselves is the degree in which we may count on seeing a sense of that freedom cultivated and bearing fruit. What else is this, indeed, but one of the most attaching elements in the great drama of our wide English-speaking life! As the novel is at any moment the most immediate and, as it were, admirably *treacherous* picture of actual manners—indirectly as well as directly, and by what it does not touch as well as by what it does—so its present situation, where we are most concerned with it, is exactly a reflection of our social changes and chances, of the signs and portents that lay most traps for most observers, and make up in general what is most "amusing" in the spectacle we offer. Nothing, I may say, for instance, strikes me more as meeting this description than the predicament finally arrived at, for the fictive energy, in consequence of our long and most respectable tradition of making it defer supremely, in the treatment, say, of a delicate case, to the inexperience of the young. The particular knot the coming novelist who shall prefer not simply to beg the question, will have here to untie may represent as-suredly the essence of his outlook. By what it shall decide to do in respect to the "young" the great prose fable will, from any serious point of view, practically see itself stand or fall. What is clear is that it has, among us, veritably never chosen—it has, mainly, always obeyed an unreason-ing instinct of avoidance in which there has often been much that was felicitous. While society was frank, was free about the incidents and accidents of the human constitution, the novel took the same robust ease as society. The young then were so very young that they were not table-high. But they began to grow, and from the moment their little chins rested on the mahogany, Richardson and Fielding began to go under it. There came into being a mistrust of any but the most guarded treatment of the great relation between men and women, the constant world-renewal, which was the conspicuous sign that whatever the prose picture of life was prepared to take upon itself, it was not prepared to take upon itself not to be superficial. Its position became very much: "There are other things, don't you know? For heaven's sake let *that* one pass!" And to this wonderful propriety of letting it pass the business has been for these so many years—with the consequences we see today—largely devoted. These consequences are of many sorts, not a few altogether charming. One of them has been that there is an immense omission in our fiction—which, though many critics will always judge that it has vitiated the whole, others will continue to speak of as signifying but a trifle. One can only talk for one's self, and of the English and American novelists of whom I am fond, I am so superlatively fond that I positively prefer to take them as they are. I cannot so much as imagine Dickens and Scott *without* the "*love-making*" left, as the phrase is, out. They were, to my perception, absolutely right—from the moment their attention to it could only be perfunctory—practically not to deal with it. In all their work it is, in spite of the number of pleasant sketches of affection gratified or crossed, the element that matters least. Why not therefore assume, it may accordingly be asked, that discriminations which have served their purpose so well in the past will continue not less successfully to meet the case? What will you have better than Scott and Dickens?

Nothing certainly *can* be, it may at least as promptly be replied, and I can imagine no more comfortable prospect than jogging along perpetually with a renewal of such blessings. The difficulty lies in the fact that two of the great conditions have changed. The novel is older, and so are the young. It would seem that everything the young can possibly do for us in the matter has been successfully done. They have kept out one thing after the other, yet there is still a certain completeness we lack, and the curious thing is that it appears to be they themselves who are making the grave discovery. "You have kindly taken," they seem to say to the fiction-mongers, "our education off the hands of our parents and pastors, and that, doubtless, has been very convenient for *them*, and left them free to amuse themselves. But what, all the while, pray, if it is a question of education, have you done with your own? These are directions in which you seem dreadfully untrained, and in which *can* it be as vain as it appears to apply to you for information?" The point is whether, from the moment it is a question of averting discredit, the novel can afford to take things quite so easily as it has, for a good while now, settled down into the way of doing. There are too many sources of interest neglected— whole categories of manners, whole corpuscular classes and provinces, museums of character and condition, un-visited; while it is on the other hand mistakenly taken for granted that safety lies in all the loose and thin material that keeps reappearing in forms at once ready-made and sadly the worse for wear. The simple themselves may finally turn against our simplifications; so that we need not, after all, be more royalist than the king or more childish than the children. It is certain that there is no real health for any art—I am not speaking, of course, of any mere industry—that does not move a step in advance of its farthest follower. It would be curious—really a great comedy—if the renewal were to spring just from the satiety of the very readers for whom the sacrifices have hitherto been supposed to be made. It bears on this that as nothing is more salient in English life today, to fresh eyes, than the revolution taking place in the position and out-look of women—and taking place much more deeply in the quiet than even the noise on the surface demonstrates

—so we may very well yet see the female elbow itself, kept in increasing activity by the play of the pen, smash with final resonance the window all this time most superstitiously closed. The particular draught that has been most deprecated will in that case take care of the question of freshness. It is the opinion of some observers that when women do obtain a free hand they will not repay their long debt to the precautionary attitude of men by unlimited consideration for the natural delicacy of the latter.

To admit, then, that the great anodyne can ever totally fail to work, is to imply, in short, that this will only be by some grave fault in some high quarter. Man rejoices in an incomparable faculty for presently mutilating and disfiguring any plaything that has helped create for him the illusion of leisure; nevertheless, so long as life retains its power of projecting itself upon his imagination, he will find the novel work off the impression better than anything he knows. Anything better for the purpose has assuredly yet to be discovered. He will give it up only when life itself too thoroughly disagrees with him. Even then, indeed, may fiction not find a second wind, or a fiftieth, in the very portrayal of that collapse? Till the world is an unpeopled void there will be an image in the mirror. What need more immediately concern us, therefore, is the care of seeing that the image shall continue various and vivid. There is much, frankly, to be said for those who, in spite of all brave pleas, feel it to be considerably menaced, for very little reflection will help to show us how the prospect strikes them. They see the whole business too divorced on the one side from observation and perception, and on the other from the art and taste. They get too little of the first-hand impression, the effort to penetrate—that effort for which the French have the admirable expression to *fouiller*—and still less, if possible, of any science of composition, any architecture, distribution, proportion. It is not a trifle, though indeed it is the concomitant of an edged force, that "mystery"

James wrote to each novel and each group of tales, describing the origin of the story and how he came to write it and throwing off, in the process, certain of the basic theories he had formulated in the creation of his art.

To be fully appreciated, these prefaces should be read in their entirety. They have been collected by R. P. Blackmur under the title The Art of the Novel *(Scribner, New York, 1934). The prefaces are, in the opinion of most critics, a veritable cornerstone of modern fictional theory. Joseph Warren Beach drew upon them for his pioneering examination of* The Method of Henry James *of 1918, and they are the scaffolding upon which Percy Lubbock erected his classic study of* The Craft of Fiction *of 1921. In 1932 the editor of this volume published a brief study of them in Paris under the title* The Prefaces of Henry James, *and in 1934 R. P. Blackmur's analysis of the prefaces appeared in the* Hound and Horn *and was later used to preface the collective volume.*

Few writers on the art of fiction in recent years have ignored these prefaces. Packed with allusion and metaphor, filled with highly imaginative imagery, they have become a kind of fount and source for the critical terminology and criticism itself of fiction. The excerpts given here are designed to illustrate certain of the central points made by James in his discussion of the aesthetic of the novel—largely as he practiced it.

THE BALLOON OF EXPERIENCE

By what art or mystery, what craft of selection, omission or commission, does a given picture of life appear to us to surround its theme, its figures and images, with the air of romance while another picture close beside it may affect us as steeping the whole matter in the element of reality? It is a question, no doubt, on the painter's part, very much more of perceived effect, effect *after* the fact, than of conscious design—though indeed I have ever failed to see how a coherent picture of anything is producible save by a complex of fine measurements. The cause of the deflexion, in one pronounced sense or the other, must lie deep, however; so that for the most part we recognize the character of our interest only after the particular magic, as I say, has thoroughly operated—and then in truth but if we be a bit critically minded, if we find our pleasure, that is, in these intimate appreciations (for which, as I am well aware, ninety-nine readers in a hundred have no use whatever). The determining condition would at any rate seem so latent that one may well doubt if the full artistic consciousness ever reaches it; leaving the matter thus a case, ever, not of an author's plotting and planning and calculating, but just of his feeling and seeing, of his conceiving, in a word, and of his thereby inevitably expressing himself, under the influence of one value or the other. These values represent different sorts and degrees of the communicable thrill, and I doubt if any novelist, for instance, ever proposed to commit himself to one kind or the other with as little mitigation as we are sometimes able to find for him. The interest is greatest—the interest of his genius, I mean, and of his general wealth—when he commits himself in both directions; not quite at the same time or to the same effect, of course, but by some need of performing his whole possible revolution, by the law of some rich passion in him for extremes.

Of the men of largest responding imagination before the human scene, of Scott, of Balzac, even of the coarse, comprehensive, prodigious Zola, we feel, I think, that the deflexion toward either quarter has never taken place; that neither the nature of the man's faculty nor the nature of his experience has ever quite determined it. His current remains therefore extraordinarily rich and mixed, washing us successively with the warm wave of the near and familiar and the tonic shock, as may be, of the far and strange. (In making which opposition I suggest not that the strange and the far are at all necessarily romantic: they happen to be simply the unknown, which is quite

a different matter. The real represents to my perception
the things we cannot possibly *not* know, sooner or later,
in one way or another; it being but one of the accidents
of our hampered state, and one of the incidents of their
quantity and number, that particular instances have not
yet come our way. The romantic stands, on the other
hand, for the things that, with all the facilities in the
world, all the wealth and all the courage and all the wit
and all the adventure, we never *can* directly know; the
things that can reach us only through the beautiful cir-
cuit and subterfuge of our thought and our desire.)
There have been, I gather, many definitions of romance,
as a matter indispensably of boats, or of caravans, or of
tigers, or of "historical characters," or of ghosts, or of
forgers, or of detectives, or of beautiful wicked women,
or of pistols and knives, but they appear for the most part
reducible to the idea of the facing of danger, the acceptance of great risks for the fascination, the very love, of
their uncertainty, the joy of success if possible and of
battle in any case. This would be a fine formula if it bore
examination; but it strikes me as weak and inadequate, as
by no means covering the true ground and yet as landing
us in strange confusions.

The panting pursuit of danger is the pursuit of life
itself, in which danger awaits us possibly at every step
and faces us at every turn; so that the dream of an
intenser experience easily becomes rather some vision of
a sublime security like that enjoyed on the flowery plains
of heaven, where we may conceive ourselves proceeding
in ecstasy from one prodigious phase and form of it to
another. And if it be insisted that the measure of the type
is then in the *appreciation* of danger—the sign of our projection of the real being the smallness of its dangers, and
that of our projection of the romantic the hugeness, the
mark of the distinction being in short, as they say of
collars and gloves and shoes, the size and "number" of the
danger—this discrimination again surely fails, since it
makes our difference not a difference of kind, which is

what we want, but a difference only of degree, and subject by that condition to the indignity of a sliding scale and a shifting measure. There are immense and flagrant dangers that are but sordid and squalid ones, as we feel, tainting with their quality the very defiances they provoke; while there are common and covert ones, that "look like nothing" and that can be but inwardly and occultly dealt with, which involve the sharpest hazards to life and honor and the highest instant decisions and intrepidities of action. It is an arbitrary stamp that keeps these latter prosaic and makes the former heroic; and yet I should still less subscribe to a mere "subjective" division—I mean one that would place the difference wholly in the temper of the imperilled agent. It would be impossible to have a more romantic temper than Flaubert's Madame Bovary, and yet nothing less resembles a romance than the record of her adventures. To classify it by that aspect—the definition of the spirit that happens to animate her—is like settling the question (as I have seen it witlessly settled) by the presence or absence of "costume." Where again then does costume begin or end?—save with the "run" of one or another sort of play? We must reserve vague labels for artless mixtures.

The only *general* attribute of projected romance that I can see, the only one that fits all its cases, is the fact of the kind of experience with which it deals—experience liberated, so to speak; experience disengaged, disembroiled, disencumbered, exempt from the conditions that we usually know to attach to it and, if we wish so to put the matter, drag upon it, and operating in a medium which relieves it, in a particular interest, of the inconvenience of a *related*, a measurable state, a state subject to all our vulgar communities. The greatest intensity may so be arrived at evidently—when the sacrifice of community, of the "related" sides of situations, has not been too rash. It must to this end not flagrantly betray itself; we must even be kept if possible, for our illusion, from suspecting any sacrifice at all. The balloon of experience is in fact of course tied

to the earth and, under that necessity we swing, thanks
to a rope of remarkable length, in the more or less com-
modious car of the imagination; but it is by the rope we
know where we are, and from the moment that cable is
cut we are at large and unrelated: we only swing apart
from the globe—though remaining as exhilarated, naturally, as we like, especially when all goes well. The art of
the romancer is, "for the fun of it," insidiously to cut the
cable, to cut it without our detecting him.

—PREFACE TO *The American*

THE HOUSE OF FICTION

. . . I have always fondly remembered a remark that
I heard fall years ago from the lips of Ivan Turgenev in
regard to his own experience of the usual origin of the
fictive picture. It began for him almost always with the
vision of some person or persons, who hovered before
him, soliciting him, as the active or passive figure, interesting him and appealing to him just as they were and by
what they were. He saw them, in that fashion, as *dis-
ponibles*, saw them subject to the chances, the complications of existence, and saw them vividly, but then had to
find for them the right relations, those that would most
bring them out; to imagine, to invent and select and piece
together the situations most useful and favorable to the
sense of the creatures themselves, the complications they
would be most likely to produce and to feel.

"To arrive at these things is to arrive at my 'story,'"
he said, "and that's the way I look for it. The result
is that I'm often accused of not having 'story' enough.
I seem to myself to have as much as I need—to show my
people, to exhibit their relations with each other; for that
is all my measure. If I watch them long enough I see them
come together, I see them *placed*, I see them engaged in
this or that act and in this or that difficulty. How they
look and move and speak and behave, always in the set-

ting I have found for them in my account of them—of
which I dare say, alas, *que cela manque souvent d'architecture*. But I would rather, I think, have too little architecture than too much—when there's danger of its interfering with my measure of the truth. The French of
course like more of it than I give—having by their own
genius such a hand for it; and indeed one must give all
one can. As for the origin of one's wind-blown germs
themselves, who shall say, as you ask, where *they* come
from? We have to go too far back, too far behind, to
say. Isn't it all we can say that they come from every
quarter of heaven, that they are *there* at almost any turn
of the road? They accumulate, and we are always picking
them over, selecting among them. They are the breath of
life—by which I mean that life, in its own way, breathes
them upon us. They are so, in a manner prescribed and
imposed—floated into our minds by the current of life.
That reduces to imbecility the vain critic's quarrel, so often,
with one's subject, when he hasn't the wit to accept it.
Will he point out then which other it should properly
have been?—his office, being, essentially *to* point out.
Il en serait bien embarrassé. Ah, when he points out what
I've done or failed to do with it, that's another matter:
there he's on his ground. I give him up my 'architecture,' "
my distinguished friend concluded, as much as he will."

So this beautiful genius, and I recall with comfort the
gratitude I drew from his reference to the intensity of
suggestion that may reside in the stray figure, the un-
attached character, the image *en disponibilité*. It gave me
higher warrant than I seemed then to have met for just
that blessed habit of one's own imagination, the trick of
investing some conceived or encountered individual, some
brace or group of individuals, with the germinal property
and authority. I was myself so much more antecedently
conscious of my figures than of their setting—a too preliminary, a preferential interest in which struck me as in
general such a putting of the cart before the horse. I
might envy, though I couldn't emulate, the imaginative

writer so constituted as to see his fable first and to make
out its agents afterwards: I could think so little of any
fable that didn't need its agents positively to launch it; I
could think so little of any situation that didn't depend
for its interest on the nature of the persons situated, and
thereby on their way of taking it. There are methods of
so-called presentation, I believe—among novelists who
have appeared to flourish—that offer the situation as different to that support; but I have not lost the sense of the
value for me, at the time, of the admirable Russian's
testimony to my not needing, all superstitiously, to try
and perform any such gymnastic. Other echoes from the
same source linger with me, I confess, as unfadingly—if
it be not all indeed one much-embracing echo. It was impossible after that not to read, for one's uses, high lucidity
into the tormented and disfigured and bemuddled question
of the objective value, and even quite into that of the
critical appreciation, of "subject" in the novel.

One had had, from an early time, for that matter, the
instinct of the right estimate of such values and of its
reducing to the inane the dull dispute over the "immoral"
subject and the moral. Recognizing so promptly the one
measure of the worth of a given subject, the question
about it that, rightly answered, disposes of all others—is
it valid, in a word, is it genuine, is it sincere, the result of
some direct impression or perception of life?—I have
found small edification, mostly, in a critical pretension
that had neglected from the first all delimitation of ground
and all definition of terms. The air of my earlier time
shows, to memory, as darkened, all round, with that
vanity—unless the difference today be just in one's own
final impatience, the lapse of one's attention. There is, I
think, no more nutritive or suggestive truth in this connection than that of the perfect dependency of the
"moral" sense of a work of art on the amount of felt life
concerned in producing it. The question comes back thus,
obviously, to the kind and the degree of the artist's prime
sensibility, which is the soil out of which his subject

springs. The quality and capacity of that soil, its ability to "grow" with due freshness and straightness any vision of life, represents, strongly or weakly, the projected morality. That element is but another name for the more or less close connection of the subject with some mark made on the intelligence, with some sincere experience. By which, at the same time, of course, one is far from contending that this enveloping air of the artist's humanity —which gives the last touch to the worth of the work—is not a widely and wondrously varying element; being on one occasion a rich and magnificent medium and on another a comparatively poor and ungenerous one. Here we get exactly the high price of the novel as a literary form—its power not only, while preserving that form with closeness, to range through all the differences of the individual relation to its subject matter, all the varieties of outlook on life, of disposition to reflect and project, created by conditions that are never the same from man to man (or, so far as that goes, from man to woman), but positively to appear more true to its character in proportion as it strains, or tends to burst, with a latent extravagance, its mould.

The house of fiction has in short not one window, but a million—a number of possible windows not to be reckoned, rather; every one of which has been pierced, or is still pierceable, in its vast front, by the need of the individual vision and by the pressure of the individual will. These apertures, of dissimilar shape and size, hang so, all together, over the human scene that we might have expected of them a greater sameness of report than we find. They are but windows at the best, mere holes in a dead wall, disconnected, perched aloft; they are not hinged doors opening straight upon life. But they have this mark of their own that at each of them stands a figure with a pair of eyes, or at least with a field glass, which forms, again and again, for observation, a unique instrument, insuring to the person making use of it an impression distinct from every other. He and his neighbors are watching the same show, but one seeing more where the other sees less, one seeing black where the other sees white, one seeing big where the other sees small, one seeing coarse where the other sees fine. And so on, and so on; there is fortunately no saying on what, for the particular pair of eyes, the window may *not* open; "fortunately" by reason, precisely, of this incalculability of range. The spreading field, the human scene, is the "choice of subject"; the pierced aperture, either broad or balconied or slitlike and low-browed, is the "literary form"; but they are, singly or together, as nothing without the posted presence of the watcher—without, in other words, the consciousness of the artist. Tell me what the artist is, and I will tell you of what he has *been* conscious. Thereby I shall express to you at once his boundless freedom and his "moral" reference.

—PREFACE TO *The Portrait of a Lady*

THE VIRUS OF SUGGESTION

What above all comes back to me with this reminiscence is the sense of the inveterate minuteness, on such happy occasions, of the precious particle—reduced, that is, to its mere fruitful essence. Such is the interesting truth about the stray suggestion, the wandering word, the vague echo, at touch of which the novelist's imagination winces as at the prick of some sharp point: its virtue is all in its needle-like quality, the power to penetrate as finely as possible. This fineness it is that communicates the virus of suggestion, anything more than the minimum of which spoils the operation. If one is given a hint at all designedly one is sure to be given too much; one's subject is in the merest grain, the speck of truth, of beauty, of reality, scarce visible to the common eye— since, I firmly hold, a good eye for a subject is anything but usual. Strange and attaching, certainly, the consistency with which the first thing to be done for the communicated and seized idea is to reduce almost to nought the form, the air as of a mere disjoined and lacerated lump of life, in which we may have happened to meet it. Life being all inclusion and confusion, and art being all discrimination and selection, the latter, in search of the hard latent *value* with which alone it is concerned, sniffs round the mass as instinctively and unerringly as a dog suspicious of some buried bone. The difference here, however, is that, while the dog desires his bone but to destroy it, the artist finds in *his* tiny nugget, washed free of awkward accretions and hammered into a sacred hardness, the very stuff for a clear affirmation, the happiest chance for the indestructible. It at the same time amuses him again and again to note how, beyond the first step of the actual case, the case that constitutes for him his germ, his vital particle, his grain of gold, life persistently blunders and deviates, loses herself in the sand. The reason is of course that life has no direct sense whatever for the subject and is capable, luckily for us, of nothing but splendid waste. Hence the opportunity for the sublime economy of art, which rescues, which saves, and hoards and "banks," investing and reinvesting these fruits of toil in wondrous useful "works" and thus making up for us, desperate spendthrifts that we all naturally are, the most princely of incomes. It is the subtle secrets of that system, however, that are meanwhile the charming study, with an endless attraction, above all, in the question—endlessly baffling indeed—of the method at the heart of the madness; the madness, I mean, of a zeal, among the reflective sort, so disinterested. If life, presenting us the germ, and left merely to herself in such a business, gives the case away, almost always, before we can stop her, what are the signs for our guidance, what the primary laws for a saving selection, how do we know when and where to intervene, where do we place the beginnings of the wrong or the right deviation? Such would be the elements of an enquiry upon which, I hasten to say, it is quite forbidden me here to embark: I but

glance at them in evidence of the rich pasture that at
every turn surrounds the ruminant critic. The answer
may be after all that mysteries here elude us, that general
considerations fail or mislead, and that even the fondest of
artists need ask no wider range than the logic of the
particular case. The particular case, or in other words
his relation to a given subject, once the relation is
established, forms in itself a little world of exercise and
agitation. Let him hold himself perhaps supremely fortunate if he can meet half the questions with which that
air alone may swarm.

—PREFACE TO *The Spoils of Poynton*

THE PROCESS OF ART

Art deals with what we see, it must first contribute
full-handed that ingredient; it plucks its material, otherwise expressed, in the garden of life—which material elsewhere grown is stale and uneatable. But it has no sooner
done this than it has to take account of a *process*—from
which only when it's the basest of the servants of man,
incurring ignominious dismissal with no "character," does
it, and whether under some muddled pretext of morality
or on any other, pusillanimously edge away. The process,
that of the expression, the literal squeezing-out, of value is
another affair—with which the happy luck of mere finding
has little to do. The joys of finding, at this stage, are
pretty well over; that quest of the subject as a whole
by "matching," as the ladies say at the shops, the big
piece with the snippet, having ended, we assume, with a
capture. The subject is found, and if the problem is then
transferred to the ground of what to do with it the field
opens out for any amount of doing. This is precisely the
infusion that, as I submit, completes the strong mixture.
It is on the other hand the part of the business that can
least be likened to the chase with horn and hound. It's all
a sedentary part—involves as much ciphering, of sorts, as

would merit the highest salary paid to a chief accountant. Not, however, that the chief accountant hasn't *his* gleams of bliss; for the felicity, or at least the equilibrium, of the artist's state wells less, surely, in the further delightful complications he can smuggle in than in those he succeeds in keeping out. He sows his seed at the risk of too thick a crop; wherefore yet again, like the gentlemen who audit ledgers, he must keep his head at any price.

—PREFACE TO *The Ambassadors*

THE VESSEL OF CONSCIOUSNESS

This in fact I have ever found rather terribly the point —that the figures in any picture, the agents in any drama, are interesting only in proportion as they feel their respective situations; since the consciousness, on their part, of the complication exhibited forms for us their link of connection with it. But there are degrees of feeling—the muffled, the faint, the just sufficient, the barely intelligent, as we may say; and the acute, the intense, the complete, in a word—the power to be finely aware and richly responsible. It is those moved in this latter fashion who "get most" out of all that happens to them and who in so doing enable us, as readers of their record, as participators by a fond attention, also to get most. Their being finely aware—as Hamlet and Lear, say, are finely aware —*makes* absolutely the intensity of their adventure, gives the maximum of sense to what befalls them. We care, our curiosity and our sympathy care, comparatively little for what happens to the stupid, the coarse and the blind; care for it, and for the effects of it, at the most as helping to precipitate what happens to the more deeply wondering, to the really sentient. Hamlet and Lear are surrounded, amid their complications, by the stupid and the blind, who minister in all sorts of ways to their recorded fate. Persons of markedly limited sense would, on such a principle as that, play a part in the career of my tormented youth; but he wouldn't be of markedly limited sense himself—he would note as many things and vibrate to as many occasions as I might venture to make him.

There wouldn't moreover simply be the question of his suffering—of which we might soon get enough; there would be the question of what, all beset and all perceptive, he should thus adventurously do, thus dream and hazard and attempt. The interest of the attitude and the act would be the actor's imagination and vision of them, together with the nature and degree of their felt return upon him. So the intelligent creature would be required and so some picture of his intelligence involved. The picture of an intelligence appears for the most part, it is true, a dead weight for the reader of the English novel to carry, this reader having so often the wondrous property of caring for the displayed tangle of human relations without caring for its intelligibility. The teller of a story is primarily, none the less, the listener to it, the reader of it, too; and, having needed thus to make it out, distinctly, on the crabbed page of life, to disengage it from the rude human character and the more or less Gothic text in which it has been packed away, the very essence of his affair has been the *imputing* of intelligence. The basis of his attention has been that such and such an imbroglio has got started—on the page of life—because of something that some one has felt and more or less understood.

I recognize at the same time, and in planning *The Princess Casamassima* felt it highly important to recognize, the danger of filling too full any supposed and above all any obviously limited vessel of consciousness. If persons either tragically or comically embroiled with life allow us the comic or tragic value of their embroilment in proportion as their struggle is a measured and directed one, it is strangely true, none the less, that beyond a certain point they are spoiled for us by this carrying of a due light. They may carry too much of it for our credence, for our compassion, for our derision. They may be shown as knowing too much and feeling too much—not certainly for their remaining remarkable, but for their remaining "natural" and typical, for their having the needful communities with our own precious liability to fall into traps and be bewildered. It seems probable that if we were never bewildered there would never be a story to tell about us; we should partake of the superior nature of the all-knowing immortals whose annals are dreadfully dull so long as flurried humans are not, for the positive relief of bored Olympians, mixed up with them. Therefore it is that the wary reader for the most part warns the novelist against making his characters too *interpretative* of the muddle of fate, or in other words too divinely, too priggishly clever. "Give us plenty of bewilderment," this monitor seems to say, "so long as there is plenty of slashing out in the bewilderment too. But don't, we beseech you, give us too much intelligence; for intelligence—well, *endangers;* endangers not perhaps the slasher himself, but the very slashing, the subject-matter of any self-respecting story. It opens up too many considerations, possibilities, issues; it *may* lead the slasher into dreary realms where slashing somehow fails and falls to the ground."

That is well reasoned on the part of the reader, who can in spite of it never have an idea—or his earnest discriminations would come to him less easily—of the extreme difficulty, for the painter of the human mixture, of reproducing that mixture aright. "Give us in the persons represented, the subjects of the bewilderment (that bewilderment without which there would be no question of an issue or of the fact of suspense, prime implications in any story) as much experience as possible, but keep down the terms in which you report that experience, because we only understand the very simplest": such in effect are the words in which the novelist constantly hears himself addressed, such the plea made him by the would-be victims of his spell on behalf of that sovereign principle the economy of interest, a principle as to which their instinct is justly strong. He listens anxiously to the charge —nothing can exceed his own solicitude for an economy of interest; but feels himself all in presence of an abyss of ambiguities, the mutual accommodations in which the reader wholly leaves to him. Experience, as I see it, is our apprehension and our measure of what happens to us as social creatures—any intelligent report of which has to be based on that apprehension. The picture of the exposed and entangled state is what is required, and there are certainly always plenty of grounds for keeping down the complexities of a picture. A picture it still has to be, however, and by that condition has to deal effectually with its subject, so that the simple device of more and more keeping down may well not see us quite to our end or even quite to our middle. One suggested way of keeping down, for instance, is not to attribute feeling, or feelings, to persons who wouldn't in all probability have had any to speak of. The less space, within the frame of the picture, their feelings take up the more space is left for their doings—a fact that may at first seem to make for a refinement of economy.

All of which is charming—yet would be infinitely more so if here at once ambiguity didn't yawn; the unreality of the sharp distinction, where the interest of observation is at stake, between doing and feeling. In the immediate field of life, for action, for application, for getting through a job, nothing may so much matter perhaps as the descent of a suspended weight on this, that or the other spot, with all its subjective concomitants quite secondary and irrelevant. But the affair of the painter is not the immediate, it is the reflected field of life, the realm not of application, but of *appreciation*—a truth that makes our measure of effect altogether different. My report of people's experience—my report as a "story-teller"—is essentially my appreciation of it, and there is no "interest" for me in what my hero, my heroine or any one else does save through that admirable process. As soon as I begin to appreciate simplification is imperiled: the sharply distinguished parts of any adventure, any case of endurance and performance, melt together as an appeal. I then see their "doing," that of the persons just mentioned, as, immensely, their feeling, their feeling as their doing; since I can have none of the conveyed sense and taste of their situation without becoming intimate with them. I can't be intimate without that sense and taste, and I can't appreciate save by intimacy, any more than I can report save by a projected light. Intimacy with a man's specific behavior, with his given case, is desperately certain to make us see it as a whole—in which event arbitrary limitations of our vision lose whatever beauty they may on occasion have pretended to. What a man thinks and what he feels are the history and the character of what he does; on all of which things the logic of intensity rests. Without intensity where is vividness, and without vividness where is presentability? If I have called the most general state of one's most exposed and assaulted figures the state of bewilderment—the condition for instance on which Thackeray so much insists in the interest of *his* exhibited careers, the condition of a humble heart, a bowed head, a patient wonder, a suspended judgment, before the "awful will" and the mysterious decrees of Providence—so it is rather witless to talk of merely getting rid of that displayed mode of reaction, one of the oft-encountered, one of the highly recommended, categories of feeling.

The whole thing comes to depend thus on the *quality* of bewilderment characteristic of one's creature, the quality involved in the given case or supplied by one's data. There are doubtless many such qualities, ranging from vague and crepuscular to sharpest and most critical; and we have but to imagine one of these latter to see how easily—from the moment it gets its head at all—it may insist on playing a part. There we have then at once a case of feeling, of ever so many possible feelings, stretched across the scene like an attached thread on which the pearls of interest are strung. There are threads shorter and less tense, and I am far from implying that the minor, the coarser and less fruitful forms and degrees of moral reaction, as we may conveniently call it, may not yield lively results. They have their subordinate, comparative, illustrative human value—that appeal of the witless which is often so penetrating. Verily even, I think, no "story" is possible without its fools—as most of the fine painters of life, Shakespeare, Cervantes and Balzac, Fielding, Scott, Thackeray, Dickens, George Meredith, George Eliot, Jane Austen, have abundantly felt. At the same time I confess I never see the *leading* interest of any human hazard but in a consciousness (on the part of the moved and moving creature) subject to fine intensification and wide enlargement. It is as mirrored in that consciousness that the gross fools, the headlong fools, the fatal fools play their part for us—they have much less to show us in themselves. The troubled life mostly at the center of our subject—whatever our subject, for the artistic hour, happens to be—embraces them and deals with them for its amusement and its anguish: they are apt largely indeed, on a near view, to be all the cause of its trouble. This means, exactly, that the person capable of feeling in the given case more than another of what is to be felt for it, and so serving in the highest degree to *record* it dramatically and objectively, is the only sort of person on whom we can count not to betray, to cheapen or, as we say, give away, the value and beauty of the thing. By so much as the affair matters *for* some such individual, by so much do we get the best there is of it, and by so much as it falls within the scope of a denser and duller, a more vulgar and more shallow capacity, do we get a picture dim and meager.

The great chroniclers have clearly always been aware of this; they have at least always either placed a mind of some sort—in the sense of a reflecting and coloring medium—in possession of the general adventure (when the latter has not been purely epic, as with Scott, say, as with old Dumas and with Zola); or else paid signally, as to the interest created, for their failure to do so. We may note moreover in passing that this failure is in almost no case intentional or part of a plan, but has sprung from their limited curiosity, their short conception of the particular sensibility projected. Edgar of Ravenswood for instance, visited by the tragic tempest of *The Bride of Lammermoor*, has a black cloak and hat and feathers more than he has a mind; just as Hamlet, while equally sabled and draped and plumed, while at least equally romantic, has yet a mind still more than he has a costume. The situation represented is that Ravenswood loves Lucy Ashton through dire difficulty and danger, and that she in the same way loves him; but the relation so created between them is by this neglect of the "feeling" question never shown us as primarily taking place. It is shown only in its secondary, its confused and disfigured aspects—where, however, luckily, it is presented with great romantic good faith. The thing has nevertheless paid for its deviation, as I say, by a sacrifice of intensity; the center of the subject is empty and the development pushed off, all round, toward the frame—which is, so to speak, beautifully rich and curious. But I mention that relation to each other of the appearances in a particular work only as a striking negative case; there are in the connection I have glanced at plenty of striking positive ones. It is very true that Fielding's hero in *Tom Jones* is but as "finely," that is but as intimately, bewildered as a young man of great health and spirits may be when he hasn't a grain of imagination: the point to be made is, at all events, that his sense of bewilderment obtains altogether on the comic, never on the tragic plane. He has so much "life" that it amounts, for the effect of comedy and application of satire, almost to his having a mind, that is to his having reactions and a full consciousness; besides which his author—*he* handsomely possessed of a mind—has such an amplitude of reflection for him and round him that we see him through the mellow air of Fielding's fine old moralism, fine old humor and fine old style, which somehow really enlarge, make every one and every thing important.

—PREFACE TO *The Princess Casamassima*

THE PICTORIAL ART

Anything that relieves responsible prose of the duty of being, while placed before us, good enough, interesting enough and, if the question be of picture, pictorial enough, above all *in itself*, does it the worst of services, and may well inspire in the lover of literature certain lively questions as to the future of that institution. That one should, as an author, reduce one's reader, "artistically" inclined, to such a state of hallucination by the images one has evoked as doesn't permit him to rest till he has noted or recorded them, set up some semblance of them in his own other medium, by his own other art—nothing could better consort than *that*, I naturally allow, with the desire or the pretension to cast a literary spell. Charming, that it, for the projector and creator of figures and scenes that are as nought from the moment they fail to become more or less visible appearances, charming for this manipulator of aspects to see such power as he may possess approved and registered by the springing of such fruit from his seed. His own garden, however, remains one thing, and the garden he has prompted the cultivation of at other hands becomes quite another; which means that the frame of one's own work no more provides place for such a plot than we expect flesh and fish to be served on the same platter. One welcomes illustration, in other words, with pride and joy; but also with the emphatic view that, might one's "literary jealousy" be duly deferred to, it would quite stand off and on its own feet and thus, as a separate and independent subject of publication, carrying its text in its spirit, just as that text correspondingly carries the plastic possibility, become a still more glorious tribute.
                                    —PREFACE TO *The Golden Bowl*

THE SCENIC VISION

I remember that in sketching my project . . . I drew
on a sheet of paper . . . the neat figure of a circle consisting of a number of small rounds disposed at equal
distance about a central object. The central object was
my situation, my subject in itself, to which the thing
would owe its title, and the small rounds represented so
many distinct lamps, as I liked to call them, the function
of each of which would be to light with all due intensity one of its aspects. I had divided it, didn't they see?
into aspects—uncanny as the little term might sound
(though not for a moment did I suggest we should use
it for the public), and by that sign we would con-
quer. . . .

The beauty of the conception was in this approximation
of the respective divisions of my form to the successive
Acts of a Play—as to which it was more than ever a case
for charmed capitals. The divine distinction of the act of
a play—and a greater than any other it easily succeeds
in arriving at—was, I reasoned, in its special, its guarded
objectivity. This objectivity, in turn, when achieving its
ideal, came from the imposed absence of that "going
behind," to compass explanations and amplifications, to
drag out odds and ends from the "mere" storyteller's
great property-shop of aids to illusion: a resource under
denial of which it was equally perplexing and delightful,
for a change, to proceed. Everything, for that matter,
becomes interesting from the moment it has closely to
consider, for full effect positively to bestride, the law of
its kind. "Kinds" are the very life of literature, and truth
and strength come from the complete recognition of them,
from abounding to the utmost in their respective senses
and sinking deep into their consistency. I myself have
scarcely to plead the cause of "going behind," which is
right and beautiful and fruitful in its place and order;

but as the confusion of kinds is the inelegance of letters and the stultification of values, so to renounce that line utterly and do something quite different instead may become in another connection the true course and the vehicle of effect. Something in the very nature, in the fine rigor, of this special sacrifice (which is capable of affecting the form lover, I think, as really more of a projected form than any other) lends it moreover a coercive charm; a charm that grows in proportion as the appeal to it tests and stretches and strains it, puts it powerfully to the touch. To make the presented occasion tell all its story itself, remain shut up in its own presence and yet on that patch of staked-out ground become thoroughly interesting and remain thoroughly clear, is a process not remarkable, no doubt, so long as a very light weight is laid on it, but difficult enough to challenge and inspire great adroitness so soon as the elements to be dealt with begin at all to "size up."

The disdainers of the contemporary drama deny, obviously, with all promptness, that the matter to be expressed by its means—richly and successfully expressed that is—*can* loom with any largeness; since from the moment it does one of the conditions breaks down. The process simply collapses under pressure, they contend, proves its weakness as quickly as the office laid on it ceases to be simple. "Remember," they say to the dramatist, "that you have to be, supremely, three things: you have to be true to your form, you have to be interesting, you have to be clear. You have in other words to prove yourself adequate to taking a heavy weight. But we defy you really to conform to your conditions with any but a light one. Make the thing you have to convey, make the picture you have to paint, at all rich and complex, and you cease to be clear. Remain clear—and with the clearness required by the infantine intelligence of any public consenting to see a play—and what becomes of the 'importance' of your subject? If it's important by any other critical measure than the little foot-rule the 'produced'

piece has to conform to, it is predestined to be a muddle. When it has escaped being a muddle the note it has succeeded in striking at the furthest will be recognized as one of those that are called high but by the courtesy, by the intellectual provinciality, of theatrical criticism, which, as we can see for ourselves any morning, is—well, an abyss even deeper than the theater itself. Don't attempt to crush us with Dumas and Ibsen, for such values are from any informed and enlightened point of view, that is measured by other high values, literary, critical, philosophic, of the most moderate order. Ibsen and Dumas are precisely cases of men, men in their degree, in their poor theatrical strait-jacket, speculative, who have *had* to renounce the finer thing for the coarser, the thick, in short, for the thin and the curious for the self-evident.
—PREFACE TO *The Awkward Age*

GHOSTS AND FAIRIES

. . . The "ghost story," as we for convenience call it, has ever been for me the most possible form of the fairy tale. It enjoys, to my eyes, this honor by being so much the neatest—neat with that neatness without which *representation*, and therewith beauty, drops. One's working of the spell is of course—decently and effectively—but by the represented thing, and the grace of the more or less closely represented state is the measure of any success; a truth by the general smug neglect of which it's difficult not to be struck. To begin to wonder, over a case, I must begin to believe—to begin to give out (that is to attend) I must begin to take in, and to enjoy *that* profit I must begin to see and hear and feel. This wouldn't seem, I allow, the general requirement—as appears from the fact that so many persons profess delight in the picture of marvels and prodigies which by any, even the easiest, critical measure *is* no picture; in the recital of wonderful horrific or beatific things that are neither represented nor,

so far as one makes out, seen as representable: a weakness
not invalidating, round about us, the most resounding
appeals to curiosity. The main condition of interest—that
of some appreciable rendering of sought effects—is absent
from them; so that when, as often happens, one is asked
how one "likes" such and such a "story" one can but
point responsively to the lack of material for a judgment.

The apprehension at work, we thus see, would be of
certain projected conditions, and its first need therefore
is that these appearances be constituted in some other and
more colorable fashion than by the author's answering
for them on his more or less gentlemanly honor. This isn't
enough; *give* me your elements, *treat* me your subject, one
has to say—I must wait till then to tell you how I like
them. I might "rave" about them all were they given and
treated; but there is no basis of opinion in such matters
without a basis of vision, and no ground for that, in
turn, without some communicated closeness of truth.
There are portentous situations, there are prodigies and
marvels and miracles as to which this communication,
whether by necessity or by chance, works comparatively
straight—works, by our measure, to some convincing
consequence; there are others as to which the report, the
picture, the plea, answers no tithe of the questions we
would put. Those questions *may* perhaps then, by the
very nature of the case, be unanswerable—though often
again, no doubt, the felt vice is but in the quality of
the provision made for them: on any showing, my own
instinct, even in the service of great adventures, is all for
the best *terms* of things; all for ground on which touches
and tricks may be multiplied, the greatest number of
questions answered, the greatest appearance of truth
conveyed. With the preference I have noted for the
"neat" evocation—the image, of any sort, with fewest
attendant vaguenesses and cheapnesses, fewest loose ends
dangling and fewest features missing, the image kept in
fine the most susceptible of intensity—with this predilection, I say, the safest arena for the play of moving

accidents and mighty mutations and strange encounters, of whatever odd matters, is the field, as I may call it, rather of their second than of their first exhibition. By which, to avoid obscurity, I mean nothing more cryptic than I feel myself show them best by showing almost exclusively the way they are felt, by recognizing as their main interest some impression strongly made by them and intensely received. We but too probably break down, I have ever reasoned, when we attempt the prodigy, the appeal to mystification, in itself; with its "objective" side too emphasized the report (it is ten to one) will practically run thin. We want it clear, goodness knows, but we also want it thick, and we get the thickness in the human consciousness that entertains and records, that amplifies and interprets it. That indeed, when the question is (to repeat) of the "supernatural," constitutes the only thickness we do get; here prodigies, when they come straight, come with an effect imperiled; they keep all their character, on the other hand, by looming through some other history—the indispensable history of somebody's *normal* relation to something. It's in such connections as these that they most interest, for what we are then mainly concerned with is their imputed and borrowed dignity. Intrinsic values they have none—as we feel for instance in such a matter as the would-be portentous climax of Edgar Poe's "Arthur Gordon Pym," where the indispensable history is absent, where the phenomena evoked, the moving accidents, coming straight, as I say, are immediate and flat, and the attempt is all at the horrific in itself. The result is that, to my sense, the climax fails—fails because it stops short, and stops short for want of connections. There *are* no connections; not only, I mean, in the sense of further statement, but of our own further relation to the elements, which hang in the void: whereby we see the effect lost, the imaginative effort wasted.

I dare say, to conclude, that whenever, in quest, as I have noted, of the amusing, I have invoked the horrific,

I have invoked it, in such air as that of "The Turn of the Screw," that of "The Jolly Corner," that of "The Friends of the Friends," that of "Sir Edmund Orme," that of "The Real Right Thing," in earnest aversion to waste and from the sense that in art economy is always beauty. The apparitions of Peter Quint and Miss Jessel, in the first of the tales just named, the elusive presence nightly "stalked" through the New York house by the poor gentleman in the second, are matters as to which in themselves, really, the critical challenge (essentially nothing ever but the spirit of fine attention) may take a hundred forms—and a hundred felt or possibly proved infirmities is too great a number. Our friends' respective minds about them, on the other hand, are a different matter—challengeable, and repeatedly, if you like, but never challengeable without some consequent further stiffening of the whole texture. Which proposition involves, I think, a moral. The moving accident, the rare conjunction, whatever it be, doesn't make the story—in the sense that the story is our excitement, our amusement, our thrill and our suspense; the human emotion and the human attestation, the clustering human conditions we expect presented, only make it. The extraordinary is most extraordinary in that it happens to you and me, and it's of value (of value for others) but so far as visibly brought home to us.

—PREFACE TO *The Altar of the Dead and Other Stories*

THE PAINTER'S SPONGE

I speak of the painter in general and of his relation to the old picture, the work of his hand, that has been lost to sight and that, when found again, is put back on the easel for measure of what time and the weather may, in the interval, have done to it. Has it too fatally faded, has it blackened or "sunk," or otherwise abdicated, or has it only, blessed thought, strengthened, for its allotted dura-

tion, and taken up, in its degree, poor dear brave thing,
some shade of the all appreciable, yet all indescribable
grace that we know as pictorial "tone"? The anxious
artist has to wipe it over, in the first place, to see; he has
to "clean it up," say, or to varnish it anew, or at the
least to place it in a light, for any right judgment of its
aspect or its worth. But the vary uncertainties themselves
yield a thrill, and if subject and treatment, working together, have had their felicity, the artist, the prime creator,
may find a strange charm in this stage of the connection.
It helps him to live back into a forgotten state, into
convictions, credulities too early spent perhaps, it breathes
upon the dead reasons of things, buried as they are in the
texture of the work, and makes them revive, so that
the actual appearances and the old motives fall together
once more, and a lesson and a moral and a consecrating
final light are somehow disengaged.

All this, I mean of course, if the case will wonderfully
take any such pressure, if the work doesn't break down
under even such mild overhauling. The author knows
well enough how easily that may happen—which he in
fact frequently enough sees it do. The old reasons then
are too dead to revive; they were not, it is plain, good
enough reasons to live. The only possible relation of the
present mind to the thing is to dismiss it altogether. On
the other hand, when it is not dismissed—as the only detachment is the detachment of aversion—the creative
intimacy is reaffirmed, and appreciation, critical apprehension, insists on becoming as active as it can. Who
shall say, granted this, where it shall not begin and where
it shall consent to end? The painter who passes over his
old sunk canvas the wet sponge that shows him what
may still come out again makes his criticism essentially
active. When having seen, while his momentary glaze
remains, that the canvas *has* kept a few buried secrets,
he proceeds to repeat the process with due care and with
a bottle of varnish and a brush, he is "living back," as I

say, to the top of his bent, is taking up the old relation, so workable apparently, yet, and there is nothing logically to stay him from following it all the way. I have felt myself then, on looking over past productions, the painter making use again and again of the tentative wet sponge. The sunk surface has here and there, beyond doubt, refused to respond: the buried secrets, the intentions, are buried too deep to rise again, and were indeed, it would appear, not much worth the burying. Not so, however, when the moistened canvas does obscurely flush and when resort to the varnish bottle is thereby immediately indicated. The simplest figure for my revision of this present array of earlier, later, larger, smaller, canvases, is to say that I have achieved it by the very aid of the varnish bottle. It is true of them throughout that, in words I have had occasion to use in another connection (where too I had revised with a view to "possible amendment of form and enhancement of meaning"), I have "nowhere scrupled to rewrite a sentence or a passage on judging it susceptible of a better turn."

—PREFACE TO *Roderick Hudson*

THE RELIGION OF DOING

All of which amounts doubtless but to saying that as the whole conduct of life consists of things done, which do other things in their turn, just so our behavior and its fruits are essentially one and continuous and persistent and unquenchable, so the act has its way of abiding and showing and testifying, and so, among our innumerable acts, are no arbitrary, no senseless separations. The more we are capable of acting the less gropingly we plead such differences; whereby, with any capability, we recognize betimes that to "put" things is very exactly and responsibly and interminably to do them. Our expression of them, and the terms on which we understand that, belong as nearly to our conduct and our life as every other feature of our freedom; these things yield in fact some of its most exquisite material to the religion of doing. More than that, our literary deeds enjoy this marked advantage over many of our acts, that, though they go forth into the world and stray even in the desert, they don't to the same extent lose themselves; their attachment and reference to us, however strained, needn't necessarily lapse—while of the tie that binds us to *them* we may make almost anything we like. We are condemned, in other words, whether we will or no, to abandon and outlive, to forget and disown and hand over to desolation, many vital or social performances—if only because the traces, records, connections, the very memorials we would fain preserve, are practically impossible to rescue for that purpose from the general mixture. We give them up even when we wouldn't—it is not a question of choice. Not so on the other hand our really "done" things of this superior and more appreciable order —which leave us indeed all licence of disconnection and disavowal, but positively impose on us no such necessity. Our relation to them is essentially traceable, and in that fact abides, we feel, the incomparable luxury of the artist. It rests altogether with himself not to break with his values, not to "give away" his importances. Not to *be* disconnected, for the tradition of behavior, he has but to feel that he is not; by his lightest touch the whole chain of relation and responsibility is reconstituted. Thus if he is always doing he can scarce, by his own measure, ever have done. All of which means for him conduct with a vengeance, since it is conduct minutely and publicly attested. Our noted behavior at large may show for ragged, because it perpetually escapes our control; we have again and again to consent to its appearing in undress—that is in no state to brook criticism. But on all the ground to which the pretension of performance by a series of exquisite laws may apply there reigns one sovereign truth—

which decrees that, as art is nothing if not exemplary, care nothing if not active, finish nothing if not consistent, the proved error is the base apologetic deed, the helpless regret is the barren commentary, and "connections" are employable for finer purposes than mere gaping contrition.

—PREFACE TO *The Golden Bowl*

PART TWO

Novels and Novelists

*

*

THREE REVIEWS

OUR MUTUAL FRIEND

OUR MUTUAL FRIEND is, to our perception, the poorest of Mr. Dickens's works. And it is poor with the poverty not of momentary embarrassment, but of permanent exhaustion. It is wanting in inspiration. For the last ten years it has seemed to us that Mr. Dickens has been unmistakably forcing himself. "Bleak House" was forced; "Little Dorrit" was labored; the present work is dug out, as with a spade and pickaxe. Of course—to anticipate the usual argument—who but Dickens could have written it? Who, indeed? Who else would have established a lady in business in a novel on the admirably solid basis of her always putting on gloves and tying a handkerchief 'round her head in moments of grief, and of her habitually addressing her family with "Peace! Hold!" It is needless to say that Mrs. Reginald Wilfer is first and last the occasion of considerable true humor. When, after conducting her daughter to Mrs. Boffin's carriage, in sight of all the envious neighbors, she is described as enjoying her triumph during the next quarter of an hour by airing herself on the doorstep "in a kind of splendidly serene trance," we laugh with as uncritical a laugh as could be desired of us. We pay the same tribute to her assertions, as she narrates the glories of the society she enjoyed at her father's table, that she has known as many as three copper-plate engravers exchanging the most exquisite sallies and retorts there at one time. But when to these we have added a dozen more happy examples of the humor which was exhaled from every line of Mr. Dickens's earlier writings, we shall have closed the list of the merits of the work before us. To say that the conduct of the story, with all its complications, betrays a long-practiced hand, is to pay no compliment worthy the author. If this were, indeed, a compliment, we should be inclined to carry it further, and congratulate him on his success in what we should call the manufacture of fiction; for in so doing we should express a feeling that has attended us throughout the book. Seldom, we reflected, had we read a book so intensely *written*, so little seen, known, or felt.

In all Mr. Dickens's works the fantastic has been his great resource; and while his fancy was lively and vigorous it accomplished great things. But the fantastic, when the fancy is dead, is a very poor business. The movement of Mr. Dickens's fancy in Mrs. Wilfer and Mr. Boffin and Lady Tippins, and the Lammles and Miss Wren, and even in Eugene Wrayburn, is, to our mind, a movement lifeless, forced, mechanical. It is the letter of his old humor without the spirit. It is hardly too much to say that every character here put before us is a mere bundle of eccentricities, animated by no principle of nature whatever. In former days there reigned in Mr. Dickens's extravagances a comparative consistency; they were exaggerated statements of types that really existed. We had, perhaps, never known a Newman Noggs, nor a Pecksniff, nor a Micawber; but we had known persons of whom these figures were but the strictly logical consummation. But among the grotesque creatures who occupy the pages before us, there is not one whom we can refer to as an existing type. In all Mr. Dickens's stories, indeed, the reader has been called upon, and has willingly consented, to accept a certain number of figures or creatures of pure fancy, for this was the author's poetry. He was, moreover, always repaid for his concession by a peculiar beauty or power in these exceptional characters. But he is now expected to make the same concession with a very inadequate reward. What do we get in return for accepting Miss Jenny Wren as a possible person? This young lady is the type of a certain class of characters of which Mr. Dickens has made a specialty, and with which he has been accustomed to draw alternate smiles and tears, according as he pressed one spring or another. But this is very cheap merriment and very cheap pathos. Miss Jenny Wren is a poor little dwarf, afflicted, as she constantly reiterates, with a "bad back" and "queer legs," who makes doll's dresses, and is forever pricking at those with whom she converses, in the air, with her needle, and assuring them that she knows their "tricks and their manners." Like all Mr. Dickens's pathetic characters, she is a little monster; she is deformed, unhealthy, unnatural; she belongs to the troop of hunchbacks, imbeciles, and precocious children who have carried on the sentimental business in all Mr. Dickens's novels; the little Nells, the Smikes, the Paul Dombeys.

Mr. Dickens goes as far out of the way for his wicked people as he does for his good ones. Rogue Riderhood, indeed, in the present story, is villainous with a sufficiently natural villainy; he belongs to that quarter of society in which the author is most at his ease. But was there ever such wickedness as that of the Lammles and Mr. Fledgeby? Not that people have not been as mischievous as they; but was any one ever mischievous in that singular fashion? Did a couple of elegant swindlers ever take such particular pains to be aggressively inhuman?—for we can find no other word for the gratuitous distortions to which they are subjected. The word *humanity* strikes us as strangely discordant, in the midst of these pages; for, let us boldly declare it, there is no humanity here. Humanity is nearer home than the Boffins, and the Lammles, and the Wilfers, and the Veneerings. It is in what men have in common with each other, and not in what they have in distinction. The people just named have nothing in common with each other, except the fact that they have nothing in common with mankind at large. What a world were this world if the world of "Our Mutual Friend" were an honest reflection of it! But a community of eccentrics is impossible. Rules alone are consistent with each other; exceptions are inconsistent. Society is maintained by natural sense and natural feeling. We cannot conceive a society in which these principles are not in some manner represented. Where in these pages are the depositaries of that intelligence without which the movement of life would cease? Who represents nature? Accepting half of Mr. Dickens's persons as intentionally grotesque, where are those exemplars of sound humanity who should afford us the proper measure of their companion's variations? We ought not, in justice to the author, to seek them among his weaker—that is, his mere conventional—characters; in John Harmon, Lizzie Hexam, or Mortimer Lightwood; but we assuredly cannot find them among his stronger—that is, his artificial creations. Suppose we take Eugene Wrayburn and Bradley Headstone. They occupy a half-way position between the habitual probable of nature and the habitual impossible of Mr. Dickens. A large portion of the story rests upon the enmity borne by Headstone to Wrayburn, both being in love with the same woman. Wrayburn is a gentleman, and Headstone is one of the people. Wrayburn is well-bred, careless, elegant, sceptical, and idle: Headstone is a high-tempered, hard-working, ambitious young schoolmaster. There lay in the opposition of these two characters a very good story. But the prime requisite was that they should *be* characters: Mr. Dickens, according to his usual plan, has made them simply figures, and between them the story that was to be, the story that should have been, has evaporated. Wrayburn lounges about with his hands in his pockets, smoking a cigar, and talking nonsense. Headstone strides about, clenching his fists and biting his lips and grasping his stick. There is one scene in which Wrayburn chaffs the schoolmaster with easy insolence, while the latter writhes impotently under his well-bred sarcasm. This scene is very clever, but it is very insufficient. If the majority of readers were not so very timid in the use of words we should call it vulgar. By this we do not mean to indicate the conventional impropriety of two gentlemen exchanging lively personalities;

we mean to emphasize the essentially small character of these personalities. In other words, the moment, dramatically, is great, while the author's conception is weak. The friction of two *men*, of two characters, of two passions, produces stronger sparks than Wrayburn's boyish repartees and Headstone's melodramatic commonplaces. Such scenes as this are useful in fixing the limits of Mr. Dickens's insight. Insight is, perhaps, too strong a word; for we are convinced that it is one of the chief conditions of his genius not to see beneath the surface of things. If we might hazard a definition of his literary character, we should, accordingly, call him the greatest of superficial novelists. We are aware that this definition confines him to an inferior rank in the department of letters which he adorns; but we accept this consequence of our proposition. It were, in our opinion, an offense against humanity to place Mr. Dickens among the greatest novelists. For, to repeat what we have already intimated, he has created nothing but figures. He has added nothing to our understanding of human character. He is master of but two alternatives: he reconciles us to what is commonplace, and he reconciles us to what is odd. The value of the former service is questionable; and the manner in which Mr. Dickens performs it sometimes conveys a certain impression of charlatanism. The value of the latter service is incontestable, and here Mr. Dickens is an honest, an admirable artist. But what is the condition of the truly great novelist? For him there are no alternatives, for him there are no oddities, for him there is nothing outside of humanity. He cannot shirk it; it imposes itself upon him. For him alone, therefore, there is a true and a false; for him alone it is possible to be right, because it is possible to be wrong. Mr. Dickens is a great observer and a great humorist, but he is nothing of a philosopher. Some people may hereupon say, so much the better; we say, so much the worse. For a novelist very soon has need of a little philosophy. In treating of Micawber, and Boffin, and Pickwick, *et hoc genus omne*, he can, indeed, dispense with it, for this—we say it with all deference—is not serious writing. But when he comes to tell the story of a passion, a story like that of Headstone and Wrayburn, he becomes a moralist as well as an artist. He must know *man* as well as *men*, and to know man is to be a philosopher. The writer who knows men alone, if he have Mr. Dickens's humor and fancy, will give us figures and pictures for which we cannot be too grateful, for he will enlarge our knowledge of the world. But when he introduces men and women whose interest is preconceived to lie not in the poverty, the weakness, the drollery of their natures, but in their complete and unconscious subjection to ordinary and healthy human emotions, all his humor, all his fancy, will avail him nothing if, out of the fullness of his sympathy, he is unable to prosecute those generalizations in which alone consists the real greatness of a work of art. This may sound like very subtle talk about a very simple matter; it is rather very simple talk about a very subtle matter. A story based upon those elementary passions in which alone we seek the true and final manifestation of character must be told in a spirit of intellectual superiority to those passions. That is, the author must understand what he is talking about. The perusal of a story so told is one of the most elevating experiences within the reach of the human mind. The perusal of a story which is not so told is infinitely depressing and unprofitable.

GEORGE ELIOT'S "MIDDLEMARCH"

MIDDLEMARCH is at once one of the strongest and one of the weakest of English novels. Its predecessors as they appeared might have been described in the same terms; *Romola* is especially a rare masterpiece, but the least *entraînant* of masterpieces. *Romola* sins by excess of analysis; there is too much description and too little drama; too much reflection (all certainly of a highly imaginative sort) and too little creation. Movement lingers in the story, and with it attention stands still in the reader. The error in *Middlemarch* is not precisely of a similar kind, but it is equally detrimental to the total aspect of the work. We can well remember how keenly we wondered, while its earlier chapters unfolded themselves, what turn in the way of form the story would take—that of an organized, molded, balanced composition, gratifying the reader with a sense of design and construction, or a mere chain of episodes, broken into accidental lengths and unconscious of the influence of a plan. We expected the actual result, but for the sake of English imaginative literature which, in this line is rarely in need of examples, we hoped for the other. If it had come we should have had the pleasure of reading, what certainly would have seemed to us in the immediate glow of attention, the first of English novels. But that pleasure has still to hover between prospect and retrospect. *Middlemarch* is a treasure-house of detail, but it is an indifferent whole.

Our objection may seem shallow and pedantic, and may even be represented as a complaint that we have had the less given us rather than the more. Certainly the greatest minds have the defects of their qualities, and as George Eliot's mind is preëminently contemplative and analytic, nothing is more natural than that her manner should be discursive and expansive. "Concentration" would doubtless have deprived us of many of the best things in the book—of Peter Featherstone's grotesquely expectant legatees, of Lydgate's medical rivals, and of Mary Garth's delightful family. The author's purpose was to be a generous rural historian, and this very redundancy of touch, born of abundant reminiscence, is one of the greatest charms of her work. It is as if her memory was crowded with antique figures, to whom for very tenderness she must grant an appearance. Her novel is a picture—vast, swarming, deep-colored, crowded with episodes, with vivid images, with lurking master-strokes, with brilliant

passages of expression; and as such we may freely accept
it and enjoy it. It is not compact, doubtless; but when was
a panorama compact? And yet, nominally, *Middlemarch*
has a definite subject—the subject indicated in the eloquent preface. An ardent young girl was to have been the
central figure, a young girl framed for a larger moral
life than circumstance often affords, yearning for a
motive for sustained spiritual effort and only wasting her
ardor and soiling her wings against the meanness of
opportunity. The author, in other words, proposed to
depict the career of an obscure St. Theresa. Her success
has been great, in spite of serious drawbacks. Dorothea
Brooke is a genuine creation, and a most remarkable one
when we consider the delicate material in which she is
wrought. George Eliot's men are generally so much better
than the usual trousered offspring of the female fancy,
that their merits have perhaps overshadowed those of her
women. Yet her heroines have always been of an exquisite
quality, and Dorothea is only that perfect flower of conception of which her predecessors were the less unfolded
blossoms. An indefinable moral elevation is the sign of
these admirable creatures; and of the representation of
this quality in its superior degrees the author seems to
have in English fiction a monopoly. To render the expression of a soul requires a cunning hand; but we seem
to look straight into the unfathomable eyes of the beautiful spirit of Dorothea Brooke. She exhales a sort of aroma
of spiritual sweetness, and we believe in her as in a
woman we might providentially meet some fine day when
we should find ourselves doubting of the immortality of
the soul. By what unerring mechanism this effect is
produced—whether by fine strokes or broad ones, by
description or by narration, we can hardly say; it is
certainly the great achievement of the book. Dorothea's
career is, however, but an episode, and though doubtless
in intention, not distinctly enough in fact, the central
one. The history of Lydgate's *ménage*, which shares
honors with it, seems rather to the reader to carry off the

lion's share. This is certainly a very interesting story, but
on the whole it yields in dignity to the record of
Dorothea's unresonant woes. The "love-problem," as the
author calls it, of Mary Garth, is placed on a rather higher
level than the reader willingly grants it. To the end we
care less about Fred Vincy than appears to be expected of
us. In so far as the writer's design has been to reproduce
the total sum of life in an English village forty years ago,
this commonplace young gentleman, with his somewhat
meager tribulations and his rather neutral egotism, has his
proper place in the picture; but the author narrates his
fortunes with a fullness of detail which the reader often
finds irritating. The reader indeed is sometimes tempted
to complain of a tendency which we are at loss exactly
to express—a tendency to make light of the serious elements of the story and to sacrifice them to the more
trivial ones. Is it an unconscious instinct or is it a deliberate plan? With its abundant and massive ingredients
Middlemarch ought somehow to have depicted a weightier
drama. Dorothea was altogether too superb a heroine to
be wasted; yet she plays a narrower part than the imagination of the reader demands. She is of more consequence
than the action of which she is the nominal center. She
marries enthusiastically a man whom she fancies a great
thinker, and who turns out to be but an arid pedant.
Here, indeed, is a disappointment with much of the
dignity of tragedy; but the situation seems to us never to
expand to its full capacity. It is analyzed with extraordinary penetration, but one may say of it, as of most of the
situations in the book, that it is treated with too much
refinement and too little breadth. It revolves too constantly on the same pivot; it abounds in fine shades, but
it lacks, we think, the great dramatic *chiaroscuro*. Mr.
Casaubon, Dorothea's husband (of whom more anon)
embittered, on his side, by matrimonial disappointment,
takes refuge in vain jealousy of his wife's relations with
an interesting young cousin of his own and registers this
sentiment in a codicil to his will, making the forfeiture

of his property the penalty of his widow's marriage with this gentleman. Mr. Casaubon's death befalls about the middle of the story, and from this point to the close our interest in Dorothea is restricted to the question, will she or will [she] not marry Will Ladislaw? The question is relatively trivial and the implied struggle slightly factitious. The author has depicted the struggle with a sort of elaborate solemnity which in the interviews related in the two last books tends to become almost ludicrously excessive.

The dramatic current stagnates; it runs between hero and heroine almost a game of hair-splitting. Our dissatisfaction here is provoked in a great measure by the insubstantial character of the hero. The figure of Will Ladislaw is a beautiful attempt, with many finely completed points; but on the whole it seems to us a failure. It is the only eminent failure in the book, and its defects are therefore the more striking. It lacks sharpness of outline and depth of color; we have not found ourselves believing in Ladislaw as we believe in Dorothea, in Mary Garth, in Rosamond, in Lydgate, in Mr. Brooke and Mr. Casaubon. He is meant, indeed, to be a light creature (with a large capacity for gravity, for he finally gets into Parliament), and a light creature certainly should not be heavily drawn. The author, who is evidently very fond of him, has found for him here and there some charming and eloquent touches; but in spite of these he remains vague and impalpable to the end. He is, we may say, the one figure which a masculine intellect of the same power as George Eliot's would not have conceived with the same complacency; he is, in short, roughly speaking, a woman's man. It strikes us as an oddity in the author's scheme that she should have chosen just this figure of Ladislaw as the creature in whom Dorothea was to find her spiritual compensations. He is really, after all, not the ideal foil to Mr. Casaubon which her soul must have imperiously demanded, and if the author of the "Key to all Mythologies" sinned by lack of order, Ladislaw too has

not the concentrated fervor essential in the man chosen
by so nobly strenuous a heroine. The impression once
given that he is a *dilettante* is never properly removed,
and there is slender poetic justice in Dorothea's marrying
a *dilettante*. We are doubtless less content with Ladislaw,
on account of the noble, almost sculptural, relief of the
neighboring figure of Lydgate, the real hero of the story.
It is an illustration of the generous scale of the author's
picture and of the conscious power of her imagination
that she has given us a hero and heroine of broadly distinct interests—erected, as it were, two suns in her firma-
ment, each with its independent solar system. Lydgate
is so richly successful a figure that we have regretted
strongly at moments, for immediate interests' sake, that
the current of his fortunes should not mingle more freely
with the occasionally thin-flowing stream of Dorothea's.
Toward the close, these two fine characters are brought
into momentary contact so effectively as to suggest a
wealth of dramatic possibility between them; but if this
train had been followed we should have lost Rosamond
Vincy—a rare psychological study. Lydgate is a really
complete portrait of a *man*, which seems to us high praise.
It is striking evidence of the altogether superior quality
of George Eliot's imagination that, though elaborately
represented, Lydgate should be treated so little from what
we may roughly (and we trust without offense) call the
sexual point of view. Perception charged with feeling has
constantly guided the author's hand, and yet her strokes
remain as firm, her curves as free, her whole manner as
serenely impersonal, as if, on a small scale, she were
emulating the creative wisdom itself. Several English
romances—notably Fielding, Thackeray, and Charles
Reade—have won great praise for their figures of women:
but they owe it, in reversed conditions, to a meaner sort
of art, it seems to us, than George Eliot has used in the
case of Lydgate; to an indefinable appeal to masculine
prejudice—to a sort of titillation of the masculine sense
of difference. George Eliot's manner is more philosophic

—more broadly intelligent, and yet her result is as concrete or, if you please, as picturesque. We have no space to dwell on Lydgate's character; we can but repeat that he is a vividly consistent, manly figure—powerful, ambitious, sagacious, with the maximum rather than the minimum of egotism, strenuous, generous, fallible, and altogether human. A work of the liberal scope of *Middlemarch* contains a multitude of artistic intentions, some of the finest of which become clear only in the meditative after-taste of perusal. This is the case with the balanced contrast between the two histories of Lydgate and Dorothea. Each is a tale of matrimonial infelicity, but the conditions in each are so different and the circumstances so broadly opposed that the mind passes from one to the other with that supreme sense of the vastness and variety of human life, under aspects apparently similar, which it belongs only to the greatest novels to produce. The most perfectly successful passages in the book are perhaps those painful fireside scenes between Lydgate and his miserable little wife. The author's rare psychological penetration is lavished upon this veritably mulish domestic flower. There is nothing more powerfully real than these scenes in all English fiction, and nothing certainly more *intelligent*. Their impressiveness and (as regards Lydgate) their pathos, is deepened by the constanly low key in which they are pitched. It is a tragedy based on unpaid butchers' bills, and the urgent need for small economies. The author has desired to be strictly real and to adhere to the facts of the common lot, and she has given us a powerful version of that typical human drama, the struggles of an ambitious soul with sordid disappointments and vulgar embarrassments. As to her catastrophe we hesitate to pronounce (for Lydgate's ultimate assent to his wife's worldly program is nothing less than a catastrophe). We almost believe that some terrific explosion would have been more probable than his twenty years of smothered aspiration. Rosamond deserves almost to rank with Tito in *Romola* as a study of a gracefully vicious, or at least of a practi-

cally baleful nature. There is one point, however, of which
we question the consistency. The author insists on her
instincts of coquetry, which seems to us a discordant note.
They would have made her better or worse—more generous or more reckless; in either case more manageable.
As it is, Rosamond represents, in a measure, the fatality of
British decorum.

In reading, we have marked innumerable passages for
quotation and comment; but we lack space and the work
is so ample that half a dozen extracts would be an in-
effective illustration. There would be a great deal to say
on the broad array of secondary figures, Mr. Casaubon,
Mr. Brooke, Mr. Bulstrode, Mr. Farebrother, Caleb Garth,
Mrs. Cadwallader, Celia Brooke. Mr. Casauban is an excellent invention; as a dusky *repoussoir* to the luminous
figure of his wife he could not have been better imagined.
There is indeed something very noble in the way in
which the author has apprehended his character. To
depict hollow pretentiousness and mouldy egotism with
so little of narrow sarcasm and so much of philosophic
sympathy, is to be a rare moralist as well as a rare storyteller. The whole portrait of Mr. Casaubon has an admirably sustained grayness of tone in which the shadows
are never carried to the vulgar black of coarser artists.
Every stroke contributes to the unwholesome, helplessly
sinister expression. Here and there perhaps (as in his
habitual diction), there is a hint of exaggeration; but we
confess we like fancy to be fanciful. Mr. Brooke and
Mr. Garth are in their different lines supremely genial
creations; they are drawn with the touch of a Dickens
chastened and intellectualized. Mrs. Cadwallader is, in
another walk of life, a match for Mrs. Poyser, and Celia
Brooke is as pretty a fool as any of Miss Austen's. Mr.
Farebrother and his delightful "womankind" belong to
a large group of figures begotten of the superabundance
of the author's creative instinct. At times they seem to
encumber the stage and to produce a rather ponderous
mass of dialogue; but they add to the reader's impression

of having walked in the Middlemarch lanes and listened to the Middlemarch accent. To but one of these accessory episodes—that of Mr. Bulstrode, with its multiplex ramifications—do we take exception. It has a slightly artificial cast, a melodramatic tinge, unfriendly to the richly natural coloring of the whole. Bulstrode himself—with the history of whose troubled conscience the author has taken great pains—is, to our sense, too diffusely treated; he never grasps the reader's attention. But the touch of genius is never idle or vain. The obscure figure of Bulstrode's comely wife emerges at the needful moment, under a few light strokes, into the happiest reality.

All these people, solid and vivid in their varying degrees, are members of a deeply human little world, the full reflection of whose antique image is the great merit of these volumes. How bravely rounded a little world the author has made it—with how dense an atmosphere of interests and passions and loves and enmities and strivings and failings, and how motley a group of great folk and small, all after their kind, she has filled it, the reader must learn for himself. No writer seems to us to have drawn from a richer stock of those long-cherished memories which one's later philosophy makes doubly tender. There are few figures in the book which do not seem to have grown mellow in the author's mind. English readers may fancy they enjoy the "atmosphere" of *Middlemarch;* but we maintain that to relish its inner essence we must —for reasons too numerous to detail—be an American. The author has commissioned herself to be real, her native tendency being that of an idealist, and the intellectual result is a very fertilizing mixture. The constant presence of thought, of generalizing instinct, of *brain*, in a word, behind her observation, gives the latter its great value and her whole manner its high superiority. It denotes a mind in which imagination is illumined by faculties rarely found in fellowship with it. In this respect—in that broad reach of vision which would make the worthy historian of solemn fact as well as wanton fiction—George Eliot seems

to us among English romancers to stand alone. Fielding
approaches her, but to our mind, she surpasses Fielding.
Fielding was didactic—the author of *Middlemarch* is
really philosophic. These great qualities imply corresponding perils. The first is the loss of simplicity. George
Eliot lost hers some time since; it lies buried (in a splendid
mausoleum) in *Romola*. Many of the discursive portions
of *Middlemarch* are, as we may say, too clever by half.
The author wishes to say too many things, and to say
them too well; to recommend herself to a scientific audi-
ence. Her style, rich and flexible as it is, is apt to betray
her on these transcendental flights; we find, in our copy,
a dozen passages marked "obscure." *Silas Marner* was a
delightful tinge of Goldsmith—we may almost call it:
Middlemarch is too often an echo of Messrs. Darwin and
Huxley. In spite of these faults—which it seems graceless
to indicate with this crude rapidity—it remains a very
splendid performance. It sets a limit, we think, to the
development of the old-fashioned English novel. Its dif-
fuseness, on which we have touched, makes it too copious
a dose of pure fiction. If we write novels so, how shall
we write History? But it is nevertheless a contribution of
the first importance to the rich imaginative department of
our literature.

NANA

M. Zola's new novel has been immensely talked about
for the last six months; but we may doubt whether, now
that we are in complete possession of it, its fame will
further increase. It is a difficult book to read; we have to
push our way through it very much as we did through
L'Assommoir, with the difference that in *L'Assommoir*
our perseverance, our patience, were constantly rewarded,
and that in *Nana*, these qualities have to content themselves with the usual recompense of virtue, the simple
sense of duty accomplished. I do not mean, indeed, by

this allusion to duty that there is any moral obligation to read *Nana;* I simply mean that such an exertion may have been felt to be due to M. Zola by those who have been interested in his general attempt. His general attempt is highly interesting, and *Nana* is the latest illustration of it. It is far from being the most successful one; the obstacles to the reader's enjoyment are numerous and constant. It is true that, if we rightly understand him, enjoyment forms no part of the emotion to which M. Zola appeals; in the eyes of "naturalism" enjoyment is a frivolous, a superficial, a contemptible sentiment. It is difficult, however, to express conveniently by any other term the reader's measure of the entertainment afforded by a work of art. If we talk of interest, instead of enjoyment, the thing does not better our case—as it certainly does not better M. Zola's. The obstacles to interest in *Nana* constitute a formidable body, and the most comprehensive way to express them is to say that the work is inconceivably and inordinately dull. M. Zola (if we again understand him) will probably say that it is a privilege, or even a duty, of naturalism to be dull, and to a certain extent this is doubtless a very lawful plea. It is not an absolutely fatal defect for a novel not to be amusing, as we may see by the example of several important works. *Wilhelm Meister* is not a sprightly composition, and yet *Wilhelm Meister* stands in the front rank of novels. *Romola* is a very easy book to lay down, and yet *Romola* is full of beauty and truth. *Clarissa Harlowe* discourages the most robust persistence, and yet, paradoxical as it seems, *Clarissa Harlowe* is deeply interesting. It is obvious, therefore, that there is something to be said for dullness; and this something is perhaps, primarily, that there is dullness and dullness. That of which *Nana* is so truly a specimen, is of a peculiarly unredeemed and unleavened quality; it lacks that human savor, that finer meaning which carries it off in the productions I just mentioned. What *Nana* means it will take a very ingenious apologist to set forth. I speak, of course, of the impression it produces on English readers; into the deep

mystery of the French taste in such matters it would be
presumptuous for one of these to attempt to penetrate.
The other element that stops the English reader's way is
that monstrous uncleanness to which—to the credit of human nature in whatever degree it may seem desirable to
determine—it is probably not unjust to attribute a part of
the facility with which the volume before us has reached,
on the day of its being offered for sale by retail, a thirty-
ninth edition. M. Zola's uncleanness is not a thing to linger
upon, but it is a thing to speak of, for it strikes us as an
extremely curious phenomenon. In this respect *Nana* has
little to envy its predecessors. The book is, perhaps
not pervaded by that ferociously bad smell which blows
through *L'Assommoir* like an emanation from an open
drain and makes the perusal of the history of Gervaise
and Coupeau very much such an ordeal as a crossing of
the Channel in a November gale; but in these matters
comparisons are as difficult as they are unprofitable, and
Nana is, in all conscience, untidy enough. To say the book
is indecent, is to make use of a term which (always, if
we understand him), M. Zola holds to mean nothing and
to prove nothing. Decency and indecency, morality and
immorality, beauty and ugliness, are conceptions with
which "naturalism" has nothing to do; in M. Zola's system
these distinctions are void, these allusions are idle. The
only business of naturalism is to be—natural, and therefore, instead of saying of *Nana* that it contains a great
deal of filth, we should simply say of it that it contains a
great deal of nature. Once upon a time a rather pretentious person, whose moral tone had been corrupted by
evil communications, and who lived among a set of people
equally pretentious, but regrettably low-minded, being in
conversation with another person, a lady of great robust-
ness of judgment and directness of utterance, made use
constantly, in a somewhat cynical and pessimistic sense,
of the expression, "the world—the world." At last the
distinguished listener could bear it no longer, and abruptly
made reply: "My poor lady, do you call that corner of

a pig-sty in which you happen to live, *the world?*" Some
such answer as this we are moved to make to M. Zola's
naturalism. Does he call that vision of things of which
Nana is a representation, *nature?* The mighty mother, in
her blooming richness, seems to blush from brow to chin
at the insult! On what authority does M. Zola represent
nature to us as a combination of the cesspool and the
house of prostitution? On what authority does he represent foulness rather than fairness as the sign that we are
to know her by? On the authority of his predilections
alone; and this is his great trouble and the weak point of
his incontestably remarkable talent. This is the point that,
as we said just now, makes the singular foulness of his
imagination worth touching upon, and which, we should
suppose, will do much towards preserving his works for
the curious contemplation of the psychologist and the
historian of literature. Never was such foulness so spon-
taneous and so complete, and never was it united with
qualities so superior to itself and intrinsically so respectable. M. Zola is an artist, and this is supposed to be a
safeguard; and, indeed, never surely was any other artist
so dirty as M. Zola! Other performers may have been so,
but they were not artists; other such exhibitions may
have taken place, but they have not taken place between
the covers of a book—and especially of a book containing
so much of vigorous and estimable effort. We have no
space to devote to a general consideration of M. Zola's
theory of the business of a novelist, or to the question of
naturalism at large—much further than to say that the
system on which the series of *Les Rougons-Macquart* has
been written, contains, to our sense, a great deal of very
solid ground. M. Zola's attempt is an extremely fine one;
it deserves a great deal of respect and deference, and
though his theory is constantly at odds with itself, we
could, at a pinch, go a long way with it without quarreling. What we quarrel with is his application of it—is
the fact that he presents us with his decoction of "nature" in a vessel unfit for the purpose, a receptacle lamen-

tably, fatally in need of scouring (though no scouring, apparently, would be really effective), and in which no article intended for intellectual consumption should ever be served up. Reality is the object of M. Zola's efforts, and it is because we agree with him in appreciating it highly that we protest against its being discredited. In a time when literary taste has turned, to a regrettable degree, to the vulgar and the insipid, it is of high importance that realism should not be compromised. Nothing tends more to compromise it than to represent it as necessarily allied to the impure. That the pure and the impure are for M. Zola, as conditions of taste, vain words, and exploded ideas, only proves that his advocacy does more to injure an excellent cause than to serve it. It takes a very good cause to carry a *Nana* on its back, and if realism breaks down, and the conventional comes in again with a rush, we may know the reason why. The real has not a single shade more affinity with an unclean vessel than with a clean one, and M. Zola's system, carried to its utmost expression, can dispense as little with taste and tact as the floweriest mannerism of a less analytic age. Go as far as we will, so long as we abide in literature, the thing remains always a question of taste, and we can never leave taste behind without leaving behind, by the same stroke, the very grounds on which we appeal, the whole human side of the business. Taste, in its intellectual applications, is the most human faculty we possess, and as the novel may be said to be the most human form of art, it is a poor speculation to put the two things out of conceit of each other. Calling it naturalism will never make it profitable. It is perfectly easy to agree with M. Zola, who has taken his stand with more emphasis than is necessary; for the matter reduces itself to a question of application. It is impossible to see why the question of application is less urgent in naturalism than at any other point of the scale, or why, if naturalism is, as M. Zola claims, a method of observation, it can be followed without delicacy or tact. There are all sorts of things to be said about it; it costs us no effort whatever to admit in the briefest terms that it is an admirable invention, and full of promise; but we stand aghast at the want of tact is has taken to make so unreadable a book as *Nana*.

To us English readers, I venture to think, the subject is very interesting, because it raises questions which no one apparently has the energy or the good faith to raise among ourselves. (It is of distinctly serious readers only that I speak, and *Nana* is to be recommended exclusively to such as have a very robust appetite for a moral.) A novelist with a system, a passionate conviction, a great plan—incontestable attributes of M. Zola—is not now to be easily found in England or the United States, where the story-teller's art is almost exclusively feminine, is mainly in the hands of timid (even when very accomplished) women, whose acquaintance with life is severely restricted, and who are not conspicuous for general views. The novel, moreover, among ourselves, is almost always addressed to young unmarried ladies, or at least always assumes them to be a large part of the novelist's public. This fact, to a French storyteller, appears, of course, a damnable restriction, and M. Zola would probably decline to take *au sérieux* any work produced under such unnatural conditions. Half of life is a sealed book to young unmarried ladies, and how can a novel be worth anything that deals only with half of life? How can a portrait be painted (in any way to be recognizable) of half a face? It is not in one eye, but in the two eyes together that the expression resides, and it is the combination of features that constitutes the human identity. These objections are perfectly valid, and it may be said that our English system is a good thing for virgins and boys, and a bad thing for the novel itself, when the novel is regarded as something more than a simple *jeu d'esprit*, and considered as a composition that treats of life at large and helps us to *know*. But under these unnatural conditions and insufferable restrictions a variety of admirable works have been produced; Thackeray, Dickens, George Eliot, have all had an eye

to the innocent classes. The fact is anomalous, and the
advocates of naturalism must make the best of it. In fact,
I believe they have little relish for the writers I have mentioned. They find that something or other is grievously
wanting in their productions—as it most assuredly is!
They complain that such writers are not serious. They are
not so, certainly, as M. Zola is so; but there are many
different ways of being serious. That of the author of
L'Assommoir, of *La Conquête de Plassans*, of *La Faute
de L'Abbé Mouret* may, as I say, with all its merits and
defects taken together, suggest a great many things to
English readers. They must admire the largeness of his
attempt and the richness of his intention. They must
admire, very often, the brilliancy of his execution. *L'Assommoir*, in spite of its fetid atmosphere, is full of magnificent passages and episodes, and the sustained power of
the whole thing, the art of carrying a weight, is extraordinary. What will strike the English reader of M. Zola at
large, however, and what will strike the English reader
of *Nana*, if he have stoutness of stomach enough to advance in the book, is the extraordinary absence of humor,
the dryness, the solemnity, the air of tension and effort. M.
Zola disapproves greatly of wit; he thinks it is an im-
pertinence in a novel, and he would probably disapprove
of humor if he *knew* what it is. There is no indication
in all his works that he has a suspicion of this; and what
tricks the absence of a sense of it plays him! What
a mess it has made of this admirable *Nana*! The presence
of it, even in a limited degree, would have operated, to
some extent, as a disinfectant, and if M. Zola had had a
more genial fancy he would also have had a cleaner one.
Is it not also owing to the absence of a sense of humor
that this last and most violent expression of the realistic
faith is extraordinarily wanting in reality? Anything less
illusory than the pictures, the people, the indecencies of
Nana, could not well be imagined. The falling-off from
L'Assommoir in this respect can hardly be exaggerated.
The human note is completely absent, the perception of

character, of the way that people feel and think and act, is helplessly, hopelessly at fault; so that it becomes almost grotesque at last to see the writer trying to drive before him a herd of figures that never for an instant stand on their legs. This is what saves us in England, in spite of our artistic levity and the presence of the young ladies—this fact that we are by disposition better psychologists, that we have, as a general thing, a deeper, more delicate perception of the play of character and the state of the soul. This is what often gives an interest to works conceived on a much narrower program than those of M. Zola—makes them more touching and more real, although the apparatus and the machinery of reality may, superficially, appear to be wanting. French novelists are at bottom, with all their extra freedom, a good deal more conventional than our own; and *Nana*, with the prodigious freedom that her author has taken, never, to my sense, leaves for a moment the region of the conventional. The figure of the brutal *fille*, without a conscience or a soul, with nothing but devouring appetites and impudences, has become the stalest of the stock properties of French fiction, and M. Zola's treatment has here imparted to her no touch of superior verity. He is welcome to draw as many figures of the same type as he finds necessary, if he will only make them human; this is as good a way of making a contribution to our knowledge of ourselves as another. It is not his choice of subject that has shocked us; it is the melancholy dryness of his execution, which gives us all the bad taste of a disagreeable dish and none of the nourishment.

*

THE LESSON OF BALZAC[1]

I HAVE found it necessary, at the eleventh hour, to sacrifice
to the terrible question of time a very beautiful and
majestic approach that I had prepared to the subject on
which I have the honor of addressing you. I recognize it
as impossible to ask you to linger with me on that pil-
lared portico—paved with marble, I beg you to believe,
and overtwined with charming flowers. I must invite you
to pass straight into the house and bear with me there as
if I had already succeeded in beginning to interest you.
Let us assume, therefore, that we have exchanged some
ideas on the question of the beneficent play of criticism,
and that I have even ingeniously struck it off that criticism
is the only gate of appreciation, just as appreciation is,
in regard to a work of art, the only gate of enjoyment.
You may wonder perhaps why I speak as if we were possessed, in our conditions, of a literary court of appeal, and
I hasten to say that the appeal I think of is precisely from
the general judgment, and not to it; is to the particular
judgment altogether: by which I mean to that quantity

[1] A lecture delivered for the first time before the Contemporary Club of Philadelphia, January 12, 1905, and repeated on various occasions elsewhere. Several passages omitted
in delivery—one of considerable length—have been restored

of opinion, very small at all times, but at all times infinitely precious, that is capable of giving some intelligible account of itself. Where, among us, at this time of day, this element of the lucid report of impressions received, of estimates formed, of intentions understood, of values attached, is exactly to be looked for—that is another branch of the question, to which I am afraid I should have to devote quite another discourse. I do not propose for a moment to invite you to blink the fact that our huge Angle-Saxon array of producers and readers—and especially our vast cis-Atlantic multitude—presents production uncontrolled, production untouched by criticism, unguided, unlighted, uninstructed, unashamed, on a scale that is really a new thing in the world. It is all the complete reversal of any proportion, between the elements, that was ever seen before. It is the biggest flock straying without shepherds, making its music without a sight of the classic crook, beribboned or other, without a sound of the sheepdog's bark—wholesome note, once in a way—that has ever found room for pasture. The very opposite has happened from what might have been expected to happen. The shepherds have diminished as the flock has increased—quite as if number and quantity had got beyond them, or even as if their charge had turned, by some uncanny process, to a pack of ravening wolves. Let us none the less assume that we may still find two or three of the fraternity hiding under a hedge or astride of some upper limb of a tree; let us even assume that if we set rightly, if we set tactfully about it, we may establish again some friendly connection with them.

Putting, on this basis, then, all our heads together, we may become aware of an intelligent gratitude, deep within our breasts, to any author who consents to fit with a certain fullness of presence and squareness of solidity into one of the conscious categories of our attention. There are literary figures in plenty that scarce fill out even the smaller of these critical receptacles; there are others, on the contrary, that almost strain the larger to breaking. It

is to these latter that interested contemplation most
fondly attaches itself—to that degree, really, that there
seems, on any good occasion, more and more about them
to be said. They have the great sign that their immediate
presence causes our ideas, whether about life in general or
about the art they have exemplified in particular, to revive
and breathe again, to multiply, more or less to swarm. I
must profess that no Novelist—since we are by common
consent confining our attention to that great Company—
no Novelist, to my sense, so rewards consideration as he
or she (and I emphasize the liberality of my "she") who
offers the critical spirit this opportunity for a certain intensity of educative practice. The lesson of Balzac, whom
we thus march straight up to, is that he offers it as no
other members of the company can pretend to do.

For there are members of the company who scarce
produce the effect in question at all. Take, to begin with,
close at Balzac's side, his illustrious contemporary Madame
George Sand, so suggestive, so affirmative, so instructive,
as a dealer with life, as an eloquent exponent of her own,
as what we call today a Personality equipped and armed,
but of an artistic complexion so comparatively smooth
and simple, so happily harmonious, that her work, taken
together, presents about as few pegs for analysis to hang
upon as if it were a large, polished, gilded Easter egg,
the pride of a sweet shop if not the treasure of a museum.
Let me add, further—so far as it is a question of the
nameable sisterhood too—that Jane Austen, with all her
light felicity, leaves us hardly more curious of her process,
or of the experience in her that fed it, than the brown
thrush who tells his story from the garden bough; and
this, I freely confess, in spite of her being one of those
of the shelved and safe, for all time, of whom I should
have liked to begin by talking; one of those in whose
favor discrimination has long since practically operated.
She is in fact a signal instance of the way it does, with all
its embarrassments, at last infallibly operate. A sharp short
cut, one of the sharpest and shortest achieved, in this

field, by the general judgment, came out, betimes, straight at her feet. Practically overlooked for thirty or forty years after her death, she perhaps really stands there for us as the prettiest possible example of that rectification of estimate, brought about by some slow clearance of stupidity, the half-century or so is capable of working round to. This tide has risen high on the opposite shore, the shore of appreciation—risen rather higher, I think, than the high-water mark, the highest, of her intrinsic merit and interest; though I grant indeed—as a point to be made—that we are dealing here in some degree with the tides so freely driven up, beyond their mere logical reach, by the stiff breeze of the commercial, in other words of the special bookselling spirit; an eager, active, interfering force which has a great many confusions of apparent value, a great many wild and wandering estimates, to answer for. For these distinctively mechanical and overdone reactions, of course, the critical spirit, even in its most relaxed mood, is not responsible. Responsible, rather, is the body of publishers, editors, illustrators, producers of the pleasant twaddle of magazines; who have found their "dear," our dear, everybody's dear, Jane so infinitely to their material purpose, so amenable to pretty reproduction in every variety of what is called tasteful, and in what seemingly proves to be saleable, form.

I do not, naturally, mean that she would be saleable if we had not more or less—beginning with Macaulay, her first slightly ponderous amoroso—lost our hearts to her; but I cannot help seeing her, a good deal, as in the same lucky box as the Brontës—lucky for the ultimate guerdon; a case of popularity (that in especial of the Yorkshire sisters), a beguiled infatuation, a sentimentalized vision, determined largely by the accidents and circumstances originally surrounding the manifestation of the genius —only with the reasons for the sentiment, in this latter connection, turned the other way. The key to Jane Austen's fortune with posterity has been in part the extraordinary grace of her facility, in fact of her uncon-

sciousness: as if, at the most, for difficulty, for embarrassment, she sometimes, over her work basket, her
tapestry flowers, in the spare, cool drawing-room of other
days, fell a-musing, lapsed too metaphorically, as one
may say, into wool gathering, and her dropped stitches,
of these pardonable, of these precious moments, were
afterwards picked up as little touches of human truth,
little glimpses of steady vision, little master-strokes of
imagination. The romantic tradition of the Brontës, with
posterity, has been still more essentially helped, I think,
by a force independent of any one of their applied faculties—by the attendant image of their dreary, their tragic
history, their loneliness and poverty of life. That picture
has been made to hang before us as insistently as the
vividest page of *Jane Eyre* or of *Wuthering Heights*. If
these things were "stories," as we say, and stories of a
lively interest, the medium from which they sprang was
above all in itself a story, such a story as has fairly
elbowed out the rights of appreciation, as has come at
last to impose itself as an expression of the power concerned. The personal position of the three sisters, of the
two in particular, had been marked, in short, with so
sharp an accent that this accent has become for us the
very tone of their united production. It covers and sup-
plants their matter, their spirit, their style, their talent,
their taste; it embodies, really, the most complete intellectual muddle, if the term be not extravagant, ever
achieved, on a literary question, by our wonderful public.
The question has scarce indeed been accepted as belonging to literature at all. Literature is an objective, a projected result; it is life that is the unconscious, the agitated,
the struggling, floundering cause. But the fashion has been,
in looking at the Brontës, so to confound the cause with
the result that we cease to know, in the presence of
such ecstasies, what we have hold of or what we are
talking about. They represent, the ecstasies, the high-water
mark of sentimental judgment.

These are but glimmering lanterns, however, you will

say, to hang in the great dusky and deserted avenue that leads up to the seated statue of Balzac; and you are so far right, I am bound to admit, as that I place them there, no doubt, in a great measure, just to render the darkness visible. We do, collectively, with all our dimness of view, arrive at rough discriminations, and by one of the roughest of these the author of the *Comédie Humaine* has in a manner profited; we have for many a year taken his greatness for granted; but in the graceless and nerveless fashion of those who edge away from a classic or a bore. "Oh, yes, he is as 'great' as you like—so let us not talk of him!" My purpose has been to "talk" of him, and I find this form of greeting, therefore, and still more this form of parting, not at all adequate; failing as I do to point my moral unless I show that a really paying acquaintance with a writer can never take place if our recognition remains perfunctory. Our indolence and our ignorance may prefer the empty form; but the penalty and the humiliation come for us with the perception that when the consecration really takes place we have been excluded, so to speak, from the fun. I see no better proof that the great interesting art of which Balzac remains the greatest master is practically, round about us, a bankrupt and discredited art (discredited, of course, I mean, for any directed and motived attention), than this very fact that we are so ready to beg off from knowing anything about him. Perfunctory rites, even, at present, are seldom rendered; and, amid the flood of verbiage for which the thousand new novels of the season find themselves a pretext in the newspapers, the name of the man who is really the father of us all, as we stand, is scarcely more mentioned than if he were not of the family.

I may at once intimate that the family strikes me as likely to recover its wasted heritage, and pull itself together for another chance, on condition only of shutting itself up, for an hour of wholesome heart-searching, with the image of its founder. He labors, I know, under the drawback of not being presentable as a classic—which

is precisely why there would have seemed to be the less
furtherance for regarding him as a bore. His situation in
this respect is all his own: it was not given him to flower,
for our convenience, into a single supreme felicity. His
"successes" hang so together that analysis is almost baffled
by his consistency, by his density. Even *Eugénie Grandet*
is not a supreme felicity in the sense that this particular
bloom is detachable from the cluster. The cluster is too
thick, the stem too tough; before we know it, when we
begin to pull, we have the whole branch about our heads
—or it would indeed be more just to say we have the
whole tree, if not the whole forest. It tells against a
great worker, for free reference, that we must take his
work in the mass; for, unfortunately, the circumstance
that nothing of it surpassingly stands forth to represent
the rest, to symbolize the whole, suggests a striking resemblance to work of other sorts. Of the mediocrities,
and the bunglers too is it true that *they* do not supremely
flower—as well as, further, of certain happy geniuses who
have flowed in an uncontrolled, an undirected, above all in
an unfiltered, current.

But the difference is that, for the most part, these loose
and easy producers, the great resounding improvisatori,
have not, in general, ended by imposing themselves; when
we deal with them conclusively and, as I have said, for
clearance of the slate, we deal with them by simplification,
by elimination: which may very well be the revenge that
time takes upon them to make up for the amount of
space they happened immediately to occupy. They are
still there, evidently: but they are there under this condition, which enters into account, as every instant, in any
pious inquiry about them, and which is attached, intimately, to the appearance they finally wear for us, that
the looseness and ease showing as their main sign in the
time of their freshness is now a quality still more striking
and often still more disconcerting. The weak sides in an
artist are weakened with time, and the strong sides
strengthened; so that it is never amiss, for duration, to

have as many strong sides as possible. It is the only way we have yet made out—even in this age of superlative study of the cheap and easy—not to have so many weak ones as will eventually betray us. Balzac stands almost alone as an extemporizer achieving closeness and weight, and whom closeness and weight have preserved. My reason for speaking of him as an extemporizer I shall presently mention; but let me meanwhile frankly say that I speak of him, and can only speak, as a man of his own craft, an emulous fellow-worker, who has learned from him more of the lessons of the engaging mystery of fiction than from any one else, and who is conscious of so large a debt to repay that it has had positively to be discharged in installments; as if one could never have at once all the required cash in hand.

When I am tempted, on occasion, to ask myself why we should, after all, so much as talk about the Novel, the wanton fable, against which, in so many ways, so showy an indictment may be drawn, I seem to see that the simplest plea is not to be sought in any attempted philosophy, in any abstract reason for our perversity or our levity. The real gloss upon these things is reflected from some great practitioner, some concrete instance of the art, some ample cloak under which we may gratefully crawl. It comes back, of course, to the example and the analogy of the Poet—with the abatement, however, that the Poet is most the Poet when he is preponderantly lyrical, when he speaks, laughing or crying, most directly from his individual heart, which throbs under the impressions of life. It is not the *image* of life that he thus expresses, so much as life itself, in its sources—so much as his own intimate, essential states and feelings. By the time he has begun to collect anecdotes, to tell stories, to represent scenes, to concern himself, that is, with the states and feelings of others, he is well on the way not to be the Poet pure and simple. The lyrical element, all the same, abides in him, and it is by this element that he is connected with what is most splendid in his expression. The

lyrical instinct and tradition are immense in Shakespeare;
which is why, great storyteller, great dramatist and
painter, great lover, in short, of the image of life though
he was, we need not press the case of his example. The
lyrical element is not great, is in fact not present at all, in
Balzac, in Scott (the Scott of the voluminous prose), nor
in Thackeray, nor in Dickens—which is precisely why
they are so essentially novelists, so almost exclusively
lovers of the image of life. It *is* great, or it is at all
events largely present, in such a writer as George Sand—
which is doubtless why we take her for a novelist in a
much looser sense than the others we have named. It
is considerable in that bright particular genius of our
own day, George Meredith, who so strikes us as hitch-
ing winged horses to the chariot of his prose—steeds
who prance and dance and caracole, who strain the
traces, attempt to quit the ground, and yearn for the
upper air. Balzac, with huge feet fairly plowing the sand
of our desert, is on the other hand the very type and
model of the projector and creator; so that when I think,
either with envy or with terror, of the nature and the
effort of the Novelist, I think of something that reaches
its highest expression in him. That is why those of us who,
as fellow-craftsmen, have once caught a glimpse of this
value in him, can never quite rest from hanging about
him; that is why he seems to have all that the others have
to tell us, with more, besides, that is all his own. He
lived and breathed in his medium, and the fact that he
was able to achieve in it, as man and as artist, so crowded
a career, remains for us one of the most puzzling problems
—I scarce know whether to say of literature or of life.
He is himself a figure more extraordinary than any he
drew, and the fascination may still be endless of all the
questions he puts to us and of the answers for which
we feel ourselves helpless.

He died, as we sufficiently remember, at fifty—worn
out with work and thought and passion; the passion, I
mean, that he had put into his mighty plan and that had

ridden him like an infliction of the gods. He began, a
friendless and penniless young provincial, to write early,
and to write very badly, and it was not till well toward
his thirtieth year, with the conception of the *Comédie
Humaine*, as we all again remember, that he found his
right ground, found his feet and his voice. This huge
distributed, divided and subdivided picture of the life of
France in his time, a picture bristling with imagination
and information, with fancies and facts and figures, a
world of special and general insight, a rank tropical forest
of detail and specification, but with the strong breath of
genius forever circulating through it and shaking the
treetops to a mighty murmur, got itself hung before us in
the space of twenty short years. The achievement remains
one of the most inscrutable, one of the unfathomable,
final facts in the history of art, and if, as I have said,
the author himself has his own surpassing objectivity, it
is just because of this challenge his figure constitutes for
any other painter of life, inflamed with ingenuity, who
should feel the temptation to represent or explain him.
How represent, how explain him, as a concrete active
energy? How depict him, we ask ourselves, *at* his huge
conceived and accepted task, how reconcile such dissemi-
nation with such intensity, the collection and possession of
so vast a number of facts with so rich a presentation of
each? The elements of the world he set up before us, with
all its insistent particulars, these elements were not, for
him, a direct revelation—of so large a part of life is it
true that we can know it only by living, and that living
is the process that, in our mortal span, makes the largest
demand on our time. How could a man have lived at
large so much if, in the service of art, he had so much
abstracted and condensed himself? How could he have so
much abstracted and condensed himself if, in the service
of life, he had felt and fought and acted, had labored and
suffered, so much as a private in the ranks? The wealth
and strength of his temperament indeed partly answer the
question and partly obscure it. He could so extend his

existence partly because he vibrated to so many kinds of contact and curiosity. To vibrate intellectually was his motive, but it magnified, all the while, it multiplied his experience. He could live at large, in short, because he was always living in the particular necessary, the particular intended connection—was always astride of his imagination, always charging, with his heavy, his heroic lance in rest, at every object that sprang up in his path. But as he was at the same time always fencing himself in against the personal adventure, the personal experience, in order to preserve himself for converting it into history, how did experience, in the immediate sense, still get itself saved?—or, to put it as simply as possible, where, with so strenuous a conception of the use of material, was material itself so strenuously quarried? Out of what mines, by what innumerable tortuous channels, in what endless winding procession of laden chariots and tugging teams and marching elephants, did the immense consignments required for his work reach him?

The point at which the emulous admirer, however diminished by comparison, may most closely approach him is, it seems to me, through the low portal of envy, so irresistibly do we lose ourselves in the vision of the quantity of life with which his imagination communicated. Quantity and intensity are at once and together his sign; the truth being that his energy did not press hard in some places only to press lightly in others, did not lay it on thick here or there to lay it on thin elsewhere, did not seek the appearance of extent and number by faintness of evocation, by shallow soundings, or by the mere sketchiness of suggestion that dispenses, for reference and verification, with the book, the total collection of human documents, with what we call "chapter and verse." He never throws dust in our eyes, save only the fine gold-dust through the haze of which his own romantic vision operates; never does it, I mean, when he is pretending not to do it, pretending to give us the full statement of his case, to deal with the facts of the spectacle sur-

rounding him. Then he goes in, as we say, for a portentous clearness, a reproduction of the real on the scale
of the real—with a definiteness actually proportionate;
though a clearness that in truth sometimes fails (like the
sight of the forest of the adage, which fails for the
presence of the trees), through the positive monstrosity
of his effort. He sees and presents too many facts,—facts
of history, of property, of genealogy, of topography, of
sociology, and has too many ideas and images about them;
their value is thus threatened with submersion by the
flood of general reference in which they float, by their
quantity of indicated relation to other facts, which break
against them like waves of a high tide. He may thus at
times become obscure from his very habit of striking too
many matches; or we may at least say of him, out of our
wondering loyalty, that the light he produces is, beyond
that of any other corner of the great planted garden of
romance, thick and rich and heavy—interesting, so to
speak, on its own account.

There would be much to say, I think, had we only a
little more time, on this question of the projected light of
the individual strong temperament in fiction—the color
of the air with which this, that or the other painter of
life (as we call them all), more or less unconsciously
suffuses his picture. I say unconsciously because I speak
here of an effect of atmosphere largely, if not wholly,
distinct from the effect sought on behalf of the special
subject to be treated; something that proceeds from the
contemplative mind itself, the very complexion of the
mirror in which the material is reflected. This is of the
nature of the man himself—an emanation of his spirit,
temper, history; it springs from his very presence, his
spiritual presence, in his work, and is, in so far, not a
matter of calculation and artistry. All a matter of his own,
in a word, for each seer of visions, the particular tone of
the medium in which each vision, each clustered group
of persons and places and objects, is bathed. Just how,
accordingly, does the light of the world, the projected,

painted, peopled, poetized, realized world, the furnished
and fitted world into which we are beguiled for the holi-
day excursion, cheap trips or dear, of the eternally amus-
able, eternally dupeable voyaging mind—just how does this
strike us as different in Fielding and in Richardson, in
Scott and in Dumas, in Dickens and in Thackeray, in
Hawthorne and in Meredith, in George Eliot and in
George Sand, in Jane Austen and in Charlotte Brontë?
Do we not feel the general landscape evoked by each of
the more or less magical wands to which I have given
name, not to open itself under the same sun that hangs
over the neighboring scene, not to receive the solar rays
at the same angle, not to exhibit its shadows with the
same intensity or the same sharpness; not, in short, to
seem to belong to the same time of day or same state of
the weather? Why is it that the life that overflows in
Dickens seems to me always to go on in the morning, or in
the very earliest hours of the afternoon at most, and in a
vast apartment that appears to have windows, large, un-
curtained, and rather unwashed windows, on all sides at
once? Why is it that in George Eliot the sun sinks forever
to the west, and the shadows are long, and the afternoon
wanes, and the trees vaguely rustle, and the color of the
day is much inclined to yellow? Why is it that in
Charlotte Brontë we move through an endless autumn?
Why is it that in Jane Austen we sit quite resigned in an
arrested spring? Why does Hawthorne give us the afternoon hour later than any one else?—oh, late, late, quite
uncannily late, and as if it were always winter outside?
But I am wasting the very minutes I pretended, at the
start, to cherish, and am only sustained though my levity
by seeing you watch for the time of day or season of
the year or state of the weather that I shall fasten upon
the complicated clockface of Thackeray. I do, I think,
see his light also—see it very much as the light (a different thing from the mere dull dusk) of rainy days in
"residential" streets; but we are not, after all, talking of
him, and, though Balzac's waiting power has proved itself,

this half-century, immense, I must not too much presume upon it.

The question of the color of Balzac's air and the time of *his* day would indeed here easily solicit our ingenuity—were I at liberty to say more than one thing about it. It is rich and thick, the mixture of sun and shade diffused through the *Comédie Humaine*—a mixture richer and thicker and representing an absolutely greater quantity of "atmosphere," than we shall find prevailing within the compass of any other suspended frame. That is how we see him, living in his garden, and it is by reason of the restless energy with which he circulated there that I hold his fortune and his privilege, in spite of the burden of his toil and the brevity of his immediate reward, to have been before any others enviable. It is strange enough, but what most abides with us, as we follow his steps, is a sense of the intellectual luxury he enjoyed. To focus him at all, for a single occasion, we have to simplify, and this wealth of his vicarious experience forms the side, more-over, on which he is most attaching for those who take an interest in the real play of the imagination. From the moment our imagination plays at all, of course, and from the moment we try to catch and preserve the pictures it throws off, from that moment we too, in our comparatively feeble way, live vicariously—succeed in opening a series of dusky passages in which, with a more or less childlike ingenuity, we can romp to and fro. Our passages are mainly short and dark, however; we soon come to the end of them—dead walls, without resonance, in presence of which the candle goes out and the game stops, and we have only to retrace our steps. Balzac's luxury, as I call it, was in the extraordinary number and length of his radiating and ramifying corridors—the labyrinth in which he finally lost himself. What it comes back to, in other words, is the intensity with which we live—and his intensity is recorded for us on every page of his work.

It is a question, you see, of *penetrating* into a subject; his corridors always went further and further and further;

which is but another way of expressing his inordinate passion for detail. It matters nothing—nothing for my present
contention—that this extravagance is also his great fault;
in spite, too, of its all being detail vivified and related,
characteristic and constructive, essentially prescribed by the
terms of his plan. The relations of parts to each other are
at moments multiplied almost to madness—which is at the
same time just why they give us the measure of his
hallucination, make up the greatness of his intellectual
adventure. His plan was to handle, primarily, not a world
of ideas, animated by figures representing these ideas; but
the packed and constituted, the palpable, provable world
before him, by the study of which ideas would inevitably
find themselves thrown up. If the happy fate is accordingly to *partake* of life, actively, assertively, not
passively, narrowly, in mere sensibility and sufferance, the
happiness has been greatest when the faculty employed has
been largest. We employ different faculties—some of us
only our arms and our legs and our stomach; Balzac
employed most what he possessed in largest quantity.
This is where his work ceases in a manner to mystify us—
this is where we make out how he did quarry his material:
it is the sole solution to an otherwise baffling problem.
He collected his experience within himself; no other
economy explains his achievement; this thrift alone, remarkable yet thinkable, embodies the necessary miracle.
His system of cellular confinement, in the interest of the
miracle, was positively that of a Benedictine monk, leading
his life within the four walls of his convent and bent, the
year round, over the smooth parchment on which, with
wondrous illumination and enhancement of gold and
crimson and blue, he inscribed the glories of the faith and
the legends of the saints. Balzac's view of himself was
indeed in a manner the monkish one; he was most at
ease, while he wrought, in the white gown and cowl—an
image of him that the friendly art of his time has handed
down to us. Only, as happened, his subject of illumination
was the legends not merely of the saints, but of the much

more numerous uncanonized strugglers and sinners, an acquaintance with whose attributes was not all to be gathered in the place of piety itself; not even from the faintest ink of old records, the mild lips of old brothers, or the painted glass of church windows.

This is where envy does follow him, for to have so many other human cases, so many other personal predicaments to get into, up to one's chin, is verily to be able to get out of one's own box. And it was up to his chin, constantly, that he sank in his illusion—not, as the weak and timid in this line do, only up to his ankles or his knees. The figures he sees begin immediately to bristle with all their characteristics. Every mark and sign, outward and inward, that they possess; every virtue and every vice, every strength and every weakness, every passion and every habit, the sound of their voices, the expression of their eyes, the tricks of feature and limb, the buttons on their clothes, the food on their plates, the money in their pockets, the furniture in their houses, the secrets in their breasts, are all things that interest, that concern, that command him, and that have, for the picture, significance, relation and value. It is a prodigious multiplication of values, and thereby a prodigious entertainment of the vision—on the condition the vision can bear it. Bearing it—that is *our* bearing it—is a serious matter; for the appeal is truly to that faculty of attention out of which we are educating ourselves, as hard as we possibly can; educating ourselves with such complacency, with such boisterous high spirits, that we may already be said to have practically lost it—with the consequence that any work of art or of criticism making a demand on it is by that fact essentially discredited. It takes attention not only to thread the labyrinth of the *Comédie Humaine*, but to keep our author himself in view, in the relations in which we thus image him. But if we can muster it, as I say, in sufficient quantity, we thus walk with him in the great glazed gallery of his thought; the long, lighted and pictured ambulatory where the endless series of windows, on one side, hangs over his revolutionized, ravaged, yet partly restored and reinstated garden of France, and where, on the other, the figures and the portraits we fancy stepping down to meet him climb back into their frames, larger and smaller, and take up position and expression as he desired they shall look out and compose.

We have lately had a literary case of the same general family as the case of Balzac, and in presence of which some of the same speculations come up: I had occasion, not long since, after the death of Émile Zola, to attempt an appreciation of *his* extraordinary performance—his series of the *Rougon-Macquart* constituting in fact, in the library of the fiction that can hope in some degree to live, a monument to the idea of plenitude, of comprehension and variety, second only to the *Comédie Humaine*. The question presented itself, in respect to Zola's ability and Zola's career, with a different proportion and value, I quite recognize, and wearing a much less distinguished face; but it was there to be met, none the less, on the very threshold, and all the more because this was just where he himself had placed it. His idea had been, from the first, in a word, to lose no time—as if one could have experience, even the mere amount requisite for showing others as having it, *without* losing time!—and yet the degree in which he too, so handicapped, has achieved valid expression is such as still to stagger us. He had had inordinately to simplify—had had to leave out the life of the soul, practically, and confine himself to the life of the instincts, of the more immediate passions, such as can be easily and promptly caught in the fact. He had had, in a word, to confine himself almost entirely to the impulses and agitations that men and women are possessed by in common, and to take them as exhibited in mass and number, so that, being writ larger, they might likewise be more easily read. He met and solved, in this manner, his difficulty—the difficulty of knowing, and of showing, of life, only what his "notes" would account for. But it is in the *waste*, I think, much rather—the waste of time, of passion, of curiosity, of contact—that true initiation resides; so that the most wonderful adventures of the artist's spirit are those, immensely quickening for his "authority," that are yet not reducible to his notes. It is exactly here that we get the difference between such a solid, square, symmetrical structure as *Les Rougon-Macquart*, vitiated, in a high degree, by its mechanical side, and the monument left by Balzac—without the example of which, I surmise, Zola's work would not have existed. The mystic process of the crucible, the transformation of the material under æsthetic heat, is, in the *Comédie Humaine*, thanks to an intenser and more submissive fusion, completer, and also finer; for if the commoner and more wayside passions and conditions are, in the various episodes there, at no time gathered into so large and so thick an illustrative bunch, yet on the other hand they are shown much more freely at play in the individual case—and the individual case it is that permits of supreme fineness. It is hard to say where Zola is fine; whereas it is often, for pages together, hard to say where Balzac is, even under the weight of his too ponderous personality, not. The most fundamental and general sign of the novel, from one desperate experiment to another, is its being everywhere an effort at *representation*—this is the beginning and the end of it: wherefore it was that one could say at last, with account taken of everything, that Zola's performance, on his immense scale, was an extraordinary show of representation imitated. The imitation, in places—notably and admirably, for instance, in *L'Assommoir*—breaks through into something that we take for reality; but, for the most part, the separating rift, the determining difference, holds its course straight, prevents the attempted process from becoming the sound, straight, whole thing that is given us by those who have really *bought* their information. This is where Balzac remains unshaken,—in our feeling that, with all his faults of pedantry, ponderosity, pretentiousness, bad taste and charmless form, his spirit has somehow paid for its knowledge. His subject is again and again the complicated human creature or human condition; and it is with these complications as if he knew them, as Shakespeare knew them, by his charged consciousness, by the history of his soul and the direct exposure of his sensibility. This source of supply he found, forever—and one may indeed say he mostly left—sitting at his fireside; where it constituted the company with which I see him shut up, and his practical intimacy with which, during such orgies and debauches of intellectual passion, might earn itself that name of high personal good fortune that I have applied.

Let me say, definitely, that I hold several of his faults to be grave, and that if there were any question of time for it I should like to speak of them; but let me add, as promptly, that they are faults, on the whole, of execution, flaws in the casting, accidents of the process: they never come back to that fault in the artist, in the novelist, that amounts most completely to a failure of dignity, the absence of saturation with his idea. When saturation fails no other presence really avails; as when, on the other hand, it operates, no failure of method fatally interferes. There is never in Balzac that damning interference which consists of the painter's not seeing, not possessing, his image; not having fixed and held his creature and his creature's conditions. "Balzac aime sa Valérie," says Taine, in his great essay,—so much the finest thing ever written on our author,—speaking of the way in which the awful little Madame Marneffe of *Les Parents Pauvres* is drawn, and of the long rope, for her acting herself out, that her creator's participation in her reality assures her. He has been contrasting her, as it happens, with Thackeray's Becky Sharp or rather with Thackeray's attitude toward Becky, and the marked jealousy of her freedom that Thackeray exhibits from the first. I remember reading at the time of the publication of Taine's study—though it was long, long ago—a phrase in an English review of the volume which seemed to my limited perception, even in extreme youth, to deserve the highest prize ever bestowed

on critical stupidity undisguised. If Balzac loved his
Valérie, said this commentator, that only showed Balzac's
extraordinary taste; the truth being really, throughout,
that it was just through this love of each seized identity,
and of the sharpest and liveliest identities most, that
Madame Marneffe's creator was able to marshal his array
at all. The love, as we call it, the joy in their communicated and exhibited movement, in their standing on their
feet and going of themselves and acting out their characters, was what rendered possible the saturation I speak
of; what supplied him, through the inevitable gaps of his
preparation and the crevices of his prison, his long prison
of labor, a short cut to the knowledge he required. It was
by loving them—as the terms of his subject and the
nuggets of his mine—that he knew them; it was not by
knowing them that he loved.

He at all events robustly loved the sense of another
explored, assumed, assimilated identity—enjoyed it as the
hand enjoys the glove when the glove ideally fits. My
image indeed is loose; for what he liked was absolutely to
get into the constituted consciousness, into all the clothes,
gloves and whatever else, into the very skin and bones, of
the habited, featured, colored, articulated form of life that
he desired to present. How do we know given persons,
for any purpose of demonstration, unless we know their
situation for themselves, unless we see it from their point
of vision, that is, from their point of pressing consciousness or sensation?—without our allowing for which there
is no appreciation. Balzac loved his Valérie then as
Thackeray did not love his Becky, or his Blanche Amory
in *Pendennis*. But his prompting was not to expose her; it
could only be, on the contrary,—intensely aware as he
was of all the lengths she might go to, and paternally,
maternally alarmed about them—to cover her up and pro-
tect her, in the interest of her special genius and freedom.
All his impulse was to *la faire valoir*, to give her all her
value, just as Thackeray's attitude was the opposite one,
a desire positively to expose and desecrate poor Becky—

to follow her up, catch her in the act, and bring her to shame: though with a mitigation, an admiration, an inconsequence, now and then wrested from him by an instinct finer, in his mind, than the so-called "moral" eagerness. The English writer wants to make sure, first of all, of your moral judgment; the French is willing, while it waits a little, to risk, for the sake of his subject and its interest, your spiritual salvation. Madame Marneffe, detrimental, fatal as she is, is "exposed," so far as anything in life, or in art, may be, by the working-out of the situation and the subject themselves; so that when they have done what they would, what they logically had to, with her, we are ready to take it from them. We do not feel, very irritatedly, very lecturedly, in other words with superfluous edification, that she has been sacrificed. Who can say, on the contrary, that Blanche Amory, in *Pendennis*, with the author's lash about her little bare white back from the first—who can feel that she has *not* been sacrificed, or that her little bareness and whiteness, and all the rest of her, have been, by such a process, presented as they had a right to demand?

It all comes back, in fine, to that respect for the liberty of the subject which I should be willing to name as *the* great sign of the painter of the first order. Such a witness to the human comedy fairly holds his breath for fear of arresting or diverting that natural license; the witness who begins to breathe so uneasily in presence of it that his respiration not only warns off the little prowling or playing creature he is supposed to be studying, but drowns, for our ears, the ingenuous sounds of the animal, as well as the general, truthful hum of the human scene at large—this demonstrator has no sufficient warrant for his task. And if such an induction as this is largely the moral of our renewed glance at Balzac, there is a lesson, of a more essential sort, I think, folded still deeper within—the lesson that there is no convincing art that is not ruinously expensive. I am unwilling to say, in the presence of such of his successors as George Eliot and Tolstoy and

Zola (to name, for convenience, only three of them), that he was the last of the novelists to do the thing handsomely; but I will say that we get the impression at least of his having had more to spend. Many of those who have followed him affect us as doing it, in the vulgar phrase, "on the cheap"; by reason mainly, no doubt, of their having been, all helplessly, foredoomed to cheapness. Nothing counts, of course, in art, but the excellent; nothing exists, however briefly, for estimation, for appreciation, but the superlative—always in its kind; and who shall declare that the severe economy of the vast majority of those apparently emulous of the attempt to "render" the human subject and the human scene proceeds from anything worse than the consciousness of a limited capital? This flourishing frugality operates happily, no doubt— given all the circumstances—for the novelist; but it has had terrible results for the novel, so far as the novel is a form with which criticism may be moved to concern itself. Its misfortune, its discredit, what I have called its bankrupt state among us, is the not unnatural consequence of its having ceased, for the most part, to be artistically interesting. It has become an object of easy manufacture, showing on every side the stamp of the machine; it has become the article of commerce, produced in quantity, and as we so see it we inevitably turn from it, under the rare visitations of the critical impulse, to compare it with those more precious products of the same general nature that we used to think of as belonging to the class of the handmade.

The lesson of Balzac, under this comparison, is extremely various, and I should prepare myself much too large a task were I to attempt a list of the separate truths he brings home. I have to choose among them, and I choose the most important; the three or four that more or less include the others. In reading him over, in opening him almost anywhere today, what immediately strikes us is the part assigned by him, in any picture, to the *conditions* of the creatures with whom he is concerned. Contrasted with him other prose painters of life scarce seem to see the conditions at all. He clearly held pretended portrayals as nothing, as less than nothing, as a most vain thing, unless it should be, in spirit and intention, the art of complete representation. "Complete" is of course a great word, and there is no art at all, we are often reminded, that is not on too many sides an abject compromise. The element of compromise is always there; it is of the essence; we live with it, and it may serve to keep us humble. The formula of the whole matter is sufficiently expressed perhaps in a reply I found myself once making to an inspired but discouraged friend, a fellow-craftsman who had declared in his despair that there was no use trying, that it was a form, the novel, absolutely too difficult. "Too difficult indeed; yet there is one way to master it—which is to pretend consistently that it isn't." We are all of us, all the while, pretending—as consistently as we can—that it isn't, and Balzac's great glory is that he pretended hardest. He never had to pretend so hard as when he addressed himself to that evocation of the medium, that distillation of the natural and social air, of which I speak, the things that most require on the part of the painter preliminary possession—so definitely require it that, terrified at the requisition, when conscious of it, many a painter prefers to beg the whole question. He has thus, this ingenious person, to invent some *other* way of making his characters interesting—some other way, that is, than the arduous way, demanding so much consideration, of presenting them to us. They are interesting, in fact, as subjects of fate, the figures round whom a situation closes, in proportion as, sharing their existence, we feel where fate comes in and just how it gets at them. In the void they are not interesting—and Balzac, like Nature herself, abhorred a vacuum. Their situation takes hold of us because it is theirs, not because it is somebody's, any one's, that of creatures unidentified. Therefore it is not superfluous that their identity shall first be established for us, and their adventures, in that measure, have a relation to it, and therewith an appreciability. There is no such thing in the world as an adventure pure and simple; there is only mine and yours, and his and hers—it being the greatest adventure of all, I verily think, just to *be* you or I, just to be he or she. To Balzac's imagination that was indeed in itself an immense adventure—and nothing appealed to him more than to show *how* we all are, and how we are placed and built-in for being so. What befalls us is but another name for the way our circumstances press upon us—so that an account of what befalls us is an account of our circumstances.

Add to this, then, that the fusion of all the elements of the picture, under his hand, is complete—of what people are with what they do, of what they do with what they are, of the action with the agents, of the medium with the action, of all the parts of the drama with each other. Such a production as *Le Père Goriot* for example, or as *Eugénie Grandet*, or as *Le Curé de Village*, has, in respect to this fusion, a kind of inscrutable perfection. The situation sits shrouded in its circumstances, and then, by its inner expansive force, emerges from them, the action marches, to the rich rustle of this great tragic and ironic train, the embroidered heroic mantle, with an art of keeping together that makes of *Le Père Goriot* in especial a supreme case of composition, a model of that high virtue that we know as economy of effect, economy of line and touch. An inveterate sense of proportion was not, in general, Balzac's distinguishing mark; but with great talents one has great surprises, and the effect of this large handling of the conditions was more often than not to make the work, whatever it might be, appear admirably composed. Of all the costly charms of a "story" this interest derived from composition is the costliest—and there is perhaps no better proof of our present penury than the fact that, in general, when one makes a plea for it, the plea might seemingly (for all it is understood!) be for trigonometry or osteology. "Composition?—what may that happen to *be*, and, whatever it is, what has it to

do with the matter?" I shall take for granted here that
every one perfectly knows, for without that assumption
I shall not be able to wind up, as I must immediately do.
The presence of the conditions, when really presented,
when made vivid, provides for the action—which is, from
step to step, constantly implied in them; whereas the
process of suspending the action in the void and dressing
it there with the tinkling bells of what is called dialogue
only makes no provision at all for the other interest.
There are two elements of the art of the novelist which,
as they present, I think, the greatest difficulty, tend
thereby most to fascinate us: in the first place that mystery of the foreshortened procession of facts and figures,
of appearances of whatever sort, which is in some lights
but another name for the picture governed by the principle of composition, and which has at any rate as little as
possible in common with the method now usual among
us, the juxtaposition of items emulating the column of
numbers of a schoolboy's sum in addition. It is the art of
the brush, I know, as opposed to the art of the slate-
pencil; but to the art of the brush the novel must return,
I hold, to recover whatever may be still recoverable of its
sacrificed honor.

The second difficulty that I commend for its fascination,
at all events, the most attaching when met and the most
rewarding when triumphantly met,—though I hasten to
add that it also strikes me as not only the least "met," in
general, but the least suspected,—this second difficulty is
that of representing, to put it simply, the lapse of time, the
duration of the subject: representing it, that is, more
subtly than by a blank space, or a row of stars, on the
historic page. With the blank space and the row of stars
Balzac's genius had no affinity, and he is therefore as
unlike as possible those narrators—so numerous, all round
us, it would appear, today in especial—the succession of
whose steps and stages, the development of whose action,
in the given case, affects us as occupying but a week or
two. No one begins, to my sense, to handle the time-

element and produce the time-effect with the authority of
Balzac in his amplest sweeps—by which I am far from
meaning in his longest passages. That study of the foreshortened image, of the neglect of which I suggest the
ill consequence, is precisely the enemy of the tiresome procession of would-be narrative items, seen all in profile,
like the rail-heads of a fence; a substitute for the baser
device of accounting for the time-quantity by mere
quantity of statement. Quality and manner of statement
account for it in a finer way—always assuming, as I say,
that unless it is accounted for nothing else really is. The
fashion of our day is to account for it almost exclusively
by an inordinate abuse of the colloquial resource, of the
report, from page to page, from chapter to chapter, from
beginning to end, of the talk, between the persons involved, in which situation and action may be conceived as
registered. Talk between persons is perhaps, of all the
parts of the novelist's plan, the part that Balzac most
scrupulously weighed and measured and kept in its place;
judging it, I think,—though he perhaps even had an undue
suspicion of its possible cheapness, as feeling it the thing
that can least afford to be cheap,—a precious and supreme
resource, the very flower of illustration of the subject
and thereby not to be inconsiderately discounted. It was
his view, discernibly, that the flower must keep its bloom,
or in other words not be too much handled, in order to
have a fragrance when nothing but its fragrance will serve.

It was his view indeed positively that there is a *law*
in these things, and that, admirable for illustration, functional for illustration, dialogue has its function perverted,
and therewith its life destroyed, when forced, all clumsily,
into the constructive office. It is in the drama, of course,
that it is constructive; but the drama lives by a law so
different, verily, that everything that is right for it seems
wrong for the prose picture, and everything that is right
for the prose picture addressed directly, in turn, to the
betrayal of the "play." These are questions, however, that
bore deep—if I have successfully braved the danger that

they absolutely do bore; so that I must content myself, as
a glance at this point, with the claim for the author of
Le Père Goriot that colloquial illustration, in his work,
suffers less, on the whole, than in any other I know, from
its attendant, its besetting and haunting penalty of springing, unless watched, a leak in its effect. It is as if the master
of the ship were keeping his eye on the pump; the pump,
I mean, of relief and alternation, the pump that keeps the
vessel free of too much water. We must always remember
that, save in the cases where "dialogue" is organic, is the
very law of the game—in which case, as I say, the game
is another business altogether—it is essentially the fluid
element: as, for instance (to cite, conveniently, Balzac's
most eminent prose contemporary) was strikingly its
character in the elder Dumas: just as its character in the
younger, the dramatist, illustrates supremely what I call the
other game. The current, in old Dumas, the large,
loose, facile flood of talked movement, talked interest, as
much as you will, is, in virtue of this fluidity, a current
indeed, with so little of wrought texture that we float and
splash in it; feeling it thus resemble much more some
capacious tepid tank than the figured tapestry, all over-
scored with objects in fine perspective, which symbolizes
to me (if one may have a symbol) the last word of the
achieved fable. Such a tapestry, with its wealth of expression of its subject, with its myriad ordered stitches, its
harmonies of tone and felicities of taste, is a work, above
all, of closeness—and therefore the more pertinent image
here, as it is in the name of closeness that I am inviting
you to let Balzac once more appeal to you.

It will strike you perhaps that I speak as if we all, as if
you all, without exception were novelists, haunting the
back shop, the laboratory, or, more nobly expressed, the
inner shrine of the temple; but such assumptions, in this
age of print—if I may not say this age of poetry—are
perhaps never too wide of the mark, and I have at any
rate taken your interest sufficiently for granted to ask you
to close up with me for an hour at the feet of the master

speaking consciousness that hold up a light of their own. Therefore I venture to follow even on a field so labored, only paying this toll to the latest and best work because the author has made it impossible to do less.

Flaubert's life is so almost exclusively the story of his literary application that to speak of his five or six fictions is pretty well to account for it all. He died in 1880 after a career of fifty-nine years singularly little marked by changes of scene, of fortune, of attitude, of occupation, of character, and above all, as may be said, of mind. He would be interesting to the race of novelists if only because, quite apart from the value of his work, he so personally gives us the example and the image, so presents the intellectual case. He was born a novelist, grew up, lived, died a novelist, breathing, feeling, thinking, speaking, performing every operation of life, only as that votary; and this though his production was to be small in amount and though it constituted all his diligence. It was not indeed perhaps primarily so much that he was born and lived a novelist as that he was born and lived literary, and that to be literary represented for him an almost overwhelming situation. No life was long enough, no courage great enough, no fortune kind enough to support a man under the burden of this character when once such a doom had been laid on him. His case was a doom because he felt of his vocation almost nothing but the difficulty. He had many strange sides, but this was the strangest, that if we argued from his difficulty to his work, the difficulty being registered for us in his letters and elsewhere, we should expect from the result but the smallest things. We should be prepared to find in it well-nigh a complete absence of the signs of a gift. We should regret that the unhappy man had not addressed himself to something he might have found at least comparatively easy. We should singularly miss the consecration supposedly given to a work of art by its having been conceived in joy. That is Flaubert's remarkable, his so far as I know unmatched distinction, that he has left works of an extraordinary art

even the conception of which failed to help him to think
in serenity. The chapter of execution, from the moment
execution gets really into the shafts, is of course always
and everywhere a troubled one—about which moreover
too much has of late been written; but we frequently find
Flaubert cursing his subjects themselves, wishing he had
not chosen them, holding himself up to derision for having
done so, and hating them in the very act of sitting down
to them. He cared immensely for the medium, the task
and the triumph involved, but was himself the last to be
able to say why. He is sustained only by the rage and the
habit of effort; the mere *love* of letters, let alone the love
of life, appears at an early age to have deserted him. Certain passages in his correspondence make us even wonder
if it be not hate that sustains him most. So, successively,
his several supremely finished and crowned compositions
came into the world, and we may feel sure that none
others of the kind, none that were to have an equal fortune, had sprung from such adversity.

I insist upon this because his at once excited and baffled
passion gives the key of his life and determines its outline. I must speak of him at least as I feel him and as in
his very latest years I had the fortune occasionally to see
him. I said just now, practically, that he is for many of our
tribe at large *the* novelist, intent and typical, and so,
gathered together and foreshortened, simplified and fixed,
the lapse of time seems to show him. It has made him in
his prolonged posture extraordinarily objective, made
him even resemble one of his own productions, constituted him as a subject, determined him as a figure; the
limit of his range, and above all of his reach, is after this
fashion, no doubt, sufficiently indicated, and yet perhaps
in the event without injury to his name. If our consideration of him cultivates a certain tenderness on the double
ground that he suffered supremely in the cause and that
there is endlessly much to be learned from him, we remember at the same time that, indirectly, the world at
large possesses him not less than the *confrère*. He has fed

and fertilized, has filtered through others, and so arrived at contact with that public from whom it was his theory that he was separated by a deep and impassable trench, the labor of his own spade. He is none the less more interesting, I repeat, as a failure however qualified than as a success however explained, and it is as so viewed that the unity of his career attaches and admonishes. Save in some degree by a condition of health (a liability to epileptic fits at times frequent, but never so frequent as to have been generally suspected), he was not outwardly hampered as the tribe of men of letters goes—an anxious brotherhood at the best; yet the fewest possible things appear to have ever succeeded in happening to him. The only son of an eminent provincial physician, he inherited a modest ease and no other incumbrance than, as was the case for Balzac, an overattentive, an importunate mother; but freedom spoke to him from behind a veil, and when we have mentioned the few apparent facts of experience that make up his landmarks over and beyond his interspaced publications we shall have completed his biography. Tall, strong, striking, he caused his friends to admire in him the elder, the florid Norman type, and he seems himself, as a man of imagination, to have found some transmission of race in his stature and presence, his light-colored salient eyes and long tawny mustache.

The central event of his life was his journey to the East in 1849 with M. Maxime Du Camp, of which the latter has left in his *Impressions littéraires* a singularly interesting and, as we may perhaps say, slightly treacherous report, and which prepared for Flaubert a state of nostalgia that was not only never to leave him, but that was to work in him as a motive. He had during that year, and just in sufficient quantity, his revelation, the particular appropriate disclosure to which the gods at some moment treat the artist unless they happen too perversely to conspire against him: he tasted of the knowledge by which he was subsequently to measure everything, appeal from everything, find everything flat. Never probably was an impression so assimilated, so positively transmuted to a function; he lived on it to the end and we may say that in *Salammbô* and *La Tentation de Saint-Antoine* he almost died of it. He made afterwards no other journey of the least importance save a disgusted excursion to the Rigi-Kaltbad shortly before his death. The Franco-German War was of course to him for the time as the valley of the shadow itself; but this was an ordeal, unlike most of his other ordeals, shared after all with millions. He never married—he declared, toward the end, to the most comprehending of his confidants, that he had been from the first "afraid of life"; and the friendliest element of his later time was, we judge, that admirable comfortable commerce, in her fullest maturity, with Madame George Sand, the confidant I just referred to; which has been preserved for us in the published correspondence of each. He had in Ivan Turgenev a friend almost as valued; he spent each year a few months in Paris, where (to mention everything) he had his natural place, so far as he cared to take it, at the small literary court of the Princess Mathilde; and, lastly, he lost toward the close of his life, by no fault of his own, a considerable part of his modest fortune. It is, however, in the long security, the almost unbroken solitude of Croisset, near Rouen, that he mainly figures for us, gouging out his successive books in the wide old room, of many windows, that, with an intervening terrace, overlooked the broad Seine and the passing boats. This was virtually a monastic cell, closed to echoes and accidents; with its stillness for long periods scarce broken save by the creak of the towing-chain of the tugs across the water. When I have added that his published letters offer a view, not very refreshing, of his youthful entanglement with Madame Louise Colet—whom we name because, apparently not a shrinking person, she long ago practically named herself—I shall have catalogued his personal vicissitudes. And I may add further that the con-

nection with Madame Colet, such as it was, rears its head
for us in something like a desert of immunity from such
complications.

His complications were of the spirit, of the literary
vision, and though he was thoroughly profane he was yet
essentially anchoretic. I perhaps miss a point, however, in
not finally subjoining that he was liberally accessible to
his friends during the months he regularly spent in Paris.
Sensitive, passionate, perverse, not less than *immediately*
sociable—for if he detested his collective contemporaries
this dropped, thanks to his humanizing shyness, before the
individual encounter—he was in particular and super-
excellently not *banal,* and he attached men perhaps more
than women, inspiring a marked, a by no means colorless
shade of respect; a respect not founded, as the air of it is
apt to be, on the vague presumption, but addressed almost
in especial to his disparities and oddities and thereby, no
doubt, none too different from affection. His friends at
all events were a rich and eager *cénacle,* among whom he
was on occasion, by his picturesque personality, a natural
and overtopping center; partly perhaps because he was
so much and so familiarly at home. He wore, up to any
hour of the afternoon, that long, colloquial dressing-gown,
with trousers to match, which one has always associated
with literature in France—the uniform really of freedom
of talk. Freedom of talk abounded by his winter fire, for
the *cénacle* was made up almost wholly of the more finely
distinguished among his contemporaries; of philosophers,
men of letters and men of affairs belonging to his own
generation and the next. He had at the time I have in
mind a small perch, far aloft, at the distant, the then
almost suburban, end of the Faubourg Saint-Honoré,
where on Sunday afternoons, at the very top of an endless
flight of stairs, were to be encountered in a cloud of conversation and smoke most of the novelists of the general
Balzac tradition. Others of a different birth and complexion were markedly not of the number, were not even
conceivable as present; none of those, unless I misre-

member, whose fictions were at that time "serialized" in
the *Revue des Deux Mondes*. In spite of Renan and Taine
and two or three more, the contributor to the *Revue*
would indeed at no time have found in the circle in
question his foot on his native heath. One could recall if
one would two or three vivid allusions to him, not of
the most quotable, on the lips of the most famous of
"naturalists"—allusions to him as represented for instance
by M. Victor Cherbuliez and M. Octave Feuillet. The
author of these pages recalls a concise qualification of
this last of his fellows on the lips of Émile Zola, which
that absorbed auditor had too directly, too rashly asked
for; but which is alas not reproducible here. There was
little else but the talk, which had extreme intensity and
variety; almost nothing, as I remember, but a painted and
gilded idol, of considerable size, a relic and a memento,
on the chimney-piece. Flaubert was huge and diffident, but
florid too and resonant, and my main remembrance is of
a conception of courtesy in him, an accessibility to the
human relation, that only wanted to be sure of the way
taken or to take. The uncertainties of the French for the
determination of intercourse have often struck me as quite
matching the sharpness of their certainties, as we for the
most part feel these latter, which sometimes in fact throw
the indeterminate into almost touching relief. I have
thought of them at such times as the people in the world
one may have to go more of the way to meet than to
meet any other, and this, as it were, through their being
seated and embedded, provided for at home, in a manner
that is all their own and that has bred them to the positive
preacceptance of interest on their behalf. We at least of
the Anglo-American race, more abroad in the world,
perching everywhere, so far as grounds of intercourse
are concerned, more vaguely and superficially, as well as
less intelligently, are the more ready by that fact with
inexpensive accommodations, rather conscious that these
themselves forbear from the claim to fascinate, and ad-
vancing with the good nature that is the mantle of our

obtuseness to any point whatever where entertainment
may be offered us. My recollection is at any rate simplified
by the fact of the presence almost always, in the little
high room of the Faubourg's end, of other persons and
other voices. Flaubert's own voice is clearest to me from
the uneffaced sense of a winter week-day afternoon when
I found him by exception alone and when something led
to his reading me aloud, in support of some judgment he
had thrown off, a poem of Théophile Gautier's. He cited
it as an example of verse intensely and distinctively
French, and French in its melancholy, which neither
Goethe nor Heine nor Leopardi, neither Pushkin nor
Tennyson nor, as he said, Byron, could at all have
matched in *kind*. He converted me at the moment to this
perception, alike by the sense of the thing and by his
large utterance of it; after which it is dreadful to have
to confess not only that the poem was then new to me,
but that, hunt as I will in every volume of its author, I
am never able to recover it. This is perhaps after all
happy, causing Flaubert's own full tone, which was the
note of the occasion, to linger the more unquenched.
But for the rhyme in fact I could have believed him to be
spouting to me something strange and sonorous of his
own. The thing really rare would have been to hear him
do that—hear him *gueuler*, as he liked to call it. Verse,
I felt, we had always with us, and almost any idiot of
goodwill could give it a value. The value of so many a
passage of *Salammbô* and of *L'Éducation* was on the other
hand exactly such as gained when he allowed himself, as
had by the legend ever been frequent *dans l'intimité*, to
"bellow" it to its fullest effect.

   One of the things that make him most exhibitional and
most describable, so that if we had invented him as an
illustration or a character we would exactly so have arranged him, is that he was formed intellectually of two
quite distinct compartments, a sense of the real and a sense
of the romantic, and that his production, for our present
cognizance, thus neatly and vividly divides itself. The

divisions are as marked as the sections on the back of a
scarab, though their distinctness is undoubtedly but the
final expression of much inward strife. M. Faguet indeed,
who is admirable on this question of our author's duality,
gives an account of the romanticism that found its way
for him into the real and of the reality that found its
way into the romantic; but he none the less strikes us as
a curious splendid insect sustained on wings of a different
coloration, the right a vivid red, say, and the left as frank
a yellow. This duality has in its sharp operation placed
Madame Bovary and *L'Éducation* on one side together
and placed together on the other *Salammbô* and *La
Tentation. Bouvard et Pécuchet* it can scarce be spoken of,
I think, as having placed anywhere or anyhow. If it was
Flaubert's way to find his subject impossible there was
none he saw so much in that light as this last-named, but
also none that he appears to have held so important for
that very reason to pursue to the bitter end. Posterity
agrees with him about the impossibility, but rather takes
upon itself to break with the rest of the logic. We may
perhaps, however, for symmetry, let *Bouvard et Pécuchet*
figure as the tail—if scarabs ever have tails—of our analo-
gous insect. Only in that case we should also append as
the very tip the small volume of the *Trois Contes*,
preponderantly of the deepest imaginative hue.

His imagination was great and splendid; in spite of
which, strangely enough, his masterpiece is not his most
imaginative work. *Madame Bovary*, beyond question, holds
that first place, and *Madame Bovary* is concerned with the
career of a country doctor's wife in a petty Norman
town. The elements of the picture are of the fewest, the
situation of the heroine almost of the meanest, the material
for interest, considering the interest yielded, of the most
unpromising; but these facts only throw into relief one of
those incalculable incidents that attend the proceedings
of genius. *Madame Bovary* was doomed by circumstances
and causes—the freshness of comparative youth and good
faith on the author's part being perhaps the chief—defi-

nitely to take its position, even though its subject was
fundamentally a negation of the remote, the splendid and
the strange, the stuff of his fondest and most cultivated
dreams. It would have seemed very nearly to exclude the
free play of the imagination, and the way this faculty on
the author's part nevertheless presides is one of those
accidents, maneuvers, inspirations, we hardly know what
to call them, by which masterpieces grow. He of course
knew more or less what he was doing for his book in
making Emma Bovary a victim of the imaginative habit,
but he must have been far from designing or measuring
the total effect which renders the work so general, so
complete an expression of himself. His separate idiosyncrasies, his irritated sensibility to the life about him,
with the power to catch it in the fact and hold it hard,
and his hunger for style and history and poetry, for the
rich and the rare, great reverberations, great adumbrations,
are here represented together as they are not in his later
writings. There is nothing of the near, of the directly observed, though there may be much of the directly perceived and the minutely detailed, either in *Salammbô* or
in *Saint-Antoine*, and little enough of the extravagance of
illusion in that indefinable last word of restrained evocation and cold execution *L'Éducation sentimentale*. M.
Faguet has of course excellently noted this—that the
fortune and felicity of the book were assured by the
stroke that made the central figure an embodiment of
helpless romanticism. Flaubert himself but narrowly escaped being such an embodiment after all, and he is thus
able to express the romantic mind with extraordinary
truth. As to the rest of the matter he had the luck of
having been in possession from the first, having begun so
early to nurse and work up his plan that, familiarity and
the native air, the native soil, aiding, he had finally made
out to the last lurking shade the small sordid sunny dusty
village picture, its emptiness constituted and peopled. It
is in the background and the accessories that the real, the
real of his theme, abides; and the romantic, the romantic

of his theme, accordingly occupies the front. Emma Bovary's poor adventures are a tragedy for the very reason that in a world unsuspecting, unassisting, unconsoling, she has herself to distill the rich and the rare. Ignorant, unguided, undiverted, ridden by the very nature and mixture of her consciousness, she makes of the business an inordinate failure, a failure which in its turn makes for Flaubert the most pointed, the most *told* of anecdotes.

There are many things to say about *Madame Bovary,* but an old admirer of the book would be but half-hearted —so far as they represent reserves or puzzlements—were he not to note first of all the circumstances by which it is most endeared to him. To remember it from far back is to have been present all along at a process of singular interest to a literary mind, a case indeed full of comfort and cheer. The finest of Flaubert's novels is today, on the French shelf of fiction, one of the first of the classics; it has attained that position, slowly but steadily, before our eyes; and we seem so to follow the evolution of the fate of a classic. We see how the thing takes place; which we rarely can, for we mostly miss either the beginning or the end, especially in the case of a consecration as complete as this. The consecrations of the past are too far behind and those of the future too far in front. That the production before us *should* have come in for the heavenly crown may be a fact to offer English and American readers a mystifying side; but it is exactly our ground and a part moreover of the total interest. The author of these remarks remembers, as with a sense of the way such things happen, that when a very young person in Paris he took up from the parental table the latest number of the periodical in which Flaubert's then duly unrecognized masterpiece was in course of publication. The moment is not historic, but it was to become in the light of history, as may be said, so unforgettable that every small feature of it yet again lives for him: it rests there like the backward end of the span. The cover of the old *Revue de Paris* was yellow, if I mistake not, like that of the new, and *Madame Bovary: Mœurs de Province*, on the inside of it, was already, on the spot, as a title, mysteriously arresting, inscrutably charged. I was ignorant of what had preceded and was not to know till much later what followed; but present to me still is the act of standing there before the fire, my back against the low beplushed and begarnished French chimney-piece and taking in what I might of that installment, taking it in with so surprised an interest, and perhaps as well such a stir of faint foreknowledge, that the sunny little salon, the autumn day, the window ajar and the cheerful outside clatter of the Rue Montaigne are all now for me more or less in the story and the story more or less in them. The story, however, was at that moment having a difficult life; its fortune was all to make; its merit was so far from suspected that, as Maxime Du Camp—though verily with no excess of contrition—relates, its cloth of gold barely escaped the editorial shears. This, with much more, contributes for us to the course of things to come. The book, on its appearance as a volume, proved a shock to the high propriety of the guardians of public morals under the second Empire, and Flaubert was prosecuted as author of a work indecent to scandal. The prosecution in the event fell to the ground, but I should perhaps have mentioned this agitation as one of the very few, of any public order, in his short list. *Le Candidat* fell at the Vaudeville Theatre, several years later, with a violence indicated by its withdrawal after a performance of but two nights, the first of these marked by a deafening uproar; only if the comedy was not to recover from this accident the misprized luster of the novel was entirely to reassert itself. It is strange enough at present—so far have we traveled since then—that *Madame Bovary* should in so comparatively recent a past have been to that extent a cause of reprobation; and suggestive above all, in such connections, as to the large unconsciousness of superior minds. The desire of the superior mind of the day—that is the governmental, official, legal—to distinguish a book

with such a destiny before it is a case conceivable, but
conception breaks down before its design of making the
distinction purely invidious. We can imagine its knowing
so little, however face to face with the object, what it
had got hold of; but for it to have been so urged on by a
blind inward spring to publish to posterity the extent of
its ignorance, that would have been beyond imagination,
beyond everything but pity.

And yet it is not after all that the place the book has
taken is so overwhelmingly explained by its inherent
dignity; for here comes in the curiosity of the matter.
Here comes in especially its fund of admonition for alien
readers. The dignity of its substance is the dignity of
Madame Bovary herself as a vessel of experience—a question as to which, unmistakably, I judge, we can only
depart from the consensus of French critical opinion. M.
Faguet for example commends the character of the heroine
as one of the most living and discriminated figures of
women in all literature, praises it as a field for the display
of the romantic spirit that leaves nothing to be desired.
Subject to an observation I shall presently make and that
bears heavily in general, I think, on Flaubert as a painter
of life, subject to this restriction he is right; which is a
proof that a work of art may be markedly open to objection and at the same time be rare in its kind, and that
when it is perfect to this point nothing else particularly
matters. *Madame Bovary* has a perfection that not only
stamps it, but that makes it stand almost alone; it holds
itself with such a supreme unapproachable assurance as
both excites and defies judgment. For it deals not in the
least, as to unapproachability, with things exalted or
refined; it only confers on its sufficiently vulgar elements
of exhibition a final unsurpassable form. The form is in
itself as interesting, as active, as much of the essence of
the subject as the idea, and yet so close is its fit and so
inseparable its life that we catch it at no moment on any
errand of its own. That verily is to *be* interesting—all
round; that is to be genuine and whole. The work is a

classic because the thing, such as it is, is ideally *done*, and because is shows that in such doing eternal beauty may dwell. A pretty young woman who lives, socially and morally speaking, in a hole, and who is ignorant, foolish, flimsy, unhappy, takes a pair of lovers by whom she is successively deserted; in the midst of the bewilderment of which, giving up her husband and her child, letting everything go, she sinks deeper into duplicity, debt, despair, and arrives on the spot, on the small scene itself of her poor depravities, at a pitiful tragic end. In especial she does these things while remaining absorbed in romantic intention and vision, and she remains absorbed in romantic intention and vision while fairly rolling in the dust. That is the triumph of the book as the triumph stands, that Emma interests us by the nature of her consciousness and the play of her mind, thanks to the reality and beauty with which those sources are invested. It is not only that they represent *her* state; they are so true, so observed and felt, and especially so shown, that they represent the state, actual or potential, of all persons like her, persons romantically determined. Then her setting, the medium in which she struggles, becomes in its way as important, becomes eminent with the eminence of art; the tiny world in which she revolves, the contracted cage in which she flutters, is hung out in space for her, and her companions in captivity there are as true as herself.

I have said enough to show what I mean by Flaubert's having in this picture expressed something of his intimate self, given his heroine something of his own imagination: a point precisely that brings me back to the restriction at which I just now hinted, in which M. Faguet fails to indulge and yet which is immediate for the alien reader. Our complaint is that Emma Bovary, in spite of the nature of her consciousness and in spite of her reflecting so much that of her creator, is really too small an affair. This, critically speaking, is in view both of the value and the fortune of her history, a wonderful circumstance.

She associates herself with Frédéric Moreau in *L'Éduca-tion* to suggest for us a question that can be answered, I hold, only to Flaubert's detriment. Emma taken alone would possibly not so directly press it, but in her com-pany the hero of our author's second study of the "real" drives it home. Why did Flaubert choose, as special conduits of the life he proposed to depict, such inferior and in the case of Frédéric such abject human specimens? I insist only in respect to the latter, the perfection of Madame Bovary scarce leaving one much warrant for wishing anything other. Even here, however, the general scale and size of Emma, who is small even of her sort, should be a warning to hyperbole. If I say that in the matter of Frédéric at all events the answer is inevitably detrimental I mean that it weighs heavily on our author's general credit. He wished in each case to make a picture of experience—middling experience, it is true—and of the world close to him; but if he imagined nothing better for his purpose than such a heroine and such a hero, both such limited reflectors and registers, we are forced to believe it to have been by a defect of his mind. And that sign of weakness remains even if it be objected that the images in question were addressed to his purpose better than others would have been: the purpose itself then shows as inferior. *L'Éducation sentimentale* is a strange, an in-describable work, about which there would be many more things to say than I have space for, and all of them of the deepest interest. It is moreover, to simplify my state-ment, very much less satisfying a thing, less pleasing whether in its unity or its variety, than its specific pred-ecessor. But take it as we will, for a success or a failure— M. Faguet indeed ranks it, by the measure of its quan-tity of intention, a failure, and I on the whole agree with him—the personage offered us as bearing the weight of the drama, and in whom we are invited to that extent to interest ourselves, leaves us mainly wondering what our entertainer could have been thinking of. He takes Frédéric Moreau on the threshold of life and conducts

him to the extreme of maturity without apparently suspecting for a moment either our wonder or our protest
—"Why, why *him?*" Frédéric is positively too poor for
his part, too scant for his charge; and we feel with a
kind of embarrassment, certainly with a kind of compassion, that it is somehow the business of a protagonist
to prevent in his designer an excessive waste of faith.
When I speak of the faith in Emma Bovary as proportionately wasted I reflect on M. Faguet's judgment that
she is from the point of view of deep interest richly or
at least roundedly representative. Representative of what?
he makes us ask even while granting all the grounds of
misery and tragedy involved. The plea for her is the plea
made for all the figures that live without evaporation
under the painter's hand—that they are not only particular
persons but types of their kind, and as valid in one light
as in the other. It is Emma's "kind" that I question for
this responsibility, even if it be inquired of me why I
then fail to question that of Charles Bovary, in its perfection, or that of the inimitable, the immortal Homais.
If we express Emma's deficiency as the poverty of her
consciousness for the typical function, it is certainly not,
one must admit, that she is surpassed in this respect either
by her platitudinous husband or by his friend the pretentious apothecary. The difference is none the less somehow in the fact that they are respectively studies but of
their character and office, which function in each expresses
adequately *all* they are. It may be, I concede, because
Emma is the only woman in the book that she is taken
by M. Faguet as *femininely* typical, typical in the larger
illustrative way, whereas the others pass with him for
images specifically conditioned. Emma is this same for
myself, I plead; she is conditioned to such an excess of the
specific, and the specific in her case leaves out so many
even of the commoner elements of conceivable life in a
woman when we are invited to see that life as pathetic,
as dramatic agitation, that we challenge both the author's
and the critic's scale of importances. The book is a picture

of the middling as much as they like, but does Emma attain even to *that?* Hers is a narrow middling even for a little imaginative person whose "social" significance is small. It is greater on the whole than her capacity of consciousness, taking this all round; and so, in a word, we feel her less illustrational than she might have been not only if the world had offered her more points of contact, but if she had had more of these to give it.

We meet Frédéric first, we remain with him long, as a *moyen,* a provincial bourgeois of the mid-century, educated and not without fortune, thereby with freedom, in whom the life of his day reflects itself. Yet the life of his day, on Flaubert's showing, hangs together with the poverty of Frédéric's own inward or for that matter outward life; so that, the whole thing being, for scale, intention and extension, a sort of epic of the usual (with the Revolution of 1848 introduced indeed as an episode), it affects us as an epic without air, without wings to lift it; reminds us in fact more than anything else of a huge balloon, all of silk pieces strongly sewn together and patiently blown up, but that absolutely refuses to leave the ground. The discrimination I here make as against our author is, however, the only one inevitable in a series of remarks so brief. What it really represents—and nothing could be more curious—is that Frédéric enjoys his position not only without the aid of a single "sympathetic" character of consequence, but even without the aid of one with whom we can directly communicate. Can we communicate with the central personage? or would we really if we could? A hundred times no, and if he himself can communicate with the people shown us as surrounding him this only proves him of their kind. Flaubert on his "real" side was in truth an ironic painter, and ironic to a tune that makes his final accepted state, his present literary dignity and "classic" peace, superficially anomalous. There is an explanation to which I shall immediately come; but I find myself feeling for a moment longer in presence of *L'Éducation* how much more interesting a writer may be on occasion by the given failure than by the given success. Successes pure and simple disconnect and dismiss him; failures—though I admit they must be a bit qualified—keep him in touch and in relation. Thus it is that as the work of a "grand écrivain" *L'Éducation*, large, labored, immensely "written," with beautiful passages and a general emptiness, with a kind of leak in its stored sadness, moreover, by which its moral dignity escapes—thus it is that Flaubert's ill-starred novel is a curiosity for a literary museum. Thus it is also that it suggests a hundred reflections, and suggests perhaps most of them directly to the intending laborer in the same field. If in short, as I have said, Flaubert is the novelist's novelist, this performance does more than any other toward making him so.

I have to add in the same connection that I had not lost sight of Madame Arnoux, the main ornament of *L'Éducation*, in pronouncing just above on its deficiency in the sympathetic. Madame Arnoux is exactly the author's one marked attempt, here or elsewhere, to represent beauty otherwise than for the senses, beauty of character and life; and what becomes of the attempt is a matter highly significant. M. Faguet praises with justice his conception of the figure and of the relation, the relation that never bears fruit, that keeps Frédéric adoring her, through hindrance and change, from the beginning of life to the end; that keeps her, by the same constraint, forever immaculately "good," from youth to age, though deeply moved and cruelly tempted and sorely tried. Her contacts with her adorer are not even frequent, in proportion to the field of time; her conditions of fortune, of association and occupation are almost sordid, and we see them with the march of the drama, such as it is, become more and more so; besides which—I again remember that M. Faguet excellently notes it—nothing in the nature of "parts" is attributed to her; not only is she not presented as clever, she is scarce invested with a character at all. Almost nothing that she says is repeated, almost nothing that she

does is shown. She is an image none the less beautiful
and vague, an image of passion cherished and abjured,
renouncing all sustenance and yet persisting in life. Only
she has for real distinction the extreme drawback that
she is offered us quite preponderantly through Frédéric's
vision of her, that we see her practically in no other light.
Now Flaubert unfortunately has not been able not so to
discredit Frédéric's vision in general, his vision of every-
one and everything, and in particular of his own life, that
it makes a medium good enough to convey adequately a
noble impression. Madame Arnoux is of course ever so
much the best thing in his life—which is saying little;
but his life is made up of such queer material that we
find ourselves displeased at her being "in" it on whatever
terms; all the more that she seems scarcely to affect,
improve or determine it. Her creator in short never had a
more awkward idea than this attempt to give us the benefit
of such a conception in such a way; and even though I
have still something else to say about that I may as well
speak of it at once as a mistake that gravely counts
against him. It is but one of three, no doubt, in all his
work; but I shall not, I trust, pass for extravagant if I
call it the most indicative. What makes it so is its being
the least superficial; the two others are, so to speak, intellectual, while this is somehow moral. It was a mistake, as
I have already hinted, to propose to register in so mean a
consciousness as that of such a hero so large and so mixed
a quantity of life as *L'Éducation* clearly intends; and it
was a mistake of the tragic sort that is a theme mainly
for silence to have embarked on *Bouvard et Pécuchet* at
all, not to have given it up sooner than be given up by
it. But these were at the worst not wholly compromising
blunders. What *was* compromising—and the great point is
that it remained so, that nothing has an equal weight
against it—is the unconsciousness of error in respect to
the opportunity that would have counted as his finest.
We feel not so much that Flaubert misses it, for that we
could bear; but that he doesn't *know* he misses it is what

stamps the blunder. We do not pretend to say how he might have shown us Madame Arnoux better—that was his own affair. What is ours is that he really thought he was showing her as well as he could, or as she might be shown; at which we veil our face. For once that he had a conception quite apart, apart I mean from the array of his other conceptions and more delicate than any, he "went," as we say, and spoiled it. Let me add in all tenderness, and to make up for possibly too much insistence, that it is the only stain on his shield; let me even confess that I should not wonder if, when all is said, it is a blemish no one has ever noticed.

Perhaps no one has ever noticed either what was present to me just above as the partial makeweight there glanced at, the fact that in the midst of this general awkwardness, as I have called it, there is at the same time a danger so escaped as to entitle our author to full credit. I scarce know how to put it with little enough of the ungracious, but I think that even the true Flaubertist finds himself wondering a little that some flaw of taste, some small but unfortunate lapse by the way, *should* as a matter of fact not somehow or somewhere have waited on the demonstration of the platonic purity prevailing between this heroine and her hero—so far as we do find that image projected. It is alike difficult to indicate without offense or to ignore without unkindness a fond reader's apprehension here of a possibility of the wrong touch, the just perceptibly false note. I would not have staked my life on Flaubert's security of instinct in such a connection—as an absolutely fine and predetermined security; and yet in the event that felicity has settled, there is not so much as the lightest wrong breath (speaking of the matter in this light of tact and taste) or the shade of a crooked stroke. One exclaims at the end of the question "Dear old Flaubert after all—!" and perhaps so risks seeming to patronize for fear of not making a point. The point made for what it is worth, at any rate, I am the more free to recover the benefit of what I mean by critical

"tenderness" in our general connection—expressing in it as
I do our general respect, and my own particular, for our
author's method and process and history, and my sense of
the luxury of such a sentiment at such a vulgar literary
time. It is a respect positive and settled and the thing
that has most to do with consecrating for us that loyalty
to him as the novelist of the novelist—unlike as it is even
the best feeling inspired by any other member of the
craft. He may stand for our operative conscience or our
vicarious sacrifice; animated by a sense of literary honor,
attached to an ideal of perfection, incapable of lapsing in
fine from a self-respect, that enable us to sit at ease, to
surrender to the age, to indulge in whatever comparative
meannesses (and no meanness in art is so mean as the
sneaking economic) we may find most comfortable or
profitable. May it not in truth be said that we practice our
industry, so many of us, at relatively little cost just *because*
poor Flaubert, producing the most expensive fictions ever
written, so handsomely paid for it? It is as if this put
it in our power to produce cheap and thereby sell dear;
as if, so expressing it, literary honor being by his example
effectively secure for the firm at large and the general
concern, on its whole esthetic side, floated once for all,
we find our individual attention free for literary and
esthetic indifference. All the while we thus lavish our
indifference the spirit of the author of *Madame Bovary*, in
the cross-light of the old room above the Seine, is trying
to the last admiration for the thing itself. That production
puts the matter into a nutshell: *Madame Bovary*, subject
to whatever qualification, as absolutely the most literary
of novels, so literary that it covers us with its mantle. It
shows us once for all that there is no *intrinsic* call for a
debasement of the type. The mantle I speak of is wrought
with surpassing fineness, and we may always, under stress
of whatever charge of illiteracy, frivolity, vulgarity, flaunt
it as the flag of the guild. Let us therefore frankly concede that to surround Flaubert with our consideration is
the least return we can make for such a privilege. The

consideration moreover is idle unless it be real, unless it be intelligent enough to measure his effort and his success. Of the effort as mere effort I have already spoken, of the desperate difficulty involved for him in making his form square with his conception; and I by no means attach general importance to these secrets of the workshop, which are but as the contortions of the fastidious muse who is the servant of the oracle. They are really rather secrets of the kitchen and contortions of the priestess of *that* tripod—they are not an upstairs matter. It is of their specially distinctive importance I am now speaking, of the light shed on them by the results before us.

They all represent the pursuit of a style, of the ideally right one for its relations, and would still be interesting if the style had not been achieved. *Madame Bovary, Salammbô, Saint-Antoine, L'Éducation* are so written and so composed (though the last-named in a minor degree) that the more we look at them the more we find in them, under this head, a beauty of intention and of effect; the more they figure in the too often dreary desert of fictional prose a class by themselves and a little living oasis. So far as that desert is of the complexion of our own English speech it supplies with remarkable rarity this particular source of refreshment. So strikingly is that the case, so scant for the most part any dream of a scheme of beauty in these connections, that a critic betrayed at artless moments into a plea for composition may find himself as blankly met as if his plea were for trigonometry. He makes inevitably his reflections, which are numerous enough; one of them being that if we turn our back so squarely, so universally to this order of considerations it is because the novel is so preponderantly cultivated among us by women, in other words by a sex ever gracefully, comfortably, enviably unconscious (it would be too much to call them even suspicious) of the requirements of form. The case is at any rate sharply enough made for us, or against us, by the circumstance that women are held to have achieved on all our ground, in spite of this weakness and others, as great results as any. The judgment is undoubtedly founded: Jane Austen was instinctive and charming, and the other recognitions—even over the heads of the ladies, some of them, from Fielding to Pater—are obvious; without, however, in the least touching my contention. For signal examples of what composition, distribution, arrangement can do, of how they intensify the life of a work of art, we have to go elsewhere; and the value of Flaubert for us is that he admirably points the moral. This is the explanation of the "classic" fortune of *Madame Bovary* in especial, though I may add that also of Hérodias and Saint-Julien l'Hospitalier in the *Trois Contes,* as well as an aspect of these works endlessly suggestive. I spoke just now of the small field of the picture in the longest of them, the small capacity, as I called it, of the vessel; yet the way the thing is done not only triumphs over the question of value but in respect to it fairly misleads and confounds us. Where else shall we find in anything proportionately so small such an air of dignity of size? Flaubert *made* things big—it was his way, his ambition and his necessity; and I say this while remembering that in *L'Éducation* (in proportion I mean again) the effect has not been produced. The subject of *L'Éducation* is in spite of Frédéric large, but an indefinable shrinkage has overtaken it in the execution. The exception so marked, however, is single; *Salammbô* and *Saint-Antoine* are both at once very "heavy" conceptions and very consistently and splendidly high applications of a manner.

It is in this assured manner that the lesson sits aloft, that the spell for the critical reader resides; and if the conviction under which Flaubert labors is more and more grossly discredited among us his compact mass is but the greater. He regarded the work of art as *existing* but by its expression, and defied us to name any other measure of its life that is not a stultification. He held style to be accordingly an indefeasible part of it, and found beauty, interest and distinction as dependent on it for emergence as a letter committed to the post office is dependent on an addressed envelope. Strange enough it may well appear to us to have to apologize for such notions as eccentric. There are persons who consider that style comes of itself —we see and hear at present, I think, enough of them; and to whom he would doubtless have remarked that it goes, of itself, still faster. The thing naturally differs in fact with the nature of the imagination; the question is one of proprieties and affinities, sympathy and proportion. The sympathy of the author of *Salammbô* was all with the magnificent, his imagination for the phrase as variously noble or ignoble in itself, contributive or destructive, adapted and harmonious or casual and common. The worse among such possibilities have been multiplied by the infection of bad writing, and he denied that the better ever do anything so obliging as to come of themselves. They scarcely indeed for Flaubert "came" at all; their arrival was determined only by fasting and prayer or by patience of pursuit, the arts of the chase, long waits and watches, figuratively speaking, among the peaks or by the waters. The production of a book was of course made inordinately slow by the fatigue of these measures; in illustration of which his letters often record that it has taken him three days[1] to arrive at one right sentence, tested by the pitch of his ideal of the right for the suggestion aimed at. His difficulties drew from the author, as I have mentioned, much resounding complaint; but those voices have ceased to trouble us and the final voice re-

---

[1] It was true, delightfully true, that, extravagance in this province of his life, though apparently in no other, being Flaubert's necessity and law, he deliberated and hung fire, wrestled, retreated and returned, indulged generally in a tragicomedy of waste; which I recall a charming expression of on the lips of Edmond de Goncourt, who quite recognized the heroic legend, but prettily qualified it: "*Il faut vous dire qu'il y avait là-dedans beaucoup de coucheries et d'école buissonière.*" And he related how on the occasion of a stay with his friend under the roof of the Princess Mathilde, the friend, missed during the middle hours of a fine afternoon, was found to have undressed himself and gone to bed to think!

mains. No feature of the whole business is more edifying than the fact that he in the first place never misses style and in the second never appears to have beaten about for it. That betrayal is of course the worst betrayal of all, and I think the way he has escaped it the happiest form of the peace that has finally visited him. It was truly a wonderful success to be so the devotee of the phrase and yet never its victim. Fine as he inveterately desired it should be he still never lost sight of the question Fine for what? It is always so related and associated, so properly part of something else that is in turn part of something other, part of a reference, a tone, a passage, a page, that the simple may enjoy it for its least bearing and the initiated for its greatest. That surely is to be a writer of the first order, to resemble when in the hand and however closely viewed a shapely crystal box, and yet to be seen when placed on the table and opened to contain innumerable compartments, springs and tricks. One is ornamental either way, but one is in the second way precious too.

The crystal box then figures the style of *Salammbô* and *Saint-Antoine* in a greater degree than that of *Bovary*, because, as the two former express the writer's romantic side, he had in them, while equally covering his tracks, still further to fare and still more to hunt. Beyond this allusion to their completing his duality I shall not attempt closely to characterize them; though I admit that in not insisting on them I press most lightly on the scale into which he had in his own view cast his greatest pressure. He lamented the doom that drove him so oddly, so ruefully, to choose his subjects, but he lamented it least when these subjects were most pompous and most exotic, feeling as he did that they had then after all most affinity with his special eloquence. In dealing with the near, the directly perceived, he had to keep down his tone, to make the eloquence small; though with the consequence, as we have seen, that in spite of such precautions the whole thing mostly insists on being ample. The familiar, that is, under his touch, took on character, importance, extension, one scarce knows what to call it, in order to carry the style or perhaps rather, as we may say, sit with proper ease in the vehicle, and there was accordingly a limit to its smallness; whereas in the romantic books, the preferred world of Flaubert's imagination, there was practically no need of compromise. The compromise gave him throughout endless trouble, and nothing would be more to the point than to show, had I space, why in particular it distressed him. It was obviously his strange predicament that the only spectacle open to him by experience and direct knowledge was the bourgeois, which on that ground imposed on him successively his three so intensely bourgeois themes. He was obliged to treat these themes, which he hated, because his experience left him no alternative; his only alternative was given by history, geography, philosophy, fancy, the world of erudition and of imagination, the world especially of this last. In the bourgeois sphere his ideal of expression labored under protest; in the other, the imagined, the projected, his need for facts, for matter, and his pursuit of them, sat no less heavily. But as his style all the while required a certain exercise of pride he was on the whole more at home in the exotic than in the familiar; he escaped above all in the former connection the associations, the disparities he detested. He could be frankly noble in *Salammbô* and *Saint-Antoine*, whereas in *Bovary* and *L'Éducation* he could be but circuitously and insidiously so. He could in the one case cut his coat according to his cloth—if we mean by his cloth his predetermined tone, while in the other he had to take it already cut. Singular enough in his life the situation so constituted: the comparatively meager human consciousness—for we must come back to that in him—struggling with the absolutely large artistic; and the large artistic half wreaking itself on the meager human and half seeking a refuge from it, as well as a revenge against it, in something quite different.

Flaubert had in fact command of two refuges which he worked in turn. The first of these was the attitude of irony, so constant in him that *L'Éducation* bristles and hardens with it and *Bouvard et Pécuchet*—strangest of "poetic" justices—is made as dry as sand and as heavy as lead; the second only was, by processes, by journeys the most expensive, to get away altogether. And we inevitably ask ourselves whether, eschewing the policy of flight, he might not after all have fought out his case a little more on the spot. Might he not have addressed himself to the human still otherwise than in *L'Éducation* and in *Bouvard*? When one thinks of the view of the life of his country, of the vast French community and its constituent creatures, offered in these productions, one declines to believe it could make up the *whole* vision of a man of his quality. Or when all was said and done was he absolutely and exclusively condemned to irony? The second refuge I speak of, the getting away from the human, the congruously and measurably human, altogether, perhaps becomes in the light of this possibility but an irony the more. Carthage and the Thebaid, Salammbô, Spendius, Matho, Hannon, Saint Anthony, Hilarion, the Paternians, the Marcosians and the Carpocratians, what are all these, inviting because queer, but a confession of supreme impatience with the actual and the near, often queer enough too, no doubt, but not consolingly, not transcendently? Last remains the question whether, even if our author's immediate as distinguished from his remote view had had more reach, the particular gift we claim for him, the perfection of arrangement and form, would have had in certain directions the acquired flexibility. States of mind, states of soul, of the simpler kind, the kinds supposable in the Emma Bovarys, the Frédérics, the Bouvards and the Pécuchets, to say nothing of the Carthaginians and the Eremites—for Flaubert's eremites are eminently artless—these conditions represent, I think, his proved psychological range. And that throws us back remarkably, almost confoundingly, upon another face of the general anomaly. The "gift" was of the greatest, a force in itself, in virtue of which he is a consummate writer; and yet

there are whole sides of life to which it was never addressed and which it apparently quite failed to suspect as
a field of exercise. If he never approached the complicated character in man or woman—Emma Bovary is
not the least little bit complicated—or the really furnished,
the finely civilized, was this because, suprisingly, he could
not? *L'âme française* at all events shows in him but ill.

This undoubtedly marks a limit, but limits are for the
critic familiar country, and he may mostly well feel the
prospect wide enough when he finds something positively
well enough done. By disposition or by obligation Flaubert
selected, and though his selection was in some respects
narrow he stops not too short to have left us three really
"cast" works and a forth of several perfect parts, to say
nothing of the element of perfection, of the superlative
for the size, in his three *nouvelles*. What he attempted he
attempted in a spirit that gives an extension to the idea of
the achievable and the achieved in a literary thing, and it
is by this that we contentedly gauge the matter. As success
goes in this world of the approximate it may pass for
success of the greatest. If I am unable to pursue the proof
of my remark in *Salammbô* and *Saint-Antoine* it is because I have also had to select and have found the
questions connected with their two companions more interesting. There are numerous judges, I hasten to mention,
who, showing the opposite preference, lose themselves
with rapture in the strange bristling archæological picture
—yet all amazingly vivified and co-ordinated—of the
Carthaginian mercenaries in revolt and the sacred veil of
the great goddess profaned and stolen; as well in the still
more peopled panorama of the ancient sects, superstitions
and mythologies that swim in the desert before the
fevered eyes of the Saint. One may be able, however, at
once to breathe more freely in *Bovary* than in *Salammbô*
and yet to hope that there is no intention of the latter
that one has missed. The great intention certainly, and
little as we may be sweetly beguiled, holds us fast; which
is simply the author's indomitable purpose of fully per-

vading his field. There are countries beyond the sea in which tracts are allowed to settlers on condition that they will really, not nominally, cultivate them. Flaubert is on his romantic ground like one of these settlers; he makes good with all his might his title to his tract, and in a way that shows how it is not only for him a question of safety but a question of honor. Honor demands that he shall set up his home and his faith there in such a way that every inch of the surface be planted or paved. He would have been ashamed merely to encamp and, after the fashion of most other adventurers, knock up a log hut among charred stumps. This was not what would have been for him taking artistic possession, it was not what would have been for him even personal honor, let alone literary; and yet the general lapse from integrity was a thing that, wherever he looked, he saw not only condoned but acclaimed and rewarded. He lived, as he felt, in an age of mean production and cheap criticism, the practical upshot of which took on for him a name that was often on his lips. He called it the hatred of literature, a hatred in the midst of which, the most literary of men, he found himself appointed to suffer. I may not, however, follow him in that direction—which would take us far; and the less that he was for himself after all, in spite of groans and imprecations, a man of resources and remedies, and that there was always his possibility of building himself in.

This he did equally in all his books—built himself into literature by means of a material put together with extraordinary art; but it leads me again to the question of what such a stiff ideal imposed on him for the element of exactitude. This element, in the romantic, was his merciless law; it was perhaps even in the romantic that—if there could indeed be degrees for him in such matters—he most despised the loose and the more-or-less. To be intensely definite and perfectly positive, to know so well what he meant that he could at every point strikingly and conclusively verify it, was the first of his needs; and if in addition to being thus synthetically final he could be strange and sad and terrible, and leave the cause of these effects inscrutable, success then had for him its highest savor. We feel the inscrutability in those memorable few words that put before us Frédéric Moreau's start upon his vain course of travel, "*Il connût alors la mélancholie des paquebots*"; an image to the last degree comprehensive and embracing, but which haunts us, in its droll pathos, without our quite knowing why. But he was really never so pleased as when he could be both rare and precise about the dreadful. His own sense of all this, as I have already indicated, was that beauty comes with expression, that expression is creation, that it *makes* the reality, and only in the degree in which it *is*, exquisitely, expression; and that we move in literature through a world of different values and relations, a blessed world in which we know nothing except by style, but in which also everything is saved by it, and in which the image is thus always superior to the thing itself. This quest and multiplication of the image, the image tested and warranted and consecrated for the occasion, was accordingly his high elegance, to which he too much sacrificed and to which *Salammbô* and partly *Saint-Antoine* are monstrous monuments. Old cruelties and perversities, old wonders and errors and terrors, endlessly appealed to him; they constitute the unhuman side of his work, and if we have not the bribe of curiosity, of a lively interest in method, or rather in evocation just *as* evocation, we tread our way among them, especially in *Salammbô*, with a reserve too dry for our pleasure. To my own view the curiosity and the literary interest are equal in dealing with the non-romantic books, and the world presented, the aspects and agents, are less deterrent and more amenable both to our own social and expressional terms. Style itself moreover, with all respect to Flaubert, never *totally* beguiles; since even when we are so queerly constituted as to be ninety-nine parts literary we are still a hundreth part something else. This hundredth part may, once we possess the book—or the book possesses us—make us imperfect as readers, and yet without it should we want or get the book at all? The curiosity at any rate, to repeat, is even greatest for me in *Madame Bovary*, say, for here I can measure, can more directly appreciate, the terms. The aspects and impressions being of an experience conceivable to me I am more touched by the beauty; my interest gets more of the benefit of the beauty even though this be not intrinsically greater. Which brings back our appreciation inevitably at last to the question of our author's lucidity.

I have sufficiently remarked that I speak from the point of view of his interest to a reader of his own craft, the point of view of his extraordinary technical wealth— though indeed when I think of the general power of *Madame Bovary* I find myself desiring not to narrow the ground of the lesson, not to connect the lesson, to its prejudice, with that idea of the "technical," that question of the way a thing is done, so abhorrent, as a call upon attention, in whatever art, to the wondrous Anglo-Saxon mind. Without proposing Flaubert as the type of the newspaper novelist, or as an easy alternative to golf or the bicycle, we should do him less than justice in failing to insist that a masterpiece like *Madame Bovary* may benefit even with the simple-minded by the way it has been done. It derives from its firm roundness that sign of all rare works that there is something in it for every one. It may be read ever so attentively, ever so freely, without a suspicion of how it is written, to say nothing of put together; it may equally be read under the excitement of these perceptions alone, one of the greatest known to the reader who is fully open to them. Both readers will have been transported, which is all any can ask. Leaving the first of them, however that may be, to state the case for himself, I state it yet again for the second, if only on this final ground. The book and its companions represent for us a practical solution, Flaubert's own troubled but settled one, of the eternal dilemma of the painter of life. From the moment this rash adventurer deals with his mysterious matter at all directly his desire is not to deal with it stintedly. It at the same time remains true that from the moment he desires to produce forms in which it shall be preserved, he desires that these forms, things of *his* creation, shall not be, as testifying to his way with them, weak or ignoble. He must make them complete and beautiful, of satisfactory production, intrinsically interesting, under peril of disgrace with those who know. Those who don't know of course don't count for him, and it neither helps nor hinders him to say that every one knows about life. Every one does not—it is distinctly the case of the few; and if it were in fact the case of the many the knowledge still might exist, on the evidence around us, even in an age of unprecedented printing, without attesting itself by a multiplication of masterpieces. The question for the artist can only be of doing the artistic utmost, and thereby of *seeing* the general task. When it is seen with the intensity with which it presented itself to Flaubert a lifetime is none too much for fairly tackling it. It must either be left alone or be dealt with, and to leave it alone is a comparatively simple matter.

To deal with it is on the other hand to produce a certain number of finished works; there being no other known method; and the quantity of life depicted will depend on this array. What will this array, however, depend on, and what will condition the number of pieces of which it is composed? The "finish," evidently, that the formula so glibly postulates and for which the novelist is thus so handsomely responsible. He has on the one side to feel his subject and on the other side to render it, and there are undoubtedly two ways in which his situation may be expressed, especially perhaps by himself. The more he feels his subject the more he *can* render it—that is the first way. The more he renders it the more he *can* feel it —that is the second way. This second way was unmistakably Flaubert's, and if the result of it for him was a bar to abundant production he could only accept such an incident as part of the game. He probably for that matter

would have challenged any easy definition of "abundance," contested the application of it to the repetition,
however frequent, of the thing not "done." What but the
"doing" makes the thing, he would have asked, and how
can a positive result from a mere iteration of negatives,
or wealth proceed from the simple addition of so many
instances of penury? We should here, in closer communion with him, have got into his highly characteristic
and suggestive view of the fertilization of subject by form,
penetration of the sense, ever, by the expression—the latter
reacting creatively on the former; a conviction in the
light of which he appears to have wrought with real
consistency and which borrows from him thus its high
measure of credit. It would undoubtedly have suffered if
his books had been things of a loose logic, whereas we
refer to it not only without shame but with an en-
couraged confidence by their showing of a logic so close.
Let the phrase, the form that the whole is at the given
moment staked on, be beautiful and related, and the rest
will take care of itself—such is a rough indication of
Flaubert's faith; which has the importance that it was a
faith sincere, active and inspiring. I hasten to add indeed
that we must most of all remember how in these matters
everything hangs on definitions. The "beautiful," with
our author, covered for the phrase a great deal of ground,
and when every sort or propriety had been gathered in
under it and every relation, in a complexity of such,
protected, the idea itself, the presiding thought, ended
surely by being pretty well provided for.

These, however, are subordinate notes, and the plain
question, in the connection I have touched upon, is of
whether we would really wish him to have written more
books, say either of the type of *Bovary* or of the type of
Salammbô, and not have written them so well. When the
production of a great artist who has lived a length of
years has been small there is always the regret; but there
is seldom, any more than here, the conceivable remedy.
For the case is doubtless predetermined by the particular

kind of great artist a writer happens to be, and this even if when we come to the conflict, to the historic case, deliberation and delay may not all have been imposed by temperament. The admirable George Sand, Flaubert's beneficent friend and correspondent, is exactly the happiest example we could find of the genius constitutionally incapable of worry, the genius for whom style "came," for whom the sought effect was ever quickly and easily struck off, the book freely and swiftly written, and who consequently is represented for us by upwards of ninety volumes. If the comparison were with this lady's great contemporary the elder Dumas the disparity would be quadrupled, but that ambiguous genius, somehow never really caught by us in the *fact* of composition, is out of our concern here: the issue is of those developments of expression which involve a style, and as Dumas never so much as once grazed one in all his long career, there was not even enough of that grace in him for a fillip of the fingernail. Flaubert is at any rate represented by six books, so that he may on that estimate figure as poor, while Madame Sand, falling so little short of a hundred, figures as rich; and yet the fact remains that I can refer the congenial mind to him with confidence and can do nothing of the sort for it in respect to Madame Sand. She is loose and liquid and iridescent, as iridescent as we may undertake to find her; but I can imagine compositions quite without virtue—the virtue I mean, of sticking together—begotten by the impulse to emulate her. She had undoubtedly herself the benefit of her facility, but are we not left wondering to what extent *we* have it? There is too little in her, by the literary connection, for the critical mind, weary of much wandering, to rest upon. Flaubert himself wandered, wandered far, went much roundabout and sometimes lost himself by the way, but how handsomely he provided for our present repose! He found the French language inconceivably difficult to write with elegance and was confronted with the equal truths that elegance is the last thing that languages, even as they most mature, seem to concern themselves with, and that at the same time taste, asserting rights, insists on it, to the effect of showing us in a boundless circumjacent waste of effort what the absence of it may mean. He saw the less of this desert of death come back to that—that everything at all saved from it for us since the beginning had been saved by a soul of elegance within, or in other words by the last refinement of selection, by the indifference on the part of the very idiom, huge quite other than "composing" agent, to the individual pretension. Recognizing thus that to carry through the individual pretension is at the best a battle, he adored a hard surface and detested a soft one—much more a muddled; regarded a style without rhythm and harmony as in a work of pretended beauty no style at all. He considered that the failure of complete expression so registered made of the work of pretended beauty a work of achieved barbarity. It would take us far to glance even at his fewest discriminations; but rhythm and harmony were for example most menaced in his scheme by repetition—when repetition had not a positive grace; and were above all most at the mercy of the bristling particles of which our modern tongues are mainly composed and which make of the desired surface a texture pricked through, from beneath, even to destruction, as by innumerable thorns.

On these lines production was of course slow work for him—especially as he met the difficulty, met it with an inveteracy which shows how it *can* be met; and full of interest for readers of English speech is the reflection he causes us to make as to the possibility of success at all comparable among ourselves. I have spoken of his groans and imprecations, his interminable waits and deep despairs; but what would these things have been, what would have become of him and what of his wrought residuum, had he been condemned to deal with a form of speech consisting, like ours, as to one part, of "that" and "which"; as to a second part, of the blessed "it," which an English sentence may repeat in three or four opposed references without in the least losing caste; as to a third face of all the "tos" of the infinite and the preposition; as to a fourth of our precious auxiliaries "be" and "do"; and as to a fifth, of whatever survives in the language for the precious art of pleasing? Whether or no the fact that the painter of "life" among us has to contend with a medium intrinsically indocile, on certain sides, like our own, whether this drawback accounts for his having failed, in our time, to treat us, arrested and charmed, to a single case of crowned classicism, there is at any rate no doubt that we in some degree owe Flaubert's counterweight for that deficiency to *his* having, on his own ground, more happily triumphed. By which I do not mean that *Madame Bovary* is a classic because the "thats," the "its" and the "tos" are made to march as Orpheus and his lute made the beasts, but because the element of order and harmony works as a symbol of everything else that is preserved for us by the history of the book. The history of the book remains the lesson and the important, the delightful thing, remains above all the drama that moves slowly to its climax. It is what we come back to for the sake of what it shows us. We see—from the present to the past indeed, never alas from the present to the future—how a classic almost inveterately grows. Unimportant, unnoticed, or, so far as noticed, contested, unrelated, alien, it has a cradle round which the fairies but scantly flock and is waited on in general by scarce a hint of significance. The significance comes by a process slow and small, the fact only that one perceptive private reader after another discovers at his convenience that the book is rare. The addition of the perceptive private readers is no quick affair, and would doubtless be a vain one did they not— while plenty of other much more remarkable books come and go—accumulate and count. The count by their quality and continuity of attention; so they have gathered for *Madame Bovary*, and so they are held. That is really once more the great circumstance. It is always in order for us to feel yet again what it is we are held by. Such is my

reason, definitely, for speaking of Flaubert as the novelist's novelist. Are we not moreover—and let it pass this
time as a happy hope!—pretty well all novelists now?

ÉMILE ZOLA

IF IT BE TRUE that the critical spirit today, in presence of
the rising tide of prose fiction, a watery waste out of
which old standards and landmarks are seen barely to
emerge, like chimneys and the tops of trees in a country
under flood—if it be true that the anxious observer, with
the water up to his chin, finds himself asking for the
reason of the strange phenomenon, for its warrant and
title, so we likewise make out that these credentials rather
fail to float on the surface. We live in a world of wanton
and importunate fable, we breathe its air and consume its
fruits; yet who shall say that we are able, when invited,
to account for our preferring it so largely to the world of
fact? To do so would be to make some adequate statement
of the good the product in question does us. What does
it do for our life, our mind, our manners, our morals—
what does it do that history, poetry, philosophy may not
do, as well or better, to warn, to comfort and command
the countless thousands for whom and by whom it comes
into being? We seem too often left with our riddle on our
hands. The lame conclusion on which we retreat is that

"stories" are multiplied, circulated, paid for, on the scale of the present hour, simply because people "like" them. As to why people *should* like anything so loose and mean as the preponderant mass of the "output," so little indebted for the magic of its action to any mystery in the making, is more than the actual state of our perceptions enables us to say.

This bewilderment might be our last word if it were not for the occasional occurrence of accidents especially appointed to straighten out a little our tangle. We are reminded that if the unnatural prosperity of the wanton fable cannot be adequately explained, it can at least be illustrated with a sharpness that is practically an argument. An abstract solution failing we encounter it in the concrete. We catch in short a new impression or, to speak more truly, recover an old one. It was always there to be had, but we ourselves throw off an oblivion, an indifference for which there are plenty of excuses. We become conscious, for our profit, of a *case*, and we see that our mystification came from the way cases had appeared for so long to fail us. None of the shapeless forms about us for the time had attained to the dignity of one. The one I am now conceiving as suddenly effective—for which I fear I must have been regarding it as somewhat in eclipse—is that of Émile Zola, whom, as a manifestation of the sort we are considering, three or four striking facts have lately combined to render more objective and, so to speak, more massive. His close connection with the most resounding of recent public quarrels; his premature and disastrous death; above all, at the moment I write, the appearance of his last-finished novel, bequeathed to his huge public from beyond the grave—these rapid events have thrust him forward and made him loom abruptly larger; much as if our pedestrian critic, treading the dusty highway, had turned a sharp corner.

It is not assuredly that Zola has ever been veiled or unapparent; he had, on the contrary been digging his field these thirty years, and for all passers to see, with an

industry that kept him, after the fashion of one of the
grand grim sowers or reapers of his brother of the brush,
or at least of the canvas, Jean-François Millet, duskily
outlined against the sky. He was there in the landscape of
labor—he had always been; but he was there as a big
natural or pictorial feature, a spreading tree, a battered
tower, a lumpish round-shouldered useful hayrick, con-
founded with the air and the weather, the rain and the
shine, the day and the dusk, merged more or less, as it
were, in the play of the elements themselves. We had got
used to him, and, thanks in a measure just to this stoutness
of his presence, to the long regularity of his performance,
had come to notice him hardly more than the dwellers in
the marketplace notice the quarters struck by the town-
clock. On top of all accordingly, for our skeptical mood,
the sense of his work—a sense determined afresh by the
strange climax of his personal history—rings out almost
with violence as a reply to our wonder. It is as if an earth-
quake or some other rude interference had shaken from
the town-clock a note of such unusual depth as to compel
attention. We therefore once more give heed, and the
result of this is that we feel ourselves after a little probably
as much enlightened as we can hope ever to be. We have
worked round to the so marked and impressive anomaly
of the adoption of the futile art by one of the stoutest
minds and stoutest characters of our time. This extraordinarily robust worker has found it good enough for him,
and if the fact is, as I say, anomalous, we are doubtless
helped to conclude that by its anomalies, in future, the
bankrupt business, as we are so often moved to pronounce
it, will most recover credit.

What is at all events striking for us, critically speaking,
is that, in the midst of the dishonor it has gradually
harvested by triumphant vulgarity of practice, its pliancy
and applicability can still plead for themselves. The
curious contradiction stands forth for our relief—the circumstance that thirty years ago a young man of extraordinary brain and indomitable purpose, wishing to give the

measure of these endowments in a piece of work supremely solid, conceived and sat down to *Les Rougon-
Macquart* rather than to an equal task in physics, mathe-
matics, politics or economics. He saw his undertaking,
thanks to his patience and courage, practically to a close;
so that it is exactly neither of the so-called constructive
sciences that happens to have had the benefit, intellectually
speaking, of one of the few most constructive achieve-
ments of our time. There then, provisionally at least, we
touch bottom; we get a glimpse of the pliancy and variety,
the ideal of vividness, on behalf of which our equivocal
form may appeal to a strong head. In the name of what
ideal on its own side, however, does the strong head yield
to the appeal? What is the logic of its so deeply com-
mitting itself? Zola's case seems to tell us, as it tells us
other things. The logic is in its huge freedom of adjust-
ment to the temperament of the worker, which it carries,
so to say, as no other vehicle can do. It expresses fully and
directly the whole man, and big as he may be it can still
be big enough for him without becoming false to its
type. We see this truth made strong, from beginning to
end, in Zola's work; we see the temperament, we see the
whole man, with his size and all his marks, stored and
packed away in the huge hold of *Les Rougon-Macquart* as
a cargo is packed away on a ship. His personality is the
thing that finally pervades and prevails, just as so often on
a vessel the presence of the cargo makes itself felt for the
assaulted senses. What has most come home to me in
reading him over is that a scheme of fiction so conducted
is in fact a capacious vessel. It can carry anything—with
art and force in the stowage; nothing in this case will
sink it. And it is the only form for which such a claim can
be made. All others have to confess to a smaller scope—to
selection, to exclusion, to the danger of distortion, explosion, combustion. The novel has nothing to fear but
sailing too light. It will take aboard all we bring in good
faith to the dock.

An intense vision of this truth must have been Zola's

comfort from the earliest time—the years, immediately
following the crash of the Empire, during which he settled himself to the tremendous task he had mapped out.
No finer act of courage and confidence, I think, is recorded in the history of letters. The critic in sympathy
with him returns again and again to the great wonder of
it, in which something so strange is mixed with something
so august. Entertained and carried out almost from the
threshold of manhood, the high project, the work of a
lifetime, announces beforehand its inevitable weakness
and yet speaks in the same voice for its admirable, its
almost unimaginable strength. The strength was in the
young man's very person—in his character, his will, his
passion, his fighting temper, his aggressive lips, his squared
shoulders (when he "sat up") and overweening confidence; his weakness was in that inexperience of life from
which he proposed not to suffer, from which he in fact
suffered on the surface remarkably little, and from which
he was never to suspect, I judge, that he had suffered
at all. I may mention for the interest of it that, meeting
him during his first short visit to London—made several
years before his stay in England during the Dreyfus trial
—I received a direct impression of him that was more
informing than any previous study. I had seen him a little,
in Paris, years before that, when this impression was a
perceptible promise, and I was now to perceive how
time had made it good. It consisted, simply stated, in his
fairly bristling with the betrayal that nothing whatever
had happened to him in life but to write *Les Rougon-
Macquart*. It was even for that matter almost more as if
Les Rougon-Macquart had written *him*, written him as he
stood and sat, as he looked and spoke, as the long, concentrated, merciless effort had made and stamped and left
him. Something very fundamental was to happen to him
in due course, it is true, shaking him to his base; fate was
not wholly to cheat him of an independent evolution. Re-
calling him from this London hour one strongly felt
during the famous "Affair" that his outbreak in connection

with it was the act of a man with arrears of personal
history to make up, the act of a spirit for which life, or
for which at any rate freedom, had been too much postponed, treating itself at last to a luxury of experience.

I welcomed the general impression at all events—I
intimately entertained it; it represented so many things, it
suggested, just as it was, such a lesson. You could neither
have everything nor be everything—you had to choose;
you could not at once sit firm at your job and wander
through space inviting initiations. The author of *Les
Rougon-Macquart* had had all those, certainly, that this
wonderful company could bring him; but I can scarce
express how it was implied in him that his time had been
fruitfully passed with *them* alone. His artistic evolution
struck one thus as, in spit of its magnitude, singularly
simple, and evidence of the simplicity seems further
offered by his last production, of which we have just come
into possession. *Vérité* truly does give the measure, makes
the author's high maturity join hands with his youth,
marks the rigid straightness of his course from point to
point. He had seen his horizon and his fixed goal from the
first, and no cross-scent, no new distance, no blue gap
in the hills to right or to left ever tempted him to stray.
Vérité, of which I shall have more to say, is in fact, as a
moral finality and the crown of an edifice, one of the
strangest possible performances. Machine-minted and
made good by an immense expertness, it yet makes us
ask how, for disinterested observation and perception, the
writer had used so much time and so much acquisition,
and how he can all along have handled so much material
without some larger subjective consequence. We really
rub our eyes in other words to see so great an intellectual
adventure as *Les Rougon-Macquart* come to its end in
deep desert sand. Difficult truly to read, because showing
him at last almost completely a prey to the danger that
had for a long time more and more dogged his steps, the
danger of the mechanical all confident and triumphant,
the book is nevertheless full of interest for a reader de-

sirous to penetrate. It speaks with more distinctness of the
author's temperament, tone and manner than if, like
several of his volumes, it achieved or enjoyed a successful
life of its own. Its heavy completeness, with all this, as
of some prodigiously neat, strong and complicated scaffolding constructed by a firm of builders for the erection
of a house whose foundations refuse to bear it and that it
is unable therefore to rise—its very betrayal of a method
and a habit more than adequate, on past occasions, to
similar ends, carries us back to the original rare exhibition,
the grand assurance and grand patience with which the
system was launched.

If it topples over, the system, by its own weight in these
last applications of it, that only makes the history of its
prolonged success the more curious and, speaking for
myself, the spectacle of its origin more attaching. Readers
of my generation will remember well the publication of
La Conquête de Plassans and the portent, indefinable but
irresistible, after perusal of the volume, conveyed in the
general rubric under which it was a first installment,
"Natural and Social History of a Family under the Second
Empire." It squared itself there at its ease, the announcement, from the first, and we were to learn promptly
enough what a fund of life it masked. It was like the
mouth of a cave with a signboard hung above, or better
still perhaps like the big booth at a fair with the name
of the show across the flapping canvas. One strange
animal after another stepped forth into the light, each in
its way a monster bristling and spotted, each a curiosity of
that "natural history" in the name of which we were
addressed, though it was doubtless not till the issue of
L'Assommoir that the true type of the monstrous seemed
to be reached. The enterprise, for those who had attention,
was even at a distance impressive, and the nearer the
critic gets to it retrospectively the more so it becomes.
The pyramid had been planned and the site staked out,
but the young builder stood there, in his sturdy strength,
with no equipment save his two hands and, as we may say,

his wheelbarrow and his trowel. His pile of material—of stone, brick and rubble or whatever—was of the smallest, but this he apparently felt as the least of his difficulties. Poor, uninstructed, unacquainted, unintroduced, he set up his subject wholly from the outside, proposing to himself wonderfully to get into it, into its depths, as he went.

If we imagine him asking himself what he knew of the "social" life of the second Empire to start with, we imagine him also answering in all honesty: "I have my eyes and my ears—I have all my senses: I have what I've seen and heard, what I've smelled and tasted and touched. And then I've my curiosity and my pertinacity; I've libraries, books, newspapers, witnesses, the material, from step to step, of an *enquête*. And then I've my genius—that is, my imagination, my passion, my sensibility to life. Lastly I've my method, and that will be half the battle. Best of all perhaps even, I've plentiful lack of doubt." Of the absence in him of a doubt, indeed of his inability, once his direction taken, to entertain so much as the shadow of one, *Vérité* is a positive monument—which again represents in this way the unity of his tone and the meeting of his extremes. If we remember that his design was nothing if not architectural, that a "majestic whole," a great balanced façade, with all its orders and parts, that a singleness of mass and a unity of effect, in fine, were before him from the first, his notion of picking up his bricks as he proceeded becomes, in operation, heroic. It is not in the least as a record of failure for him that I note this particular fact of the growth of the long series as on the whole the liveliest interest it has to offer. "I don't know my subject, but I must live into it; I don't know life, but I must learn it as I work"—that attitude and program represent, to my sense, a drama more intense on the worker's own part than any of the dramas he was to invent and put before us.

It was the fortune, it was in a manner the doom, of *Les Rougon-Macquart* to deal with things almost always in gregarious form, to be a picture of *numbers*, of classes,

crowds, confusions, movements, industries—and this for
a reason of which it will be interesting to attempt some
account. The individual life is, if not wholly absent, reflected in coarse and common, in generalized terms;
whereby we arrive precisely at the oddity just named, the
circumstance that, looking out somewhere, and often
woefully athirst, for the taste of fineness, we find it not
in the fruits of our author's fancy, but in a different
matter altogether. We get it in the very history of his
effort, the image itself of his lifelong process, comparatively so personal, so spiritual even, and, through all its
patience and pain, of a quality so much more distinguished
than the qualities he succeeds in attributing to his figures
even when he most aims at distinction. There can be no
question in these narrow limits of my taking the successive
volumes one by one—all the more that our sense of the
exhibition is as little as possible an impression of parts and
books, of particular "plots" and persons. It produces the
effect of a mass of imagery in which shades are sacrificed,
the effect of character and passion in the lump or by the
ton. The fullest, the most characteristic episodes affect us
like a sounding chorus or procession, as with a hubbub of
voices and a multitudinous tread of feet. The setter of the
mass into motion, he himself, in the crowd, figures best,
with whatever queer idiosyncrasies, excrescences and gaps,
a being of a substance akin to our own. Taking him as we
must, I repeat, for quite heroic, the interest of detail in
him is the interest of his struggle at every point with his
problem.

The sense for crowds and processions, for the gross and
the general, was largely the *result* of this predicament, of
the disproportion between his scheme and his material—
though it was certainly also in part an effect of his particular turn of mind. What the reader easily discerns in
him is the sturdy resolution with which breadth and
energy supply the place of penetration. He rests to his
utmost on his documents, devours and assimilates them,
makes them yield him extraordinary appearances of life;

but in his way he too improvises in the grand manner, the manner of Walter Scott and of Dumas the elder. We feel that he *has* to improvise for his moral and social world, the world as to which vision and opportunity must come, if they are to come at all, unhurried and unhustled—must take their own time, helped undoubtedly more or less by blue-books, reports and interviews, by inquiries "on the spot," but never wholly replaced by such substitutes without a general disfigurement. Vision and opportunity reside in a personal sense and a personal history, and no short cut to them in the interest of plausible fiction has ever been discovered. The short cut, it is not too much to say, was with Zola the subject of constant ingenious experiment, and it is largely to this source, I surmise, that we owe the celebrated element of his grossness. He was *obliged* to be gross, on his system, or neglect to his cost an invaluable aid to representation, as well as one that apparently struck him as lying close at hand; and I cannot withhold my frank admiration from the courage and consistency with which he faced his need.

His general subject in the last analysis was the nature of man; in dealing with which he took up, obviously, the harp of most numerous strings. His business was to make these strings sound true, and there were none that he did not, so far as his general economy permitted, persistently try. What happened then was that many—say about half, and these, as I have noted, the most silvered, the most golden—refused to give out their music. They would only sound false, since (as with all his earnestness he must have felt) he could command them, through want of skill, of practice, of ear, to none of the right harmony. What therefore was more natural than that, still spendidly bent on producing his illusion, he should throw himself on the strings he might thump with effect, and should work them, as our phrase is, for all they were worth? The nature of man, he had plentiful warrant for holding, is an extraordinary mixture, but the great thing was to represent a sufficient part of it to show that it was solidly, palpably,

commonly the nature. With this preoccupation he doubtless fell into extravagance—there was clearly so much to
lead him on. The coarser side of his subject, based on the
community of all the instincts, was for instance the more
practicable side, a sphere the vision of which required but
the general human, scarcely more than the plain physical,
initiation, and dispensed thereby conveniently enough
with special introductions or revelations. A free entry into
this sphere was undoubtedly compatible with a youthful
career as hampered right and left even as Zola's own.

He was in prompt possession thus of the range of
sympathy that he *could* cultivate, though it must be added
that the complete exercise of that sympathy might have
encountered an obstacle that would somewhat undermine
his advantage. Our friend might have found himself able,
in other words, to pay to the instinctive, as I have called
it, only such tribute as protesting taste (his own dose
of it) permitted. Yet there it was again that fortune and
his temperament served him. Taste as he knew it, taste
as his own constitution supplied it, proved to have nothing
to say to the matter. His own dose of the precious elixir
had no perceptible regulating power. Paradoxical as the
remark may sound, this accident was positively to operate
as one of his greatest felicities. There are parts of his
work, those dealing with romantic or poetic elements,
in which the inactivity of the principle in question is
sufficiently hurtful; but it surely should not be described
as hurtful to such pictures as *Le Ventre de Paris*, as
L'Assommoir, as *Germinal*. The conception on which
each of these productions rests is that of a world with
which taste has nothing to do, and though the act of
representation may be justly held, as an artistic act, to
involve its presence, the discrimination would probably
have been in fact, given the particular illusion sought,
more detrimental than the deficiency. There was a great
outcry, as we all remember, over the rank materialism
of *L'Assommoir*, but who cannot see today how much a
milder infusion of it would have told against the close

embrace of the subject aimed at? *L'Assommoir* is the
nature of man—but not his finer, nobler, cleaner or more
cultivated nature; it is the image of his free instincts, the
better and the worse, the better struggling as they can,
gasping for light and air, the worse making themselves
at home in darkness, ignorance and poverty. The whole
handling makes for emphasis and scale, and it is not to
be measured how, as a picture of conditions, the thing
would have suffered from timidity. The qualification of
the painter was precisely his stoutness of stomach, and
we scarce exceed in saying that to have taken in and
given out again less of the infected air would, with such
a resource, have meant the waste of a faculty.

I may add in this connection moreover that refinement
of intention did on occasion and after a fashion of its
own unmistakably preside at these experiments; making
the remark in order to have done once for all with a feature of Zola's literary physiognomy that appears to have
attached the gaze of many persons to the exclusion of
every other. There are judges in these matters so perversely preoccupied that for them to see anywhere the
"improper" is for them straightway to cease to see anything else. The said improper, looming supremely large
and casting all the varieties of the proper quite into the
shade, suffers thus in their consciousness a much greater
extension than it ever claimed, and this consciousness
becomes, for the edification of many and the information
of a few, a colossal reflector and record of it. Much
may be said, in relation to some of the possibilities of the
nature of man, of the nature in especial of the "people,"
on the defect of our author's sense of proportion. But
the sense of proportion of many of those he has scandal-
ized would take us further yet. I recall at all events as
relevant—for it comes under a very attaching general
head—two occasions of long ago, two Sunday afternoons
in Paris, on which I found the question of intention very
curiously lighted. Several men of letters of a group in
which almost every member either had arrived at re-

nown or was well on his way to it, were assembled
under the roof of the most distinguished of their number, where they exchanged free confidences on current
work, on plans and ambitions, in a manner full of interest
for one never previously privileged to see artistic conviction, artistic passion (at least on the literary ground) so
systematic and so articulate. "Well, I on my side," I
remember Zola's saying, "am engaged on a book, a study
of the *mœurs* of the people, for which I am making a
collection of all the 'bad words,' the *gros mots*, of the
language, those with which the vocabulary of the people,
those with which their familiar talk, bristles." I was
struck with the tone in which he made the announcement
—without bravado and without apology, as an interesting
idea that had come to him and that he was working,
really to arrive at character and particular truth, with
all his conscience; just as I was struck with the unqualified
interest that his plan excited. It was *on* a plan that he
was working—formidably, almost grimly, as his fatigued
face showed; and the whole consideration of this interesting element partook of the general seriousness.

But there comes back to me also as a companion-piece
to this another day, after some interval, on which the
interest was excited by the fact that the work for love of
which the brave license had been taken was actually under
the ban of the daily newspaper that had engaged to
"serialize" it. Publication had definitively ceased. The
thing had run a part of its course, but it had outrun the
courage of editors and the curiosity of subscribers—that
stout curiosity to which it had evidently in such good
faith been addressed. The chorus of contempt for the ways
of such people, their pusillanimity, their superficiality,
vulgarity, intellectual platitude, was the striking note on
this occasion; for the journal impugned had declined to
proceed and the serial, broken off, been obliged, if I
am not mistaken, to seek the hospitality of other columns,
secured indeed with no great difficulty. The composition
so qualified for future fame was none other, as I was later

to learn, than *L'Assommoir;* and my reminiscence has perhaps no greater point than in connecting itself with a matter always dear to the critical spirit, especially when the latter has not too completely elbowed out the romantic—the matter of the "origins," the early consciousness, early steps, early tribulations, early obscurity, as so often happens of productions finally crowned by time.

Their greatness is for the most part a thing that has originally begun so small; and this impression is particularly strong when we have been in any degree present, so to speak, at the birth. The course of the matter is apt to tend preponderantly in that case to enrich our stores of irony. In the eventual conquest of consideration by an abused book we recognize, in other terms, a drama of romantic interest, a drama often with large comic no less than with fine pathetic interweavings. It may of course be said in this particular connection that *L'Assommoir* had not been one of the literary things that creep humbly into the world. Its "success" may be cited as almost insolently prompt, and the fact remains true if the idea of success be restricted, after the inveterate fashion, to the idea of circulation. What remains truer still, however, is that for the critical spirit circulation mostly matters not the least little bit, and it is of the success with which the history of Gervaise and Coupeau nestles in *that* capacious bosom, even as the just man sleeps in Abraham's, that I here speak. But it is a point I may better refer to a moment hence.

Though a summary study of Zola need not too anxiously concern itself with book after book—always with a partial exception from this remark for *L'Assommoir*—groups and varieties none the less exist in the huge series, aids to discrimination without which no measure of the presiding genius is possible. These divisions range themselves to my sight, roughly speaking, however, as scarce more than three in number—I mean if the ten volumes of the *Œuvres critiques* and the *Théâtre* be left out of account. The critical volumes in especial abound in the

characteristic, as they were also a wondrous addition to
his sum of achievement during his most strenuous years.
But I am forced not to consider them. The two groups
constituted after the close of *Les Rougon-Macquart—
Les Trois Villes* and the incomplete *Quatre Évangiles—*
distribute themselves easily among the three types, or, to
speak more exactly, stand together under one of the three.
This one, so comprehensive as to be the author's main
exhibition, includes to my sense all his best volumes—to
the point in fact of producing an effect of distinct inferiority for those outside of it, which are, luckily for his
general credit, the less numerous. It is so inveterately
pointed out in any allusion to him that one shrinks, in
repeating it, from sounding flat; but as he was admirably
equipped from the start for the evocation of number and
quantity, so those of his social pictures that most easily
surpass the others are those in which appearances, the
appearances familiar to him, are at once most magnified
and most multiplied.

To make his character swarm, and to make the great
central thing they swarm about "as large as life," porten-
tously, heroically big, that was the task he set himself
very nearly from the first, that was the secret he triumphantly mastered. Add that the big central thing was
always some highly representative institution or industry
of the France of his time, some seated Moloch of custom,
of commerce, of faith, lending itself to portrayal through
its abuses and excesses, its idol-face and great devouring
mouth, and we embrace the main lines of his attack. In
Le Ventre de Paris he had dealt with the life of the huge
Halles, the general markets and their supply, the personal
forces, personal situations, passions, involved in (strangest
of all subjects) the alimentation of the monstrous city,
the city whose victualing occupies so inordinately much
of its consciousness. Paris richly gorged, Paris sublime and
indifferent in her assurance (so all unlike poor Oliver's)
of "more," figures here the theme itself, lies across the
scene like some vast ruminant creature breathing in a

cloud of parasites. The book was the first of the long
series to show the full freedom of the author's hand,
though *La Curée* had already been symptomatic. This
freedom, after an interval, broke out on a much bigger
scale in *L'Assommoir*, in *Au bonheur des dames*, in *Germinal*, in *La Bête humaine*, in *L'Argent*, in *La Débâcle*,
and then again, though more mechanically and with much
of the glory gone, in the more or less wasted energy of
Lourdes, Rome, Paris, of *Fécondité, Travail* and *Vérité*.

Au bonheur des dames handles the colossal modern
shop, traces the growth of such an organization as the
Bon Marché or the Magasin-du-Louvre, sounds the abysses
of its inner life, marshals its population, its hierarchy
of clerks, counters, departments, divisions and subdi-
visions, plunges into the labyrinth of the mutual relations
of its staff, and above all traces its ravage amid the
smaller fry of the trade, of all the trades, pictures these
latter gasping for breath in an air pumped clean by its
mighty lungs. *Germinal* revolves about the coal mines of
Flemish France, with the subterranean world of the pits
for its central presence, just as *La Bête humaine* has for
its protagonist a great railway and *L'Argent* presents in
terms of human passion—mainly of human baseness—the
fury of the Bourse and the monster of Credit. *La Débâcle*
takes up with extraordinary breadth the first act of the
Franco-Prussian war, the collapse at Sedan, and the titles
of the six volumes of The Three Cities and the Four
Gospels sufficiently explain them. I may mention, however,
for the last lucidity, that among these *Fécondité* manipu-
lates, with an amazing misapprehension of means to ends,
of remedies to ills, no less thickly peopled a theme than
that of the decline in the French birth rate, and that
Vérité presents a fictive equivalent of the Dreyfus case,
with a vast and elaborate picture of the battle in France
between lay and clerical instruction. I may even further
mention, to clear the ground, that with the close of *Les
Rougon-Macquart* the diminution of freshness in the
author's energy, the diminution of intensity and, in short,

of quality, becomes such as to render sadly difficult a happy life with some of the later volumes. Happiness of the purest strain never indeed, in old absorptions of Zola, quite sat at the feast; but there was mostly a measure of coercion, a spell without a charm. From these last-named productions of the climax everything strikes me as absent but quantity (*Vérité*, for instance, is, with the possible exception of *Nana*, the longest of the list); though indeed there is something impressive in the way his quantity represents his patience.

There are efforts here at stout perusal that, frankly, I have been unable to carry through, and I should verily like, in connection with the vanity of these, to dispose on the spot of the sufficiently strange phenomenon constituted by what I have called the climax. It embodies in fact an immense anomaly; it casts back over Zola's prime and his middle years the queerest gray light of eclipse. Nothing moreover—nothing "literary"—was ever so odd as in this matter the whole turn of the case, the consummation so logical yet so unexpected. Writers have grown old and withered and failed; they have grown weak and sad; they have lost heart, lost ability, yielded in one way or another—the possible ways being so numerous—to the cruelty of time. But the singular doom of this genius, and which began to multiply its symptoms ten years before his death, was to find, with life, at fifty, still rich in him, strength only to undermine all the "authority" he had gathered. He had not grown old and he had not grown feeble; he had only grown all too wrongly insistent, setting himself to wreck, poetically, his so massive identity —to wreck it in the very waters in which he had formally arrayed his victorious fleet. (I say "poetically" on purpose to give him the just benefit of all the beauty of his power.) The process of the disaster, so full of the effect, though so without the intention, of perversity, is difficult to trace in a few words; it may best be indicated by an example or two of its action.

The example that perhaps most comes home to me is

again connected with a personal reminiscence. In the course of some talk that I had with him during his first visit to England I happened to ask him what opportunity to travel (if any) his immense application had ever left him, and whether in particular he had been able to see Italy, a country from which I had either just returned or which I was luckily—not having the "Natural History of a Family" on my hands—about to revisit. "All I've done, alas," he replied, "was, the other year, in the course of a little journey to the south, to my own *pays*—all that has been possible was then to make a little dash as far as Genoa, a matter of only a few days." *Le Docteur Pascal*, the conclusion of *Les Rougon-Macquart*, had appeared shortly before, and it further befell that I asked him what plans he had for the future, now that, still *dans la force de l'âge*, he had so cleared the ground. I shall never forget the fine promptitude of his answer— "Oh, I shall begin at once *Les Trois Villes*." "And which cities are they to be?" The reply was finer still—"Lourdes, Paris, Rome."

It was splendid for confidence and cheer, but it left me, I fear, more or less gaping, and it was to give me afterwards the key, critically speaking, to many a mystery. It struck me as breathing to an almost tragic degree the fatuity of those in whom the gods stimulate that vice to their ruin. He was an honest man—he had always bristled with it at every pore; but no artistic reverse was inconceivable for an adventurer who, stating in one breath that his knowledge of Italy consisted of a few days spent at Genoa, was ready to declare in the next that he had planned, on a scale, a picture of Rome. It flooded his career, to my sense, with light; it showed how he had marched from subject to subject and had "got up" each in turn—showing also how consummately he had reduced such getting-up to an artifice. He had success and a rare impunity behind him, but nothing would now be so interesting as to see if he could again play the trick. One would leave him, and welcome, Lourdes and Paris—he had

already dealt, on a scale, with his own country and
people. But was the adored Rome also to be his on such
terms, the Rome he was already giving away before possessing an inch of it? One thought of one's own frequenta-
tions, saturations—a history of long years, and of how the
effect of them had somehow been but to make the subject
too august. Was *he* to find it easy through a visit of a
month or two with "introductions" and a Baedeker?

It was not indeed that the Baedeker and the introductions didn't show, to my sense, at that hour, as extremely suggestive; they were positively a part of the light
struck out by his announcement. They defined the system
on which he had brought *Les Rougon-Macquart* safely
into port. He had had his Baedeker and his introductions
for *Germinal,* for *L'Assommoir,* for *L'Argent,* for *La
Débâcle,* for *Au bonheur des dames;* which advantages,
which researches, had clearly been all the more in character for being documentary, extractive, a matter of
renseignements, published or private, even when most
mixed with personal impressions snatched, with *enquêtes
sur les lieux,* with facts obtained from the best authorities,
proud and happy to co-operate in so famous a connection.
That was, as we say, all right, all the more that the
process, to my imagination, became vivid and was wonderfully reflected back from its fruits. There *were* the fruits
—so it hadn't been presumptuous. Presumption, however,
was now to begin, and what omen mightn't there be in
its beginning with such complacency? Well, time would
show—as time in due course effectually did. *Rome,* as
the second volume of *The Three Cities,* appeared with
high punctuality a year or two later; and the interesting
question, an occasion really for the moralist, was by that
time not to recognize in it the mere triumph of a mechanical art, a "receipt" applied with the skill of long
practice, but to do much more than this—that is really
to give a name to the particular shade of blindness that
could constitute a trap for so great an artistic intelligence.
The presumptuous volume, without sweetness, without

antecedents, superficial and violent, has the minimum instead of the maximum of *value;* so that it betrayed or "gave away" just in this degree the state of mind on the author's part responsible for its inflated hollowness. To put one's finger on the state of mind was to find out accordingly what was, as we say, the matter with him.

It seemed to me, I remember, that I found out as never before when, in its turn, *Fécondité* began the work of crowning the edifice. *Fécondité* is physiological, whereas *Rome* is not, whereas *Vérité* likewise is not; yet these three productions joined hands at a given moment to fit into the lock of the mystery the key of my meditation. They came to the same thing, to the extent of permitting me to read into them together the same precious lesson. This lesson may not, barely stated, sound remarkable; yet without being in possession of it I should have ventured on none of these remarks. "The matter with" Zola then, so far as it goes, was that, as the imagination of the artist is in the best cases not only clarified but intensified by his equal possession of Taste (deserving here if ever the old-fashioned honor of a capital), so when he has luck-lessly never inherited that auxiliary blessing the imagina-tion itself inevitably breaks down as a consequence. There is simply no limit, in fine, to the misfortune of being taste-less; it does not merely disfigure the surface and the fringe of your performance—it eats back into the very heart and enfeebles the sources of life. When you have no taste you have no discretion, which is the conscience of taste, and when you have no discretion you perpetrate books like *Rome*, which are without intellectual modesty, books like *Fécondité*, which are without a sense of the ridiculous, books like *Vérité*, which are without the finer vision of human experience.

It is marked that in each of these examples the de-ficiency has been directly fatal. No stranger doom was ever appointed for a man so plainly desiring only to be just than the absurdity of not resting till he had buried the felicity of his past, such as it was, under a great flat leaden slab. *Vérité* is a plea for science, as science, to Zola, is *all* truth, the mention of any other kind being mere imbecility; and the simplification of the human picture to which his negations and exasperations have here conducted him was not, even when all had been said, credible in advance. The result is amazing when we consider that the finer observation is the supposed basis of all such work. It is not that even here the author has not a queer idealism of his own; this idealism is on the contrary so present as to show positively for the falsest of his simplifications. In *Fécondité* it becomes grotesque, makes of the book the most muscular mistake of *sense* probably ever committed. Where was the judgment of which experience is supposed to be the guarantee when the perpetrator could persuade himself that the lesson he wished in these pages to convey could be made immediate and direct, chalked, with loud taps and a still louder commentary, the sexes and generations all convoked, on the blackboard of the "family sentiment"?

I have mentioned, however, all this time but one of his categories. The second consists of such things as *La Fortune des Rougon* and *La Curée*, as *Eugène Rougon* and even *Nana*, as *Pot-Bouille*, as *L'Œuvre* and *La Joie de vivre*. These volumes may rank as social pictures in the narrowest sense, studies, comprehensively speaking, of the manners, the morals, the miseries—for it mainly comes to that—of a bourgeoisie grossly materialized. They deal with the life of individuals in the liberal professions and with that of political and social adventures, and offer the personal character and career, more or less detached, as the center of interest. *La Curée* is an evocation, violent and "romantic," of the extravagant appetites, the fever of the senses, supposedly fostered, for its ruin, by the hapless second Empire, upon which general ills and turpitudes at large were at one time so freely and conveniently fathered. *Eugène Rougon* carries out this view in the high color of a political portrait, not other than scandalous, for which one of the ministerial *âmes damnées*

of Napoleon III, M. Rouher, is reputed, I know not how
justly, to have sat. *Nana*, attaching itself by a hundred
strings to a prearranged table of kinships, heredities,
transmissions, is the vast crowded *epos* of the daughter
of the people filled with poisoned blood and sacrificed as
well as sacrificing on the alter of luxury and lust; the
panorama of such a "progress" as Hogarth would more
definitely have named—the progress across the high
plateau of "pleasure" and down the facile descent on the
other side. *Nana* is truly a monument to Zola's patience;
the subject being so ungrateful, so formidably special,
that the multiplication of illustrative detail, the plunge
into pestilent depths, represents a kind of technical
intrepidity.

There are other plunges, into different sorts of darkness;
of which the esthetic, even the scientific, even the ironic
motive fairly escapes us—explorations of stagnant pools
like that of *La Joie de vivre*, as to which, granting the
nature of the curiosity and the substance labored in, the
patience is again prodigious, but which make us wonder
what pearl of philosophy, of suggestion or just of homely
recognition, the general picture, as of rats dying in a
hole, has to offer. Our various senses, sight, smell, sound,
touch, are, as with Zola always, more or less convinced;
but when the particular effect upon each of these is added
to the effect upon the others the mind still remains be-
wilderedly unconscious of any use for the total. I am not
sure indeed that the case is in this respect better with the
productions of the third order—*La Faute de l'Abbé
Mouret, Une Page d'amour, Le Rêve, Le Docteur Pascal*
—in which the appeal is more directly, is in fact quite
earnestly, to the moral vision; so much, on such ground,
was to depend precisely on those discriminations in which
the writer is least at home. The volumes whose names I
have just quoted are his express tribute to the "ideal,"
to the select and the charming—fair fruits of invention
intended to remove from the mouth so far as possible
the bitterness of the ugly things in which so much of the

rest of his work had been condemned to consist. The subjects in question then are "idyllic" and the treatment poetic, concerned essentially to please on the largest lines and involving at every turn that salutary need. They are matters of conscious delicacy, and nothing might interest us more than to see what, in the shock of the potent forces enlisted, becomes of this shy element. Nothing might interest us more, literally, and might positively affect us more, even very nearly to tears, though indeed sometimes also to smiles, than to see the constructor of *Les Rougon-Macquart* trying, "for all he is worth," to be fine with fineness, finely tender, finely true —trying to be, as it is called, distinguished—in face of constitutional hindrance.

The effort is admirably honest, the tug at his subject splendidly strong; but the consequences remain of the strangest, and we get the impression that—as representing discriminations unattainable—they are somehow the price he paid. *Le Docteur Pascal*, for instance, which winds up the long chronicle on the romantic note, on the note of invoked beauty, in order to sweeten, as it were, the total draught—*Le Docteur Pascal*, treating of the erotic ardor entertained for each other by an uncle and his niece, leaves us amazed at such a conception of beauty, such an application of romance, such an estimate of sweetness, a sacrifice to poetry and passion so little in order. Of course, we definitely remind ourselves, the whole long chronicle is explicitly a scheme, solidly set up and intricately worked out, lighted, according to the author's pretension, by "science," high, dry, and clear, and with each part involved and necessitated in all the other parts, each block of the edifice, each "morceau de vie," *physiologically* determined by previous combinations. "How can I help it," we hear the builder of the pyramid ask, "if experience (by which alone I proceed) shows me certain plain results —if, holding up the torch of my famous 'experimental method' I find it stare me in the face that the union of certain types, the conflux of certain strains of blood, the intermarriage, in a word, of certain families, produces nervous conditions, conditions temperamental, psychical and pathological, in which nieces *have* to fall in love with uncles and uncles with nieces? Observation and imagination, for any picture of life," he as audibly adds, "know no light but science, and are false to all intellectual decency, false to their own honor, when they fear it, dodge it, darken it. To pretend to any other guide or law is mere base humbug."

That is very well, and the value, in a hundred ways, of a mass of production conceived in such a spirit can never (when robust execution has followed) be small. But the formula really sees us no further. It offers a definition which is no definition. "Science" is soon said—the whole thing depends on the ground so covered. Science accepts surely *all* our consciousness of life; even, rather, the latter closes maternally round it—so that, becoming thus a force within us, not a force outside, it exists, it illuminates only as we apply it. We do emphatically apply it in art. But Zola would apparently hold that it much more applies *us*. On the showing of many of his volumes then it makes but a dim use of us, and this we should still consider the case even were we sure that the article offered us in the majestic name is absolutely at one with its own pretension. This confidence we can on too many grounds never have. The matter is one of appreciation, and when an artist answers for science who answers for the artist—who at the least answers for art? Thus it is with the mistakes that affect us, I say, as Zola's penalties. We are reminded by them that the game of art has, as the phrase is, to be played. It may not with any sure felicity for the result be both taken and left. If you insist on the common you must submit to the common; if you discriminate, on the contrary, you must, however invidious your discriminations may be called, trust to them to see you through.

To the common then Zola, often with splendid results, inordinately sacrifices, and this fact of its overwhelming him is what I have called his paying for it. In *L'Assom-*

moir, in *Germinal,* in *La Débâcle,* productions in which he
must most survive, the sacrifice is ordered and fruitful,
for the subject and the treatment harmonize and work
together. He describes what he best feels, and feels it more
and more as it naturally comes to him—quite, if I may
allow myself the image, as we zoologically see some
mighty animal, a beast of a corrugated hide and a portentous snout, soaking with joy in the warm ooze of an
African riverside. In these cases everything matches, and
"science," we may be permitted to believe, has had little in
the business. The author's perceptions go straight, and the
subject, grateful and responsive, gives itself wholly up.
It is no longer a case of an uncertain smoky torch, but of
a personal vision, the vision of genius, springing from an
inward source. Of this genius *L'Assommoir* is the most
extraordinary record. It contains, with the two companions I have given it, all the best of Zola, and the three
books together are solid ground—or would be could I
now so take them—for a study of the particulars of his
power. His strongest marks and features abound in them;
L'Assommoir above all is (not least in respect to its bold
free linguistic reach, already glanced at) completely genial,
while his misadventures, his unequipped and delusive
pursuit of the life of the spirit and the tone of culture,
are almost completely absent.

It is a singular sight enough this of a producer of
illusions whose interest for us is so independent of our
pleasure or at least of our complacency—who touches
us deeply even while he most "puts us off," who makes us
care for his ugliness and yet himself at the same time
pitilessly (pitilessly, that is, for *us*) makes a mock of it,
who fills us with a sense of the rich which is none the less
never the rare. Gervaise, the most immediately "felt," I
cannot but think, of all his characters, is a lame washer-
woman, loose and gluttonous, without will, without any
principle of cohesion, the sport of every wind that assaults
her exposed life, and who, rolling from one gross mistake
to another, finds her end in misery, drink and despair. But

her career, as presented, has fairly the largeness that, throughout the chronicle, we feel as epic, and the intensity of her creator's vision of it and of the dense sordid life hanging about it is one of the great things the modern novel has been able to do. It has done nothing more completely constitutive and of a tone so rich and full and sustained. The tone of *L'Assommoir* is, for mere "keeping up," unsurpassable, a vast deep steady tide on which every object represented is triumphantly borne. It never shrinks nor flows thin, and nothing for an instant drops, dips or catches; the high-water mark of sincerity, of the genial, as I have called it, is unfailingly kept.

For the artist in the same general "line" such a production has an interest almost inexpressible, a mystery as to origin and growth over which he fondly but rather vainly bends. How after all does it so get itself *done?*— the "done" being admirably the sign and crown of it. The light of the richer mind has been elsewhere, as I have sufficiently hinted, frequent enough, but nothing truly in all fiction was ever built so strong or made so dense as here. Needless to say there are a thousand things with more charm in their truth, with more beguilement of every sort, more prettiness of pathos, more innocence of drollery, for the spectator's sense of truth. But I doubt if there has ever been a more totally *represented* world, anything more founded and established, more provided for all round, more organized and carried on. It is a world practically workable, with every part as functional as every other, and with the parts all chosen for direct mutual aid. Let it not be said either that the equal constitution of parts makes for repletion or excess; the air circulates and the subject blooms; deadness comes in these matters only when the right parts are absent and there is vain beating of the air in their place—the refuge of the fumbler incapable of the thing "done" at all.

The mystery I speak of, for the reader who reflects as he goes, is the wonder of the scale and energy of Zola's assimilations. This wonder besets us above all throughout the three books I have placed first. How, all sedentary and "scientific," did he get so *near?* By what art, inscrutable, immeasurable, indefatigable, did he arrange to make of his documents, in these connections, a use so vivified? Say he was "near" the subject of *L'Assommoir* in imagination, in more or less familiar impression, in temperament and humor, he could not after all have been near it in personal experience, and the copious personalism of the picture, not to say its frank animalism, yet remains its note and its strength. When the note had been struck in a thousand forms we had, by multiplication, as a kind of cumulative consequence, the finished and rounded book; just as we had the same result by the same process in *Germinal.* It is not of course that multiplication and accumulation, the extraordinary pair of legs on which he walks, are easily or directly consistent with his projecting himself morally; this immense diffusion, with its appropriation of everything it meets, affects us on the contrary as perpetually delaying access to what we may call the private world, the world of the individual. Yet since the individual—for it so happens—is simple and shallow our author's dealings with him, as met and measured, maintain their resemblance to those of the lusty bee who succeeds in plumping for an instant, of a summer morning, into every flower-cup of the garden.

Grant—and the generalization may be emphatic—that the shallow and the simple are *all* the population of his richest and most crowded pictures, and that his "psychology," in a psychologic age, remains thereby comparatively coarse, grant this and we but get another view of the miracle. We see enough of the superficial among novelists at large, assuredly, without deriving from it, as we derive from Zola at his best, the concomitant impression of the solid. It is in general—I mean among the novelists at large—the impression of the *cheap*, which the author of *Les Rougon-Macquart*, honest man, never faithless for a moment to his own stiff standard, manages to spare us even in the prolonged sandstorm of *Vérité*. The

Common is another matter; it is one of the forms of the superficial—pervading and consecrating all things in such a book as *Germinal*—and it only adds to the number of our critical questions. How in the world is it made, this deplorable democratic malodorous Common, so strange and so interesting? How is it taught to receive into its loins the stuff of the epic and still, in spite of that association with poetry, never depart from its nature? It is in the great lusty game he plays with the shallow and the simple that Zola's mastery resides, and we see of course that when values are small it takes innumerable items and combinations to make up the sum. In *L'Assommoir* and in *Germinal*, to some extent even in *La Débâcle*, the values are all, morally, personally, of the lowest—the highest is poor Gervaise herself, richly human in her generosities and follies—yet each is as distinct as a brass-headed nail.

What we come back to accordingly is the unprecedented case of such a combination of parts. Painters, of great schools, often of great talent, have responded liberally on canvas to the appeal of ugly things, of Spanish beggars, squalid and dusty-footed, of martyred saints or other convulsed sufferers, tortured and bleeding, of boors and louts soaking a Dutch proboscis in perpetual beer; but we had never before had to reckon with so literary a treatment of the mean and vulgar. When we others of the Anglo-Saxon race are vulgar we are, handsomely and with the best conscience in the world, vulgar all through, too vulgar to be in any degree literary, and too much so therefore to be critically reckoned with at all. The French are different—they separate their sympathies, multiply their possibilities, observe their shades, remain more or less outside of their worst disasters. They mostly contrive to get the *idea*, in however dead a faint, down into the lifeboat. They may lose sight of the stars, but they save in some such fashion as that their intellectual souls. Zola's own reply to all puzzlements would have been, at any rate, I take it, a straight summary of his inveterate professional habits. "It is all very simple—I produce, roughly speaking, a volume a year, and of this time some five months go to preparation, to special study. In the other months, with all my *cadres* established, I write the book. And I can hardly say which part of the job is stiffest."

The story was not more wonderful for him than that, nor the job more complex; which is why we must say of his whole process and its results that they constitute together perhaps the most extraordinary *imitation* of observation that we possess. Balzac appealed to "science" and proceeded by her aid; Balzac had *cadres* enough and a tabulated world, rubrics, relationships and genealogies; but Balzac affects us in spite of everything as personally overtaken by life, as fairly hunted and run to earth by it. He strikes us as struggling and all but submerged, as beating over the scene such a pair of wings as were not soon again to be wielded by any visitor of his general air and as had not at all events attached themselves to Zola's rounded shoulders. His bequest is in consequence immeasurably more interesting, yet who shall declare that his adventure was in its greatness more successful? Zola "pulled it off," as we say, supremely, in that he never but once found himself obliged to quit, to our vision, his magnificent treadmill of the pigeonholed and documented —the region we may qualify as that of experience by imitation. His splendid economy saw him through, he labored to the end within sight of his notes and his charts.

The extraordinary thing, however, is that on the single occasion when, publicly—as his whole manifestation was public—life did swoop down on him, the effect of the visitation was quite perversely other than might have been looked for. His courage in the Dreyfus connection testified admirably to his ability to live for himself and out of the order of his volumes—little indeed as living at all might have seemed a question for one exposed, when his crisis was at its height and he was found guilty of "insulting" the powers that were, to be literally torn to pieces in the precincts of the Palace of Justice. Our point is that nothing was ever so odd as that these great moments should appear to have been wasted, when all was said, for his creative intelligence. *Vérité*, as I have intimated, the production in which they might most have been reflected, is a production unrenewed and unrefreshed by them, spreads before us as somehow flatter and grayer, not richer and more relieved, by reason of them. They really arrived, I surmise, too late in the day; the imagination they might have vivified was already fatigued and spent.

I must not moreover appear to say that the power to evoke and present has not even on the dead level of *Vérité* its occasional minor revenges. There are passages, whole pages, of the old full-bodied sort, pictures that elsewhere in the series would in all likelihood have seemed abundantly convincing. Their misfortune is to have been discounted by our intensified, our finally fatal sense of the *procédé*. Quarreling with all conventions, defiant of them in general, Zola was yet inevitably to set up his own group of them—as, for that matter, without a sufficient collection, without their aid in simplifying and making possible, how could he ever have seen his big ship into port? Art welcomes them, feeds upon them always; no sort of form is practicable without them. It is only a question of what particular ones we use—to wage war on certain others and to arrive at particular forms. The convention of the blameless being, the thoroughly "scientific" creature possessed impeccably of all truth and serving as the mouthpiece of it and of the author's highest complacencies, this character is for instance a convention inveterate and indispensable, without whom the "sympathetic" side of the work could never have been achieved. Marc in *Vérité*, Pierre Froment in *Lourdes* and in *Rome*, the wondrous representatives of the principle of reproduction in *Fécondité*, the exemplary painter of *L'Œuvre*, sublime in his modernity and paternity, the patient Jean Macquart of *La Débâcle*, whose patience is as guaranteed as the exactitude of a well-made watch,

the supremely enlightened Docteur Pascal even, as I
recall him, all amorous nepotism but all virtue too and
all beauty of life—such figures show us the reasonable and
the good not merely in the white light of the old George
Sand novel and its improved moralities, but almost in
that of our childhood's nursery and schoolroom, that
of the moral tale of Miss Edgeworth and Mr. Thomas
Day.

Yet let not these restrictions be my last word. I had
intended, under the effect of a reperusal of *La Débâcle*,
Germinal and *L'Assommoir*, to make no discriminations
that should not be in our hero's favor. The long-drawn
incident of the marriage of Gervaise and Cadet-Cassis
and that of the Homeric birthday feast later on in the
laundress's workshop, each treated from beginning to end
and in every item of their coarse comedy and humanity,
still show the unprecedented breadth by which they
originally made us stare, still abound in the particular
kind and degree of vividness that helped them, when they
appeared, to mark a date in the portrayal of manners.
Nothing had then been so sustained and at every moment
of its grotesque and pitiful existence lived into as the nup-
tial day of the Coupeau pair in especial, their fantastic pro-
cessional pilgrimage through the streets of Paris in the rain,
their bedraggled exploration of the halls of the Louvre
museum, lost as in the labyrinth of Crete, and their arrival at last, ravenous and exasperated, at the *guinguette*
where they sup at so much a head, each paying, and
where we sit down with them in the grease and the per-
spiration and succumb, half in sympathy, half in shame, to
their monstrous pleasantries, acerbities and miseries. I
have said enough of the mechanical in Zola; here in truth
is, given the elements, almost insupportably the sense of
life. That effect is equally in the historic chapter of the
strike of the miners in *Germinal*, another of those illustrative episodes, viewed as great passages to be "rendered," for which our author established altogether a new
measure and standard of handling, a new energy and

veracity, something since which the old trivialities and poverties of treatment of such aspects have become incompatible, for the novelist, with either rudimentary intelligence or rudimentary self-respect.

As for *La Débâcle*, finally, it takes its place with Tolstoy's very much more universal but very much less composed and condensed epic as an incomparably human picture of war. I have been rereading it, I confess, with a certain timidity, the dread of perhaps impairing the deep impression received at the time of its appearance. I recall the effect it then produced on me as a really luxurious act of submission. It was early in the summer; I was in an old Italian town; the heat was oppressive, and one could but recline, in the lightest garments, in a great dim room and give one's self up. I like to think of the conditions and the emotion, which melt for me together into the memory I fear to imperil. I remember that in the glow of my admiration there was not a reserve I had ever made that I was not ready to take back. As an application of the author's system and his supreme faculty, as a triumph of what these things could do for him, how could such a performance be surpassed? The long, complex, horrific, pathetic battle, embraced, mastered, with every crash of its squadrons, every pulse of its thunder and blood resolved for us, by reflection, by communication from two of the humblest and obscurest of the military units, into immediate vision and contact, into deep human thrills of terror and pity—this bristling center of the book was such a piece of "doing" (to come back to our word) as could only shut our mouths. That doubtless is why a generous critic, nursing the sensation, may desire to drop for a farewell no term into the other scale. That our author was clearly great at congruous subjects—this may well be our conclusion. If the others, subjects of the private and intimate order, gave him more or less inevitably "away," they yet left him the great distinction that the more he could be promiscuous and collective, the more even he could (to repeat my imputation) illustrate our

than the doctrine. M. Guy de Maupassant has lately traversed with a firm and rapid step a literary crisis of this kind; he has clambered safely up the bank at the further end of the morass. If he has relieved himself in the preface to *Pierre et Jean*, the last-published of his tales, he has also rendered a service to his friends; he has not only come home in a recognizable plight, escaping gross disaster with a success which even his extreme good sense was far from making in advance a matter of course, but he has expressed in intelligible terms (that by itself is a ground of felicitation) his most general idea, his own sense of his direction. He has arranged, as it were, the light in which he wishes to sit. If it is a question of attempting, under however many disadvantages, a sketch of him, the critic's business therefore is simplified: there will be no difficulty in placing him, for he himself has chosen the spot, he has made the chalk mark on the floor.

I may as well say at once that in dissertation M. de Maupassant does not write with his best pen; the philosopher in his composition is perceptibly inferior to the storyteller. I would rather have written half a page of *Boule de Suif* than the whole of the introduction to Flaubert's *Letters to Madame Sand;* and his little disquisition on the novel in general, attached to that particular example of it which he has just put forth,[1] is considerably less to the point than the masterpiece which it ushers in. In short, as a commentator M. de Maupassant is slightly common, while as an artist he is wonderfully rare. Of course we must, in judging a writer, take one thing with another, and if I could make up my mind that M. de Maupassant is weak in theory, it would almost make me like him better, render him more approachable, give him the touch of softness that he lacks, and show us a human flaw. The most general quality of the author of *La Maison Tellier* and *Bel-Ami*, the impression that remains last, after the others have been accounted for, is an essential hardness—hardness of form, hardness of na-

[1] *Pierre et Jean* (Paris: Ollendorff, 1888).

ture; and it would put us more at ease to find that if the fact with him (the fact of execution) is so extraordinarily definite and adequate, his explanations, after it, were a little vague and sentimental. But I am not sure that he must even be held foolish to have noticed the race of critics: he is at any rate so much less foolish than several of that fraternity. He has said his say concisely and as if he were saying it once for all. In fine, his readers must be grateful to him for such a passage as that in which he remarks that whereas the public at large very legitimately says to a writer, "Console me, amuse me, terrify me, make me cry, make me dream, or make me think," what the sincere critic says is, "Make me something fine in the form that shall suit you best, according to your temperament." This seems to me to put into a nutshell the whole question of the different classes of fiction, concerning which there has recently been so much discourse. There are simply as many different kinds as there are persons practicing the art, for if a picture, a tale, or a novel be a direct impression of life (and that surely constitutes its interest and value), the impression will vary according to the plate that takes it, the particular structure and mixture of the recipient.

I am not sure that I know what M. de Maupassant means when he says, "The critic shall appreciate the result only according to the nature of the effort; he has no right to concern himself with tendencies." The second clause of that observation strikes me as rather in the air, thanks to the vagueness of the last word. But our author adds to the definiteness of his contention when he goes on to say that any form of the novel is simply a vision of the world from the standpoint of a person constituted after a certain fashion, and that it is therefore absurd to say that there is, for the novelist's use, only one reality of things. This seems to me commendable, not as a flight of metaphysics, hovering over bottomless gulfs of controversy, but, on the contrary, as a just indication of the vanity of certain dogmatisms. The particular way we see the world is our particular illusion about it, says M. de Maupassant, and this illusion fits itself to our organs and senses; our receptive vessel becomes the furniture of *our* little plot of the universal consciousness.

"How childish, moreover, to believe in reality, since we each carry our own in our thought and in our organs. Our eyes, our ears, our sense of smell, of taste, differing from one person to another, create as many truths as there are men upon earth. And our minds, taking instruction from these organs, so diversely impressed, understand, analyze, judge, as if each of us belonged to a different race. Each one of us, therefore, forms for himself an illusion of the world, which is the illusion poetic, or sentimental, or joyous, or melancholy, or unclean, or dismal, according to his nature. And the writer has no other mission than to reproduce faithfully this illusion, with all the contrivances of art that he has learned and has at his command. The illusion of beauty, which is a human convention! The illusion of ugliness, which is a changing opinion! The illusion of truth, which is never immutable! The illusion of the ignoble, which attracts so many! The great artists are those who make humanity accept their particular illusion. Let us, therefore, not get angry with any one theory, since every theory is the generalized expression of a temperament asking itself questions."

What is interesting in this is not that M. de Maupassant happens to hold that we have no universal measure of the truth, but that it is the last word on a question of art from a writer who is rich in experience and has had success in a very rare degree. It is of secondary importance that our impression should be called, or not called, an illusion; what is excellent is that our author has stated more neatly than we have lately seen it done that the value of the artist resides in the clearness with which he gives forth that impression. His particular organism constitutes a *case*, and the critic is intelligent in proportion as he apprehends and enters into that case. To quarrel with it because it is not another, which it could not possibly have been without a wholly different outfit, appears to M. de Maupassant a deplorable waste of time. If this appeal to our disinterestedness may strike some readers as chilling (through their inability to conceive of any other form than the one they like—a limitation excellent for a reader but poor for a judge), the occasion happens to be none of the best for saying so, for M. de Maupassant himself precisely presents all the symptoms of a "case" in the most striking way, and shows us how far the consideration of them may take us. Embracing such an opportunity as this, and giving ourselves to it freely, seems to me indeed to be a course more fruitful in valid conclusions, as well as in entertainment by the way, than the more common method of establishing one's own premises. To make clear to ourselves those of the author of *Pierre et Jean*—those to which he is committed by the very nature of his mind—is an attempt that will both stimulate and repay curiosity. There is no way of looking at his work less dry, less academic, for as we proceed from one of his peculiarities to another, the whole horizon widens, yet without our leaving firm ground, and we see ourselves landed, step by step, in the most general questions—those explanations of things which reside in the race, in the society. Of course there are cases and cases, and it is the salient ones that the disinterested critic is delighted to meet.

What makes M. de Maupassant salient is two facts: the first of which is that his gifts are remarkably strong and definite, and the second that he writes directly *from* them, as it were: holds the fullest, the most uninterrupted —I scarcely know what to call it—the boldest communication with them. A case is poor when the cluster of the artist's sensibilities is small, or they themselves are wanting in keenness, or else when the personage fails to admit them—either through ignorance, or diffidence, or stupidity, or the error of a false ideal—to what may be called a legitimate share in his attempt. It is, I think, among

English and American writers that this latter accident is most liable to occur; more than the French we are apt to be misled by some convention or other as to the sort of feeler we *ought* to put forth, forgetting that the best one will be the one that nature happens to have given us. We have doubtless often enough the courage of our opinions (when it befalls that we have opinions), but we have not so constantly that of our perceptions. There is a whole side of our perceptive apparatus that we in fact neglect, and there are probably many among us who would erect this tendency into a duty. M. de Maupassant neglects nothing that he possesses; he cultivates his garden with admirable energy; and if there is a flower you miss from the rich parterre, you may be sure that it could not possibly have been raised, his mind not containing the soil for it. He is plainly of the opinion that the first duty of the artist, and the thing that makes him most useful to his fellow-men, is to master his instrument, whatever it may happen to be.

His own is that of the senses, and it is through them alone, or almost alone, that life appeals to him; it is almost alone by their help that he describes it, that he produces brilliant works. They render him this great assistance because they are evidently, in his constitution, extraordinarily alive; there is scarcely a page in all his twenty volumes that does not testify to their vivacity. Nothing could be further from his thought than to disavow them and to minimize their importance. He accepts them frankly, gratefully, works them, rejoices in them. If he were told that there are many English writers who would be sorry to go with him in this, he would, I imagine, staring, say that that is about what was to have been expected of the Anglo-Saxon race, or even that many of them probably could not go with him if they would. Then he would ask how our authors can be so foolish as to sacrifice such a *moyen*, how they can afford to, and exclaim, "They must be pretty works, those they produce, and give a fine, true, complete account of life, with such

omissions, such lacunæ!" M. de Maupassant's productions
teach us, for instance, that his sense of smell is exception-
ally acute—as acute as that of those animals of the field
and forest whose subsistence and security depend upon it.
It might be thought that he would, as a student of the
human race, have found an abnormal development of this
faculty embarrassing, scarcely knowing what to do with
it, where to place it. But such an apprehension betrays
an imperfect conception of his directness and resolution,
as well as of his constant economy of means. Nothing
whatever prevents him from representing the relations of
men and women as largely governed by the scent of the
parties. Human life in his pages (would this not be the
most general description he would give of it?) appears for
the most part as a sort of concert of odors, and his
people are perpetually engaged, or he is engaged on their
behalf, in sniffing up and distinguishing them, in some
pleasant or painful exercise of the nostril. "If everything
in life speaks to the nostril, why on earth shouldn't we say
so?" I suppose him to inquire; "and what a proof of the
empire of poor conventions and hypocrisies, *chez vous
autres*, that you should pretend to describe and characterize, and yet take no note (or so little that it comes to
the same thing) of that essential sign!"

Not less powerful is his visual sense, the quick, direct
discrimination of his eye, which explains the singularly
vivid concision of his descriptions. These are never prolonged nor analytic, have nothing of enumeration, of the
quality of the observer, who counts the items to be sure
he has made up the sum. His eye *selects* unerringly, un-
scrupulously, almost impudently—catches the particular
thing in which the character of the object or the scene
resides, and, by expressing it with the artful brevity of a
master, leaves a convincing, original picture. If he is inveterately synthetic, he is never more so than in the way
he brings this hard, short, intelligent gaze to bear. His
vision of the world is for the most part a vision of ugliness, and even when it is not, there is in his easy power to

generalize a certain absence of love, a sort of bird's-eye-view contempt. He has none of the superstitions of observation, none of our English indulgences, our tender and often imaginative superficialities. If he glances into a railway carriage bearing its freight into the Parisian suburbs of a summer Sunday, a dozen dreary lives map themselves out in a flash.

"There were stout ladies in farcical clothes, those middle-class goodwives of the *banlieue* who replace the distinction they don't possess by an irrelevant dignity; gentlemen weary of the office, with sallow faces and twisted bodies, and one of their shoulders a little forced up by perpetual bending at work over a table. Their anxious, joyless faces spoke moreover of domestic worries, incessant needs for money, old hopes finally shattered; for they all belonged to the army of poor threadbare devils who vegetate frugally in a mean little plaster house, with a flower-bed for a garden."

Even in a brighter picture, such as the admirable vignette of the drive of Madame Tellier and her companions, the whole thing is an impression, as painters say nowadays, in which the figures are cheap. The six women at the station clamber into a country cart and go jolting through the Norman landscape to the village.

"But presently the jerky trot of the nag shook the vehicle so terribly that the chairs began to dance, tossing up the travelers to right, to left, with movements like puppets, scared grimaces, cries of dismay suddenly interrupted by a more violent bump. They clutched the sides of the trap, their bonnets turned over on to their backs, or upon the nose or the shoulder; and the white horse continued to go, thrusting out his head and straightening the little tail, hairless like that of a rat, with which from time to time he whisked his buttocks. Joseph Rivet, with one foot stretched upon the shaft, the other leg bent under him, and his elbows very high, held the reins and emitted from his throat every moment a kind of cluck which caused the animal to prick up his ears and quicken his pace. On either side of the road the green country stretched away. The colza, in flower, produced in spots a great carpet of undulating yellow, from which there rose a strong, wholesome smell, a smell penetrating and pleasant, carried very far by the breeze. In the tall rye the cornflowers held up their little azure heads, which the women wished to pluck; but M. Rivet refused to stop. Then, in some place, a whole field looked as if it were sprinkled with blood, it was so crowded with poppies. And in the midst of the great level, taking color in this fashion from the flowers of the soil, the trap passed on with the jog of the white horse, seeming itself to carry a nosegay of richer hues; it disappeared behind the big trees of a farm, to come out again where the foliage stopped and parade afresh through the green and yellow crops, pricked with red or blue, its blazing cartload of women, which receded in the sunshine."

As regards the other sense, the sense *par excellence*, the sense which we scarcely mention in English fiction, and which I am not very sure I shall be allowed to mention in an English periodical, M. de Maupassant speaks for that, and of it, with extraordinary distinctness and authority. To say that it occupies the first place in his picture is to say too little; it covers in truth the whole canvas, and his work is little else but a report of its innumerable manifestations. These manifestations are not, for him, so many incidents of life; they are life itself, they represent the standing answer to any question that we may ask about it. He describes them in detail, with a familiarity and a frankness which leave nothing to be added; I should say with singular truth, if I did not consider that in regard to this article he may be taxed with a certain exaggeration. M. de Maupassant would doubtless affirm that where the empire of the sexual sense is concerned, no exaggeration is possible: nevertheless it may be said that whatever depths may be discovered by those who dig for them, the impression of the human spectacle for him who takes it as it comes has less analogy with that of the monkeys' cage than this admirable writer's account of it. I speak of the human spectacle as we Anglo-Saxons see it—as we Anglo-Saxons pretend we see it, M. de Maupassant would possibly say.

At any rate, I have perhaps touched upon this peculiarity sufficiently to explain my remark that his point of view is almost solely that of the senses. If he is a very interesting case, this makes him also an embarrassing one, embarrassing and mystifying for the moralist. I may as well admit that no writer of the day strikes me as equally so. To find M. de Maupassant a lion in the path—that may seem to some people a singular proof of want of courage; but I think the obstacle will not be made light of by those who have really taken the measure of the animal. We are accustomed to think, we of the English faith, that a cynic is a living advertisement of his errors, especially in proportion as he is a thoroughgoing one; and M. de Maupassant's cynicism, unrelieved as it is, will not be disposed of off-hand by a critic of a competent literary sense. Such a critic is not slow to perceive, to his no small confusion, that though, judging from usual premises, the author of *Bel-Ami* ought to be a warning, he somehow is not. His baseness, as it pervades him, ought to be written all over him; yet somehow there are there certain aspects —and those commanding, as the house agents say—in which it is not in the least to be perceived. It is easy to exclaim that if he judges life only from the point of view of the senses, many are the noble and exquisite things that he must leave out. What he leaves out has no claim to get itself considered till after we have done justice to what he takes in. It is this positive side of M. de Maupassant that is most remarkable—the fact that his literary character is so complete and edifying. "Auteur à peu près irréprochable dans un genre qui ne l'est pas," as that excellent critic M. Jules Lemaître says of him, he disturbs us by associ-

ating a conscience and a high standard with a temper long
synonymous, in our eyes, with an absence of scruples. The
situation would be simpler certainly if he were a bad
writer; but none the less it is possible, I think, on the
whole, to circumvent him, even without attempting to
prove that after all he is one.

The latter part of his introduction to *Pierre et Jean* is
less felicitous than the beginning, but we learn from it—
and this is interesting—that he regards the analytic fashion
of telling a story, which has lately begotten in his own
country some such remarkable experiments (few votaries
as it has attracted among ourselves), as very much less
profitable than the simple epic manner which "avoids
with care all complicated explanations, all dissertations
upon motives, and confines itself to making persons and
events pass before our eyes." M. de Maupassant adds that
in his view "psychology should be hidden in a book, as it
is hidden in reality under the facts of existence. The novel
conceived in this manner gains interest, movement, color,
the bustle of life." When it is a question of an artistic
process, we must always mistrust very sharp distinctions,
for there is surely in every method a little of every other
method. It is as difficult to describe an action without
glancing at its motive, its moral history, as it is to describe
a motive without glancing at its practical consequence.
Our history and our fiction are what we do; but it surely
is not more easy to determine where what we do begins
than to determine where it ends—notoriously a hopeless
task. Therefore it would take a very subtle sense to draw
a hard and fast line on the borderland of explanation
and illustration. If psychology be hidden in life, as, according to M. de Maupassant, it should be in a book, the
question immediately comes up, "From whom is it hidden?" From some people, no doubt, but very much less
from others; and all depends upon the observer, the nature
of one's observation, and one's curiosity. For some people
motives, reasons, relations, explanations, are a part of the
very surface of the drama, with the footlights beating

full upon them. For me an act, an incident, an attitude, may be a sharp, detached, isolated thing, of which I give a full account in saying that in such and such a way it came off. For you it may be hung about with implications, with relations, and conditions as necessary to help you to recognize it as the clothes of your friends are to help you know them in the street. You feel that they would seem strange to you without petticoats and trousers.

M. de Maupassant would probably urge that the right thing is to know, or to guess, how events come to pass, but to say as little about it as possible. There are matters in regard to which he feels the importance of being explicit, but that is not one of them. The contention to which I allude strikes me as rather arbitrary, so difficult is it to put one's finger upon the reason why, for instance, there should be so little mystery about what happened to Christiane Andermatt, in *Mont-Oriol*, when she went to walk on the hills with Paul Brétigny, and so much, say, about the forces that formed her for that gentleman's convenience, or those lying behind any other odd collapse that our author may have related. The rule misleads, and the best rule certainly is the tact of the individual writer, which will adapt itself to the material as the material comes to him. The cause we plead is ever pretty sure to be the cause of our idiosyncrasies, and if M. de Maupassant thinks meanly of "explanations," it is, I suspect, that they come to him in no great affluence. His view of the conduct of man is so simple as scarcely to require them; and indeed so far as they are needed he *is*, virtually, explanatory. He deprecates reference to motives, but there is one, covering an immense ground in his horizon, as I have already hinted, to which he perpetually refers. If the sexual impulse be not a moral antecedent, it is none the less the wire that moves almost all M. de Maupassant's puppets, and as he has not hidden it, I cannot see that he has eliminated analysis or made a sacrifice to discretion. His pages are studded with that particular analysis; he is constantly peeping behind the curtain. telling us what he discovers there. The truth is that the admirable system of simplification which makes his tales so rapid and so concise (especially his shorter ones, for his novels in some degree, I think, suffer from it) strikes us as not in the least a conscious intellectual effort, a selective, comparative process. He tells us all he knows, all he suspects, and if these things take no account of the moral nature of man, it is because he has no window looking in that direction, and not because artistic scruples have compelled him to close it up. The very compact mansion in which he dwells presents on that side a perfectly dead wall.

This is why, if his axiom that you produce the effect of truth better by painting people from the outside than from the inside has a large utility, his example is convincing in a much higher degree. A writer is fortunate when his theory and his limitations so exactly correspond, when his curiosities may be appeased with such precision and promptitude. M. de Maupassant contends that the most that the analytic novelist can do is to put himself— his own peculiarities—into the costume of the figure analyzed. This may be true, but if it applies to one manner of representing people who are not ourselves, it applies also to any other manner. It is the limitation, the difficulty of the novelist, to whatever clan or camp he may belong. M. de Maupassant is remarkably objective and impersonal, but he would go too far if he were to entertain the belief that he has kept himself out of his books. They speak of him eloquently, even if it only be to tell us how easy —how easy, given his talent of course—he has found this impersonality. Let us hasten to add that in the case of describing a character it is doubtless more difficult to convey the impression of something that is not one's self (the constant effort, however delusive at bottom, of the novelist) than in the case of describing some object more immediately visible. The operation is more delicate, but that circumstance only increases the beauty of the problem.

On the question of style our author has some excellent

remarks; we may be grateful indeed for every one of them, save an odd reflection about the way to "become original" if we happen not to be so. The recipe for this transformation, it would appear, is to sit down in front of a blazing fire, or a tree in a plain, or any object we encounter in the regular way of business, and remain there until the tree, or the fire, or the object, whatever it be, become different for us from all other specimens of the same class. I doubt whether this system would always answer, for surely the resemblance is what we wish to discover, quite as much as the difference, and the best way to preserve it is not to look for something opposed to it. Is not this indication of the road to take to become, as a writer, original touched with the same fallacy as the recommendation about eschewing analysis? It is the only *naïveté* I have encountered in M. de Maupassant's many volumes. The best originality is the most unconscious, and the best way to describe a tree is the way in which it has struck us. "Ah, but we don't always know how it has struck us," the answer to that may be, "and it takes some time and ingenuity—much fasting and prayer—to find out." If we do not know, it probably has not struck us very much: so little indeed that our inquiry had better be relegated to that closed chamber of an artist's meditations, that sacred back kitchen, which no *a priori* rule can light up. The best thing the artist's adviser can do in such a case is to trust him and turn away, to let him fight the matter out with his conscience. And be this said with a full appreciation of the degree in which M. de Maupassant's observations on the whole question of a writer's style, at the point we have come to today, bear the stamp of intelligence and experience. His own style is of so excellent a tradition that the presumption is altogether in favor of what he may have to say.

He feels oppressively, discouragingly, as many another of his countrymen must have felt—for the French have worked their language as no other people have done—the penalty of coming at the end of three centuries of litera-

ture, the difficulty of dealing with an instrument of expression so worn by friction, of drawing new sounds from
the old familiar pipe. "When we read, so saturated with
French writing as we are that our whole body gives us
the impression of being a paste made of words, do we
ever find a line, a thought, which is not familiar to us, and
of which we have not had at least a confused presenti-
ment?" And he adds that the matter is simple enough for
the writer who only seeks to amuse the public by means
already known; he attempts little, and he produces "with
confidence, in the candor of his mediocrity," works which
answer no question and leave no trace. It is he who wants
to do more than this that has less and less an easy time of
it. Everything seems to him to have been done, every
effect produced, every combination already made. If he
be a man of genius, his trouble is lightened, for mysterious
ways are revealed to him, and new combinations spring
up for him even after novelty is dead. It is to the simple
man of taste and talent, who has only a conscience and a
will, that the situation may sometimes well appear desperate; he judges himself as he goes, and he can only go
step by step over ground where every step is already a
footprint.

If it be a miracle whenever there is a fresh tone, the
miracle has been wrought for M. de Maupassant. Or is
he simply a man of genius to whom short cuts have been
disclosed in the watches of the night? At any rate he has
had faith—religion has come to his aid; I mean the religion
of his mother tongue, which he has loved well enough to
be patient for her sake. He has arrived at the peace
which passeth understanding, at a kind of conservative
piety. He has taken his stand on simplicity, on a studied
sobriety, being persuaded that the deepest science lies in
that direction rather than in the multiplication of new
terms, and on this subject he delivers himself with superlative wisdom.

"There is no need of the queer, complicated, numerous,

and Chinese vocabulary which is imposed on us today under the name of artistic writing, to fix all the shades of thought; the right way is to distinguish with an extreme clearness all those modifications of the value of a word which come from the place it occupies. Let us have fewer nouns, verbs and adjectives of an almost imperceptible sense, and more different phrases variously constructed, ingeniously cast, full of the science of sound and rhythm. Let us have an excellent general form rather than be collectors of rare terms."

M. de Maupassant's practice does not fall below his exhortation (though I must confess that in the foregoing passage he makes use of the detestable expresion "stylist," which I have not reproduced). Nothing can exceed the masculine firmness, the quiet force of his own style, in which every phrase is a close sequence, every epithet a paying piece, and the ground is completely cleared of the vague, the ready-made and the second-best. Less than any one today does he beat the air; more than any one does he hit out from the shoulder.

II

He has produced a hundred short tales and only four regular novels; but if the tales deserve the first place in any candid appreciation of his talent it is not simply because they are so much the more numerous: they are also more characteristic; they represent him best in his originality, and their brevity, extreme in some cases, does not prevent them from being a collection of masterpieces. (They are very unequal, and I speak of the best.) The little story is but scantily relished in England, where readers take their fiction rather by the volume than by the page, and the novelist's idea is apt to resemble one of those old-fashioned carriages which require a wide court to turn round. In America, where it is associated pre-eminently with Hawthorne's name, with Edgar Poe's, and with that of Mr. Bret Harte, the short tale has had a better fortune. France, however, has been the land of its great prosperity, and M. de Maupassant had from the first the advantage of addressing a public accustomed to catch on, as the modern phrase is, quickly. In some respects, it may be said, he encountered prejudices too friendly, for he found a tradition of indecency ready made to his hand. I say indecency with plainness, though my indication would perhaps please better with another word, for we suffer in English from a lack of roundabout names for the *conte leste*—that element for which the French, with their *grivois*, their *gaillard*, their *égrillard*, their *gaudriole*, have so many convenient synonyms. It is an honored tradition in France that the little story, in verse or in prose, should be liable to be more or less obscene (I can think only of that alternative epithet), though I hasten to add that among literary forms it does not monopolize the privilege. Our uncleanness is less producible—at any rate it is less produced.

For the last ten years our author has brought forth with regularity these condensed compositions, of which, probably, to an English reader, at a first glance, the most universal sign will be their licentiousness. They really partake of this quality, however, in a very differing degree, and a second glance shows that they may be divided into numerous groups. It is not fair, I think, even to say that what they have most in common is their being extremely *lestes*. What they have most in common is their being extremely strong, and after that their being extremely brutal. A story may be obscene without being brutal, and *vice versa*, and M. de Maupassant's contempt for those interdictions which are supposed to be made in the interest of good morals is but an incident—a very large one indeed—of his general contempt. A pessimism so great that its alliance with the love of good work, or even with the calculation of the sort of work that pays best in a country of style, is, as I have intimated, the most puzzling of anomalies (for it would seem in the light of such sentiments that nothing is worth anything); this cynical strain is the sign of such gems of narration as *La Maison Tellier*, *L'Histoire d'une fille de ferme*, *L'Ane*, *Le Chien*, *Mademoiselle Fifi*, *Monsieur Parent*, *L'Héritage*, *En Famille*, *Le Baptême*, *Le Père Amable*. The author fixes a hard eye on some small spot of human life, usually some ugly, dreary, shabby, sordid one, takes up the particle, and squeezes it either till it grimaces or till it bleeds. Sometimes the grimace is very droll, sometimes the wound is very horrible; but in either case the whole thing is real, observed, noted, and represented, not an invention or a castle in the air. M. de Maupassant sees human life as a terribly ugly business relieved by the comical, but even the comedy is for the most part the comedy of misery, of avidity, of ignorance, helplessness, and grossness. When his laugh is not for these things, it is for the little *saletés* (to use one of his own favorite words) of luxurious life, which are intended to be prettier, but which can scarcely be said to brighten the picture. I like *La Bête à Maître Belhomme*, *La Ficelle*, *Le Petit Fût*, *Le Cas de Madame Luneau*, *Tribuneaux rustiques*, and many others of this category much better than his anecdotes of the mutual confidences of his little *marquises* and *baronnes*.

Not counting his novels for the moment, his tales may be divided into the three groups of those which deal with the Norman peasantry, those which deal with the *petit employé* and small shopkeeper, usually in Paris, and the miscellaneous, in which the upper walks of life are represented, and the fantastic, the whimsical, the weird, and even the supernatural, figure as well as the unexpurgated. These last things range from *Le Horla* (which is not a specimen of the author's best vein—the only occasion on which he has the weakness of imitation is when he strikes us as emulating Edgar Poe) to *Miss Harriet*, and from *Boule de Suif* (a triumph) to that almost inconceivable little growl of Anglophobia, *Découverte*—inconceivable I mean in its irresponsibility and ill-nature on the part of a man of M. de Maupassant's distinction; passing by such little perfections as *Petit Soldat*, *L'Abandonné*, *Le Collier* (the list is too long for complete enumeration), and such gross imperfections (for it once in a while befalls our author to go woefully astray) as *La Femme de Paul, Châli, Les Sœurs Rondoli.* To these might almost be added as a special category the various forms in which M. de Maupassant relates adventures in railway carriages. Numerous, to his imagination, are the pretexts for enlivening fiction afforded by first, second, and third class compartments; the accidents (which have nothing to do with the conduct of the train) that occur there constitute no inconsiderable part of our earthly transit.

It is surely by his Norman peasant that his tales will live; he knows this worthy as if he had made him, understands him down to the ground, puts him on his feet with a few of the freest, most plastic touches. M. de Maupassant does not admire him, and he is such a master of the subject that it would ill become an outsider to suggest a revision of judgment. He is a part of the contemptible furniture of the world, but on the whole, it would appear, the most grotesque part of it. His caution, his canniness, his natural astuteness, his stinginess, his general grinding sordidness, are as unmistakable as that quaint and brutish dialect in which he expresses himself, and on which our author plays like a virtuoso. It would be impossible to demonstrate with a finer sense of the humor of the thing the fatuities and densities of his ignorance, the bewilderments of his opposed appetites, the overreachings of his caution. His existence has a gay side, but it is apt to be the barbarous gaiety commemorated in *Farce Normande,* an anecdote which, like many of M. de Maupassant's anecdotes, it is easier to refer the reader to than to repeat. If it is most convenient to place *La Maison Tellier* among the tales of the peasantry, there is no doubt that it stands at the head of the list. It is absolutely unadapted to the perusal of ladies and young persons, but it shares this peculiarity with most of its fellows, so that to ignore it on that account would be to imply that we must forswear M. de Maupassant altogether, which is an incongruous and insupportable conclusion. Every good story is of course both a picture and an idea, and the more they are interfused the better the problem is solved. In *La Maison Tellier* they fit each other to perfection; the capacity for sudden innocent delights latent in natures which have lost their innocence is vividly illustrated by the singular scenes to which our acquaintance with Madame and her staff (little as it may be a thing to boast of) successively introduces us. The breadth, the freedom, and brightness of all this give the measure of the author's talent, and of that large, keen way of looking at life which sees the pathetic and the droll, the stuff of which the whole piece is made, in the queerest and humblest patterns. The tone of *La Maison Tellier* and the few compositions which closely resemble it, expresses M. de Maupassant's nearest approach to geniality. Even here, however, it is the geniality of the showman exhilarated by the success with which he feels that he makes his mannikins (and especially his womankins) caper and squeak, and who after the performance tosses them into their box with the irreverence of a practiced hand. If the pages of the author of *Bel-Ami* may be searched almost in vain for a manifestation of the sentiment of respect, it is naturally not by Mme. Tellier and her charges that we must look most to see it called forth; but they are among the things that please him most.

Sometimes there is a sorrow, a misery, or even a little heroism, that he handles with a certain tenderness (*Une Vie* is the capital example of this), without insisting on the poor, the ridiculous, or, as he is fond of saying, the bestial side of it. Such an attempt, admirable in its sobriety and delicacy, is the sketch, in *L'Abandonné*, of the old lady and gentleman, Mme. de Cadour and M. d'Apreval, who, staying with the husband of the former at a little watering-place on the Normandy coast, take a long, hot walk on a summer's day, on a straight, white road, into the interior, to catch a clandestine glimpse of a young farmer, their illegitimate son. He has been

pensioned, he is ignorant of his origin, and is a common-
place and unconciliatory rustic. They look at him, in his
dirty farmyard, and no sign passes between them; then
they turn away and crawl back, in melancholy silence,
along the dull French road. The manner in which this
dreary little occurrence is related makes it as large as a
chapter of history. There is tenderness in *Miss Harriet,*
which sets forth how an English old maid, fantastic,
hideous, sentimental, and tract-distributing, with a smell of
india rubber, fell in love with an irresistible French
painter, and drowned herself in the well because she saw
him kissing the maidservant; but the figure of the lady
grazes the farcical. Is it because we know Miss Harriet
(if we are not mistaken in the type the author has had
in his eye) that we suspect the good spinster was not so
weird and desperate, addicted though her class may be,
as he says, to "haunting all the *tables d'hôte* in Europe, to
spoiling Italy, poisoning Switzerland, making the charming
towns of the Mediterranean uninhabitable, carrying everywhere their queer little manias, their *mœurs de vestales
pétrifiées,* their indescribable garments, and that odor of
india rubber which makes one think that at night they
must be slipped into a case?" What would Miss Harriet
have said to M. de Maupassant's friend, the hero of the
Découverte, who, having married a little Anglaise because
he thought she was charming when she spoke broken
French, finds she is very flat as she becomes more fluent,
and has nothing more urgent than to denounce her to a
gentleman he meets on the steamboat, and to relieve his
wrath in ejaculations of "Sales Anglais"?

M. de Maupassant evidently knows a great deal about
the army of clerks who work under government, but it is
a terrible tale that he has to tell of them and of the *petit
bourgeois* in general. It is true that he has treated the
petit bourgeois in *Pierre et Jean* without holding him up
to our derision, and the effort has been so fruitful, that
we owe to it the work for which, on the whole, in the
long list of his successes, we are most thankful. But of

Pierre et Jean, a production neither comic nor cynical (in the degree, that is, of its predecessors), but serious and fresh, I will speak anon. In *Monsieur Parent, L'Héritage, En Famille, Une Partie de campagne, Promenade,* and many other pitiless little pieces, the author opens the window wide to his perception of everything mean, narrow, and sordid. The subject is ever the struggle for existence in hard conditions, lighted up simply by more or less *polissonnerie.* Nothing is more striking to an Anglo-Saxon reader than the omission of all the other lights, those with which our imagination, and I think it ought to be said our observation, is familiar, and which our own works of fiction at any rate do not permit us to forget: those of which the most general description is that they spring from a certain mixture of good humor and piety —piety, I mean, in the civil and domestic sense quite as much as in the religious. The love of sport, the sense of decorum, the necessity for action, the habit of respect, the absence of irony, the pervasiveness of childhood, the expansive tendency of the race, are a few of the qualities (the analysis might, I think, be pushed much further) which ease us off, mitigate our tension and irritation, rescue us from the nervous exasperation which is almost the commonest element of life as depicted by M. de Maupassant. No doubt there is in our literature an immense amount of conventional blinking, and it may be questioned whether pessimistic representation in M. de Maupassant's manner does not follow his particular original more closely than our perpetual quest of pleasantness (does not Mr. Rider Haggard make even his African carnage pleasant?) adheres to the lines of the world we ourselves know.

Fierce indeed is the struggle for existence among even our pious and good-humored millions, and it is attended with incidents as to which after all little testimony is to be extracted from our literature of fiction. It must never be forgotten that the optimism of that literature is partly the optimism of women and of spinsters; in other words the optimism of ignorance as well as of delicacy. It might

be supposed that the French, with their mastery of the
arts d'agrément, would have more consolations than we,
but such is not the account of the matter given by the
new generation of painters. To the French we seem superficial, and we are certainly open to the reproach; but none
the less even to the infinite majority of readers of good
faith there will be a wonderful want of correspondence
between the general picture of *Bel-Ami*, of *Mont-Oriol*,
of *Une Vie*, *Yvette* and *En Famille*, and our own vision
of reality. It is an old impression of course that the satire
of the French has a very different tone from ours; but few
English readers will admit that the feeling of life is less
in ours than in theirs. The feeling of life is evidently, *de
part et d'autre*, a very different thing. If in ours, as the
novel illustrates it, there are superficialities, there are also
qualities which are far from being negatives and omissions: a large imagination and (is it fatuous to say?) a
large experience of the positive kind. Even those of our
novelists whose manner is most ironic pity life more and
hate it less than M. de Maupassant and his great initiator
Flaubert. It comes back I suppose to our good humor
(which may apparently also be an artistic force); at any
rate, we have reserves about our shames and our sorrows,
indulgences and tolerances about our Philistinism, for-
bearances about our blows, and a general friendliness of
conception about our possibilities, which take the cruelty
from our self-derision and operate in the last resort as a
sort of tribute to our freedom. There is a horrible, admirable scene in *Monsieur Parent*, which is a capital example of triumphant ugliness. The harmless gentleman
who gives his name to the tale has an abominable wife, one
of whose offensive attributes is a lover (unsuspected by
her husband), only less impudent than herself. M. Parent
comes in from a walk with his little boy, at dinner time,
to encounter suddenly in his abused, dishonored, deserted
home, convincing proof of her misbehavior. He waits and
waits dinner for her, giving her the benefit of every doubt;
but when at last she enters, late in the evening, accom-

panied by the partner of her guilt, there is a tremendous domestic concussion. It is to the peculiar vividness of this scene that I allude, the way we hear it and see it, and its most repulsive details are evoked for us: the sordid confusion, the vulgar noise, the disordered table and ruined dinner, the shrill insolence of the wife, her brazen mendacity, the scared inferiority of the lover, the mere momentary heroics of the weak husband, the scuffle and somersault, the eminently unpoetic justice with which it all ends.

When Thackeray relates how Arthur Pendennis goes home to take pot luck with the insolvent Newcomes at Boulogne, and how the dreadful Mrs. Mackenzie receives him, and how she makes a scene, when the frugal repast is served, over the diminished mutton bone, we feel that the notation of that order of misery goes about as far as we can bear it. But this is child's play to the history of M. and Mme. Caravan and their attempt, after the death (or supposed death) of the husband's mother, to transfer to their apartment before the arrival of the other heirs certain miserable little articles of furniture belonging to the deceased, together with the frustration of the maneuver not only by the grim resurrection of the old woman (which is a sufficiently fantastic item), but by the shock of battle when a married daughter and her husband appear. No one gives us like M. de Maupassant the odious words exchanged on such an occasion as that: no one depicts with so just a hand the feelings of small people about small things. These feelings are very apt to be "fury"; that word is of strikingly frequent occurrence in his pages. *L'Héritage* is a drama of private life in the little world of the Ministère de la Marine—a world, according to M. de Maupassant, of dreadful little jealousies and ineptitudes. Readers of a robust complexion should learn how the wretched M. Lesable was handled by his wife and her father on his failing to satisfy their just expectations, and how he comported himself in the singular situation thus prepared for him. The story is a model of narration, but

it leaves our poor average humanity dangling like a beaten
rag.

Where does M. de Maupassant find the great multitude
of his detestable women? or where at least does he find,
the courage to represent them in such colors? Jeanne de
Lamare, in *Une Vie*, receives the outrages of fate with a
passive fortitude; and there is something touching in Mme.
Roland's *âme tendre de caissière*, as exhibited in *Pierre et
Jean*. But for the most part M. de Maupassant's heroines
are a mixture of extreme sensuality and extreme mendacity. They are a large element in that general disfigurement, that *illusion de l'ignoble, qui attire tant d'êtres*,
which makes the perverse or the stupid side of things the
one which strikes him first, which leads him, if he glances
at a group of nurses and children sunning themselves in
a Parisian square, to notice primarily the *yeux de brute* of
the nurses; or if he speaks of the longing for a taste of
the country which haunts the shopkeeper fenced in behind his counter, to identify it as the *amour bête de la
nature;* or if he has occasion to put the boulevards before
us on a summer's evening, to seek his effect in these
terms: "The city, as hot as a stew, seemed to sweat in the
suffocating night. The drains puffed their pestilential
breath from their mouths of granite, and the underground
kitchens poured into the streets, through their low windows, the infamous miasmas of their dishwater and old
sauces." I do not contest the truth of such indications, I
only note the particular selection and their seeming to the
writer the most *apropos.*

Is it because of the inadequacy of these indications when
applied to the long stretch that M. de Maupassant's novels,
strike us as less complete, in proportion to the talent
expended upon them, than his *contes* and *nouvelles?* I
make this invidious distinction in spite of the fact that
Une Vie (the first of the novels in the order of time) is
a remarkably interesting experiment, and that *Pierre et
Jean* is, so far as my judgment goes, a faultless production.
Bel-Ami is full of the bustle and the crudity of life (its

energy and expressiveness almost bribe one to like it), but it has the great defect that the physiological explanation of things here too visibly contracts the problem in order to meet it. The world represented is too special, too little inevitable, too much to take or to leave as we like—a world in which every man is a cad and every woman a harlot. M. de Maupassant traces the career of a finished blackguard who succeeds in life through women, and he represents him primarily as succeeding in the profession of journalism. His colleagues and his mistresses are as depraved as himself, greatly to the injury of the ironic idea, for the real force of satire would have come from seeing him engaged and victorious with natures better than his own. It may be remarked that this was the case with the nature of Mme. Walter; but the reply to that is —hardly! Moreover the author's whole treatment of the episode of Mme. Walter is the thing on which his admirers have least to congratulate him. The taste of it is so atrocious, that it is difficult to do justice to the way it is made to stand out. Such an instance as this pleads with irresistible eloquence, as it seems to me, the cause of that salutary diffidence or practical generosity which I mentioned on a preceding page. I know not the English or American novelist who could have written this portion of the history of *Bel-Ami* if he would. But I also find it impossible to conceive of a member of that fraternity who would have written it if he could. The subject of *Mont-Oriol* is full of queerness to the English mind. Here again the picture has much more importance than the idea, which is simply that a gentleman, if he happen to be a low animal, is liable to love a lady very much less if she presents him with a pledge of their affection. It need scarcely be said that the lady and gentleman who in M. de Maupassant's pages exemplify this interesting truth are not united in wedlock—that is with each other.

M. de Maupassant tells us that he has imbibed many of his principles from Gustave Flaubert, from the study of his works as well as, formerly, the enjoyment of his words.

It is in *Une Vie* that Flaubert's influence is most directly traceable, for the thing has a marked analogy with *L'Éducation sentimentale*. That is, it is the presentation of a simple piece of a life (in this case a long piece), a series of observations upon an episode *quelconque*, as the French say, with the minimum of arrangement of the given objects. It is an excellent example of the way the impression of truth may be conveyed by that form, but it would have been a still better one if in his search for the effect of dreariness (the effect of dreariness may be said to be the subject of *Une Vie*, so far as the subject is reducible) the author had not eliminated excessively. He has arranged, as I say, as little as possible; the necessity of a "plot" has in no degree imposed itself upon him, and his effort has been to give the uncomposed, unrounded look of life, with its accidents, its broken rhythm, its queer resemblance to the famous description of "Bradshaw"—a compound of trains that start but don't arrive, and trains that arrive but don't start. It is almost an arrangement of the history of poor Mme. de Lamare to have left so many things out of it, for after all she is described in very few of the relations of life. The principal ones are there certainly; we see her as a daughter, a wife, and a mother, but there is a certain accumulation of secondary experience that marks any passage from youth to old age which is a wholly absent element in M. de Maupassant's narrative, and the suppression of which gives the thing a tinge of the arbitrary. It is in the power of this secondary experience to make a great difference, but nothing makes any difference for Jeanne de Lamare as M. de Maupassant puts her before us. Had she no other points of contact than those he describes?—no friends, no phases, no episodes, no chances, none of the miscellaneous *remplissage* of life? No doubt M. de Maupassant would say that he has had to select, that the most comprehensive enumeration is only a condensation, and that, in accordance with the very just principles enunciated in that preface to which I have perhaps too repeatedly referred, he has sacrificed what is uncharacteristic to what is characteristic. It characterizes the career of this French country lady of fifty years ago that its long gray expanse should be seen as peopled with but five or six figures. The essence of the matter is that she was deceived in almost every affection, and that essence is given if the persons who deceived her are given.

The reply is doubtless adequate, and I have only intended my criticism to suggest the degree of my interest. What it really amounts to is that if the subject of this artistic experiment had been the existence of an English lady, even a very dull one, the air of verisimilitude would have demanded that she should have been placed in a denser medium. *Une Vie* may after all be only a testimony to the fact of the melancholy void of the coast of Normandy, even within a moderate drive of a great seaport, under the Restoration and Louis Philippe. It is especially to be recommended to those who are interested in the question of what constitutes a "story," offering as it does the most definite sequences at the same time that it has nothing that corresponds to the usual idea of a plot, and closing with an implication that finds us prepared. The picture again in this case is much more dominant than the idea, unless it be an idea that loneliness and grief are terrible. The picture, at any rate, is full of truthful touches, and the work has the merit and the charm that it is the most delicate of the author's productions and the least hard. In none other has he occupied himself so continuously with so innocent a figure as his soft, bruised heroine; in none other has he paid our poor blind human history the compliment (and this is remarkable, considering the flatness of so much of the particular subject) of finding it so little *bête*. He may think it, here, but comparatively he does not say it. He almost betrays a sense of moral things. Jeanne is absolutely passive, she has no moral spring, no active moral life, none of the edifying attributes of character (it costs her apparently as little as may be in the way of a shock, a complication of feeling, to discover, by letters, after her mother's death, that this lady has not been the virtuous woman she has supposed); but her chronicler has had to handle the immaterial forces of patience and renunciation, and this has given the book a certain purity, in spite of two or three "physiological" passages that come in with violence—a violence the greater as we feel it to be a result of selection. It is very much a mark of M. de Maupassant that on the most striking occasion, with a single exception, on which his picture is not a picture of libertinage it is a picture of unmitigated suffering. Would he suggest that these are the only alternatives?

The exception that I here allude to is for *Pierre et Jean*, which I have left myself small space to speak of. Is it because in this masterly little novel there is a show of those immaterial forces which I just mentioned, and because Pierre Roland is one of the few instances of operative character that can be recalled from so many volumes, that many readers will place M. de Maupassant's latest production altogether at the head of his longer ones? I am not sure, inasmuch as after all the character in question is not extraordinarily distinguished, and the moral problem not presented in much complexity. The case is only relative. Perhaps it is not of importance to fix the reasons of preference in respect to a piece of writing so essentially a work of art and of talent. *Pierre et Jean* is the best of M. de Maupassant's novels mainly because M. de Maupassant has never before been so clever. It is a pleasure to see a mature talent able to renew itself, strike another note, and appear still young. This story suggests the growth of a perception that everything has not been said about the actors on the world's stage when they are represented either as helpless victims or as mere bundles of appetites. There is an air of responsibility about Pierre Roland, the person on whose behalf the tale is mainly told, which almost constitutes a pledge. An inquisitive critic may ask why in this particular case M. de Maupassant should have stuck to the *petit bourgeois*, the circumstances not being such as to typify that class more than another. There are reasons indeed which on reflection are perceptible; it was necessary that his people should be poor, and necessary even that to attenuate Madame Roland's misbehavior she should have had the excuse of the contracted life of a shopwoman in the Rue Montmartre. Were the inquisitive critic slightly malicious as well, he might suspect the author of a fear that he should seem to give way to the *illusion du beau* if in addition to representing the little group in *Pierre et Jean* as persons of about the normal conscience he had also represented them as of the cultivated class. If they belong to the humble life this belittles and—I am still quoting the supposedly malicious critic—M. de Maupassant *must*, in one way or the other, belittle. To the English reader it will appear, I think, that Pierre and Jean are rather more of the cultivated class than two young Englishmen in the same social position. It belongs to the drama that the struggle of the elder brother—educated, proud, and acute—should be partly with the pettiness of his opportunities. The author's choice of a *milieu*, moreover, will serve to English readers as an example of how much more democratic contemporary French fiction is than that of his own country. The greater part of it—almost all the work of Zola and of Daudet, the best of Flaubert's novels, and the best of those of the brothers De Goncourt—treat of that vast, dim section of society which, lying between those luxurious walks on whose behalf there are easy presuppositions and that darkness of misery which, in addition to being picturesque, brings philanthropy also to the writer's aid, constitutes really, in extent and expressiveness, the substance of any nation. In England, where the fashion of fiction still sets mainly to the country house and the hunting-field, and yet more novels are published than anywhere else in the world, that thick twilight of mediocrity of condition has been little explored. May it yield triumphs in the years to come!

It may seem that I have claimed little for M. de

Maupassant, so far as English readers are concerned with him, in saying that after publishing twenty improper volumes he has at last published a twenty-first, which is neither indecent nor cynical. It is not this circumstance that has led me to dedicate so many pages to him, but the circumstance that in producing all the others he yet remained, for those who are interested in these matters, a writer with whom it was impossible not to reckon. This is why I called him, to begin with, so many ineffectual names: a rarity, a "case," an embarrassment, a lion in the path. He is still in the path as I conclude these observations, but I think that in making them we have discovered a legitimate way round. If he is a master of his art and it is discouraging to find what low views are compatible with mastery, there is satisfaction, on the other hand, in learning on what particular condition he holds his strange success. This condition, it seems to me, is that of having totally omitted one of the items of the problem, an omission which has made the problem so much easier that it may almost be described as a short cut to a solution. The question is whether it be a fair cut. M. de Maupassant has simply skipped the whole reflective part of his men and women—that reflective part which governs conduct and produces character. He may say that he does not see it, does not know it; to which the answer is, "So much the better for you, if you wish to describe life without it. The strings you pull are by so much the less numerous, and you can therefore pull those that remain with greater promptitude, consequently with greater firmness, with a greater air of knowledge." Pierre Roland, I repeat, shows a capacity for reflection, but I cannot think who else does, among the thousand figures who compete with him—I mean for reflection addressed to anything higher than the gratification of an instinct. We have an impression that M. d'Apreval and Madame de Cadour reflect, as they trudge back from their mournful excursion, but that indication is not pushed very far. An aptitude for this exercise is a part of disciplined manhood, and disciplined manhood M. de Maupassant has simply not attempted to represent. I can remember no instance in which he sketches any considerable capacity for conduct, and his women betray that capacity as little as his men. I am much mistaken if he has once painted a gentleman, in the English sense of the term. His gentlemen, like Paul Brétigny and Gontran de Ravenel, are guilty of the most extraordinary deflections. For those who are conscious of this element in life, look for it and like it, the gap will appear to be immense. It will lead them to say, "No wonder you have a contempt if that is the way you limit the field. No wonder you judge people roughly if that is the way you see them. Your work, on your premisses, remains the admirable thing it is, but is your 'case' not adequately explained?"

The erotic element in M. de Maupassant, about which much more might have been said, seems to me to be explained by the same limitation, and explicable in a similar way wherever else its literature occurs in excess. The carnal side of man appears the most characteristic if you look at it a great deal; and you look at it a great deal if you do not look at the other, at the side by which he reacts against his weaknesses, his defeats. The more you look at the other, the less the whole business to which French novelists have ever appeared to English readers to give a disproportionate place—the business, as I may say, of the senses—will strike you as the only typical one. Is not this the most useful reflection to make in regard to the famous question of the morality, the decency, of the novel? It is the only one, it seems to me, that will meet the case as we find the case today. Hard and fast rules, *a priori* restrictions, mere interdictions (you shall not speak of this, you shall not look at that) have surely served their time, and will in the nature of the case never strike an energetic talent as anything but arbitrary. A healthy, living and growing art, full of curiosity and fond of exercise, has an indefeasible mistrust of rigid prohibitions. Let us then leave this magnificent art of the novelist to itself and to its perfect freedom, in the faith that one example is at good as another, and that our fiction will always be decent enough if it be sufficiently general. Let us not be alarmed at this prodigy (though prodigies are alarming) of M. de Maupassant, who is at once so licentious and so impeccable, but gird ourselves up with the conviction that another point of view will yield another perfection.

TURGENEV AND TOLSTOY

THERE IS perhaps no novelist of alien race who more naturally than Ivan Turgenev inherits a niche in a Library for English readers; and this not because of any advance or concession that in his peculiar artistic independence he ever made, or could dream of making, such readers, but because it was one of the effects of his peculiar genius to give him, even in his lifetime, a special place in the regard of foreign publics. His position is in this respect singular; for it is his Russian savor that as much as anything has helped generally to domesticate him.

Born in 1818, at Orel in the heart of Russia, and dying in 1883, at Bougival near Paris, he had spent in Germany and France the latter half of his life; and had incurred in his own country in some degree the reprobation that is apt to attach to the absent—the penalty they pay for such extension or such beguilement as they may have happened to find over the border. He belonged to the class of large rural proprietors of land and of serfs; and with his ample patrimony, offered one of the few examples of literary labor achieved in high independence of the question of gain—a character that he shares with his illustrious contemporary Tolstoy, who is of a type in other respects so different. It may give us an idea of his primary situation to imagine some large Virginian or Carolinian slaveholder, during the first half of the century, inclining to "Northern" views; and becoming (though not predominantly under pressure of these, but rather by the operation of an exquisite genius) the great American novelist—one of the great novelists of the world. Born under a social and political order sternly repressive, all Turgenev's deep instincts, all his moral passion, placed him on the liberal side; with the consequence that early in life, after a period spent at a German university, he found himself, through the accident of a trifling public utterance, under such suspicion in high places as to be sentenced to a term of tempered exile—confinement to his own estate. It was partly under these circumstances perhaps that he gathered material for the work from the appearance of which his reputation dates—*A Sportsman's Sketches*, published in two volumes in 1852. This admirable collection of impressions of homely country life, as the old state of servitude had made it, is often spoken of as having borne to the great decree of Alexander II the relation borne by Mrs. Beecher Stowe's famous novel to the emancipation of the Southern slaves. Incontestably, at any rate, Turgenev's rustic studies sounded, like *Uncle Tom's Cabin*, a particular hour: with the difference, however, of not having at the time produced an agitation—of having rather presented the case with an art too insidious for instant recognition, an art that stirred the depths more than the surface.

The author was designated promptly enough, at any

rate, for such influence as might best be exercised at a distance: he traveled, he lived abroad; early in the sixties he was settled in Germany; he acquired property at Baden-Baden, and spent there the last years of the prosperous period—in the history of the place—of which the Franco-Prussian War was to mark the violent term. He cast in his lot after that event mainly with the victims of the lost cause; setting up a fresh home in Paris—near which city he had, on the Seine, a charming alternate residence—and passing in it, and in the country, save for brief revisitations, the remainder of his days. His friendships, his attachments, in the world of art and of letters, were numerous and distinguished; he never married; he produced, as the years went on, without precipitation or frequency; and these were the years during which his reputation gradually established itself as, according to the phrase, European—a phrase denoting in this case, perhaps, a public more alert in the United States even than elsewhere.

Tolstoy, his junior by ten years, had meanwhile come to fruition; though, as in fact happened, it was not till after Turgenev's death that the greater fame of *War and Peace* and of *Anna Karénina* began to be blown about the world. One of the last acts of the elder writer, performed on his deathbed, was to address to the other (from whom for a considerable term he had been estranged by circumstances needless to reproduce) an appeal to return to the exercise of the genius that Tolstoy had already so lamentably, so monstrously forsworn. "I am on my deathbed; there is no possibility of my recovery. I write you expressly to tell you how happy I have been to be your contemporary, and to utter my last, my urgent prayer. Come back, my friend, to your literary labors. That gift came to you from the source from which all comes to us. Ah, how happy I should be could I think you would listen to my entreaty! My friend, great writer of our Russian land, respond to it, obey it!" These words, among the most touching surely ever addressed by one

great spirit to another, throw an indirect light—perhaps
I may even say a direct one—upon the nature and
quality of Turgenev's artistic temperament; so much so
that I regret being without opportunity, in this place, to
gather such aid for a portrait of him as might be supplied
by following out the unlikeness between the pair. It
would be too easy to say that Tolstoy was, from the
Russian point of view, for home consumption, and
Turgenev for foreign: *War and Peace* has probably had
more readers in Europe and America than *A House of
Gentlefolk* or *On the Eve* or *Smoke*,—a circumstance
less detrimental than it may appear to my claim of our
having, in the Western world, supremely adopted the
author of the latter works. Turgenev is in a peculiar
degree what I may call the novelists' novelist—an artistic
influence extraordinarily valuable and ineradicably established. The perusal of Tolstoy—a wonderful mass of life
—is an immense event, a kind of splendid accident, for
each of us: his name represents nevertheless no such
eternal spell of method, no such quiet irresistibility of
presentation, as shines, close to us and lighting our possible
steps, in that of his precursor. Tolstoy is a reflector as
vast as a natural lake; a monster harnessed to his great
subject—all human life!—as an elephant might be harnessed, for purposes of traction, not to a carriage, but to a
coach-house. His own case is prodigious, but his example
for others dire: disciples not elephantine he can only
mislead and betray.

One by one, for thirty years, with a firm, deliberate
hand, with intervals and patiences and waits, Turgenev
pricked in his sharp outlines. His great external mark is
probably his concision: an ideal he never threw over—
it shines most perhaps even when he is least brief—and
that he often applied with a rare felicity. He has masterpieces of a few pages; his perfect things are sometimes
his least prolonged. He abounds in short tales, episodes
clipped as by the scissors of Atropos; but for a direct
translation of the whole we have still to wait—depending

meanwhile upon the French and German versions, which have been, instead of the original text (thanks to the paucity among us of readers of Russian), the source of several published in English. For the novels and *A Sportsman's Sketches* we depend upon the nine volumes (1897) of Mrs. Garnett. We touch here upon the remarkable side, to our vision, of the writer's fortune—the anomaly of his having constrained to intimacy even those who are shut out from the enjoyment of his medium, for whom that question is positively prevented from existing. Putting aside extrinsic intimations, it is impossible to read him without the conviction of his being, in the vividness of his own tongue, of the strong type of those made to bring home to us the happy truth of the unity, in a generous talent, of material and form—of their being inevitable faces of the same medal; the type of those, in a word, whose example deals death to the perpetual clumsy assumption that subject and style are—æsthetically speaking, or in the living work—different and separable things. We are conscious, reading him in a language not his own, of not being reached by his personal tone, his individual accent.

It is a testimony therefore to the intensity of his presence, that so much of his particular charm does reach us; that the mask turned to us has, even without his expression, still so much beauty. It is the beauty (since we must try to formulate) of the finest presentation of the familiar. His vision is of the world of character and feeling, the world of the relations life throws up at every hour and on every spot; he deals little, on the whole, in the miracles of chance,—the hours and spots over the edge of time and space; his air is that of the great central region of passion and motive, of the usual, the inevitable, the intimate—the intimate for weal or woe. No theme that he ever chooses but strikes us as full; yet with all have we the sense that their animation comes from within, and is not pinned to their backs like the pricking objects used of old in the horse races of the Roman carnival, to make the animals run. Without a patch of "plot" to draw blood, the story he mainly tells us, the situation he mainly gives, runs as if for dear life. His first book was practically full evidence of what, if we have to specify, is finest in him—the effect, for the commonest truth, of an exquisite envelope of poetry. In this medium of feeling—full, as it were, of all the echoes and shocks of the universal danger and need—everything in him goes on; the sense of fate and folly and pity and wonder and beauty. The tenderness, the humor, the variety of *A Sportsman's Sketches* revealed on the spot an observer with a rare imagination. These faculties had attached themselves, together, to small things and to great: to the misery, the simplicity, the piety, the patience, of the unemancipated peasant; to all the natural wonderful life of earth and air and winter and summer and field and forest; to queer apparitions of country neighbors, of strange local eccentrics; to old-world practices and superstitions; to secrets gathered and types disinterred and impressions absorbed in the long, close contacts with man and nature involved in the passionate pursuit of game. Magnificent in stature and original vigor, Tugenev, with his love of the chase, or rather perhaps of the inspiration he found in it, would have been the model of the mighty hunter, had not such an image been a little at variance with his natural mildness, the softness that often accompanies the sense of an extraordinary reach of limb and play of muscle. He was in person the model rather of the strong man at rest: massive and towering, with the voice of innocence and the smile almost of childhood. What seemed still more of a contradiction to so much of him, however, was that his work was all delicacy and fancy, penetration and compression.

If I add, in their order of succession, *Rudin, Fathers and Children, Spring Floods,* and *Virgin Soil,* to the three novels I have (also in their relation of time) named above, I shall have indicated the larger blocks of the compact monument, with a base resting deep and interstices well filled, into which that work disposes itself. The list of his minor productions is too long to draw out: I can only mention, as a few of the most striking—"A Correspondence," "The Wayside Inn," "The Brigadier," "The Dog," "The Jew," "Visions," "Mumu," "Three Meetings," "A First Love," "The Forsaken," "Assia," "The Journal of a Superfluous Man," "The Story of Lieutenant Yergunov," "A King Lear of the Steppe." The first place among his novels would be difficult to assign: general opinion probably hesitates between *A House of Gentlefolk* and *Fathers and Children*. My own predilection is great for the exquisite *On the Eve*; though I admit that in such a company it draws no supremacy from being exquisite. What is less contestable is that *Virgin Soil*—published shortly before his death, and the longest of his fictions—has, although full of beauty, a minor perfection.

Character, character expressed and exposed, is in all these things what we inveterately find. Turgenev's sense of it was the great light that artistically guided him; the simplest account of him is to say that the mere play of it constitutes in every case his sufficient drama. No one has had a closer vision, or a hand at once more ironic and more tender, for the individual figure. He sees it with its minutest signs and tricks—all its heredity of idiosyncrasies, all its particulars of weakness and strength, of ugliness and beauty, of oddity and charm; and yet it is of his essence that he sees it in the general flood of life, steeped in its relations and contacts, struggling or submerged, a hurried particle in the stream. This gives him, with his quiet method, his extraordinary breadth; dissociates his rare power to particularize from dryness or hardness, from any peril of caricature. He understands so much that we almost wonder he can express anything; and his expression is indeed wholly in absolute projection, in illustration, in giving of everything the unexplained and irresponsible specimen. He is of a spirit so human that we almost wonder at his control of his matter; of a pity so deep and so general that we almost wonder at his curiosity. The element of poetry in him is constant, and yet reality stares through it without the loss of a wrinkle. No one has more of that sign of the born novelist which resides in a respect unconditioned for the freedom and vitality, the absoluteness when summoned, of the creatures he invokes; or is more superior to the strange and second-rate policy of explaining or presenting them by reprobation or apology,—of taking the short cuts and anticipating the emotions and judgments about them that should be left, at the best, to the perhaps not most intelligent reader. And yet his system, as it may summarily be called, of the mere particularized report, has a lucidity beyond the virtue of the cruder moralist.

If character, as I say, is what he gives us at every turn, I should speedily add that he offers it not in the least as a synonym, in our Western sense, of resolution and prosperity. It wears the form of the almost helpless detachment of the short-sighted individual soul; and the perfection of his exhibition of it is in truth too often but the intensity of what, for success, it just does not produce. What works in him most is the question of the will; and the most constant induction he suggests, bears upon the sad figure that principle seems mainly to make among his countrymen. He had seen—he suggests to us—its collapse in a thousand quarters; and the most general tragedy, to his view, is that of its desperate adventures and disasters, its inevitable abdication and defeat. But if the men, for the most part, let it go, it takes refuge in the other sex; many of the representatives of which, in his pages, are supremely strong—in wonderful addition, in various cases, to being otherwise admirable. This is true of such a number—the younger women, the girls, the "heroines" in especial—that they form in themselves, on the ground of moral beauty, of the finest distinction of soul, one of the most striking groups the modern novel has given us. They are heroines to the letter, and of a heroism obscure and undecorated: it is almost they alone who have the energy to determine and to act. Elena, Lisa, Tatyana,

so much to elevate the art of the novelist. The author of *The Warden,* of *Barchester Towers,* of *Framley Parsonage,* does not, to our mind, stand on the very same level as Dickens, Thackeray and George Eliot; for his talent was of a quality less fine than theirs. But he belonged to the same family—he had as much to tell us about English life; he was strong, genial and abundant. He published too much; the writing of novels had ended by becoming, with him, a perceptibly mechanical process. Dickens was prolific, Thackeray produced with a freedom for which we are constantly grateful; but we feel that these writers had their periods of gestation. They took more time to look at their subject; relatively (for today there is not much leisure, at best, for those who undertake to entertain a hungry public), they were able to wait for inspiration. Trollope's fecundity was prodigious; there was no limit to the work he was ready to do. It is not unjust to say that he sacrificed quality to quantity. Abundance, certainly, is in itself a great merit; almost all the greatest writers have been abundant. But Trollope's fertility was gross, importunate; he himself contended, we believe, that he had given to the world a greater number of printed pages of fiction than any of his literary contemporaries. Not only did his novels follow each other without visible intermission, overlapping and treading on each other's heels, but most of these works are of extraordinary length. *Orley Farm, Can You Forgive Her? He Knew He Was Right,* are exceedingly voluminous tales. *The Way We Live Now* is one of the longest of modern novels. Trollope produced, moreover, in the intervals of larger labor a great number of short stories, many of them charming, as well as various books of travel, and two or three biographies. He was the great *improvisatore* of these latter years. Two distinguished storytellers of the other sex —one in France and one in England—have shown an extraordinary facility of composition; but Trollope's pace was brisker even than that of the wonderful Madame Sand and the delightful Mrs. Oliphant. He had taught himself to keep this pace, and had reduced his admirable faculty to a system. Every day of his life he wrote a certain number of pages of his current tale, a number sacramental and invariable, independent of mood and place. It was once the fortune of the author of these lines to cross the Atlantic in his company, and he has never forgotten the magnificent example of plain persistence that it was in the power of the eminent novelist to give on that occasion. The season was unpropitious, the vessel overcrowded, the voyage detestable; but Trollope shut himself up in his cabin every morning for a purpose which, on the part of a distinguished writer who was also an invulnerable sailor, could only be communion with the muse. He drove his pen as steadily on the tumbling ocean as in Montague Square; and as his voyages were many, it was his practice before sailing to come down to the ship and confer with the carpenter, who was instructed to rig up a rough writing-table in his small sea-chamber. Trollope has been accused of being deficient in imagination, but in the face of such a fact as that the charge will scarcely seem just. The power to shut one's eyes, one's ears (to say nothing of another sense), upon the scenery of a pitching Cunarder and open them upon the loves and sorrows of Lily Dale or the conjugal embarrassments of Lady Glencora Palliser, is certainly a faculty which could take to itself wings. The imagination that Trollope possessed he had at least thoroughly at his command. I speak of all this in order to explain (in part) why it was that, with his extraordinary gift, there was always in him a certain infusion of the common. He abused his gift, overworked it, rode his horse too hard. As an artist he never took himself seriously; many people will say this was why he was so delightful. The people who take themselves seriously are prigs and bores; and Trollope, with his perpetual "story," which was the only thing he cared about, his strong good sense, hearty good nature, generous appreciation of life in all its varieties, responds in perfection to a certain English ideal. According to that ideal it is rather dangerous to be explicitly or consciously an artist—to have a system, a doctrine, a form. Trollope, from the first, went in, as they say, for having as little form as possible; it is probably safe to affirm that he had no "views" whatever on the subject of novel writing. His whole manner is that of a man who regards the practice as one of the more delicate industries, but has never troubled his head nor clogged his pen with theories about the nature of his business. Fortunately he was not obliged to do so, for he had an easy road to success; and his honest, familiar, deliberate way of treating his readers as if he were one of them, and shared their indifference to a general view, their limitations of knowledge, their love of a comfortable ending, endeared him to many persons in England and America. It is in the name of some chosen form that, of late years, things have been made most disagreeable for the novel reader, who has been treated by several votaries of the new experiments in fiction to unwonted and bewildering sensations. With Trollope we were always safe; there were sure to be no new experiments.

His great, his inestimable merit was a complete appreciation of the usual. This gift is not rare in the annals of English fiction; it would naturally be found in a walk of literature in which the feminine mind has labored so fruitfully. Women are delicate and patient observers; they hold their noses close, as it were, to the texture of life. They feel and perceive the real with a kind of personal tact, and their observations are recorded in a thousand delightful volumes. Trollope, therefore, with his eyes comfortably fixed on the familiar, the actual, was far from having invented a new category; his great distinction is that in resting there his vision took in so much of the field. And then he *felt* all daily and immediate things as well as saw them; felt them in a simple, direct, salubrious way, with their sadness, their gladness, their charm, their comicality, all their obvious and measurable meanings. He never wearied of the pre-established round of English customs—never needed a respite or a change—

was content to go on indefinitely watching the life that surrounded him, and holding up his mirror to it. Into this mirror the public, at first especially, grew very fond of looking—for it saw itself reflected in all the most credible and supposable ways, with that curiosity that people feel to know how they look when they are represented, "just as they are," by a painter who does not desire to put them into an attitude, to drape them for an effect, to arrange his light and his accessories. This exact and on the whole becoming image, projected upon a surface without a strong intrinsic tone, constitutes mainly the entertainment that Trollope offered his readers. The striking thing to the critic was that his robust and patient mind had no particular bias, his imagination no light of its own. He saw things neither pictorially and grotesquely like Dickens; nor with that combined disposition to satire and to literary form which gives such "body," as they say of wine, to the manner of Thackeray; nor with anything of the philosophic, the transcendental cast—the desire to follow them to their remote relations—which we associate with the name of George Eliot. Trollope had his elements of fancy, of satire, of irony; but these qualities were not very highly developed, and he walked mainly by the light of his good sense, his clear, direct vision of the things that lay nearest, and his great natural kindness. There is something remarkably tender and friendly in his feeling about all human perplexities; he takes the good-natured, temperate, conciliatory view—the humorous view, perhaps, for the most part, yet without a touch of pessimistic prejudice. As he grew older, and had sometimes to go farther afield for his subjects, he acquired a savor of bitterness and reconciled himself sturdily to treating of the disagreeable. A more copious record of disagreeable matters could scarcely be imagined, for instance, than *The Way We Live Now*. But, in general, he has a wholesome mistrust of morbid analysis, an aversion to inflicting pain. He has an infinite love of detail, but his details are, for the most part, the innumerable items of the expected. When the French are disposed to pay a compliment to the English mind they are so good as to say that there is in it something remarkably *honnête*. If I might borrow this epithet without seeming to be patronizing, I should apply it to the genius of Anthony Trollope. He represents in an eminent degree this natural decorum of the English spirit, and represents it all the better that there is not in him a grain of the mawkish or the prudish. He writes, he feels, he judges like a man, talking plainly and frankly about many things, and is by no means destitute of a certain saving grace of coarseness. But he has kept the purity of his imagination and held fast to old-fashioned reverences and preferences. He thinks it a sufficient objection to several topics to say simply that they are unclean. There was nothing in his theory of the storyteller's art that tended to convert the reader's or the writer's mind into a vessel for polluting things. He recognized the right of the vessel to protest, and would have regarded such a protest as conclusive. With a considerable turn for satire, though this perhaps is more evident in his early novels than in his later ones, he had as little as possible of the quality of irony. He never played with a subject, never juggled with the sympathies or the credulity of his reader, was never in the least paradoxical or mystifying. He sat down to his theme in a serious, businesslike way, with his elbows on the table and his eye occasionally wandering to the clock.

To touch successively upon these points is to attempt a portrait, which I shall perhaps not altogether have failed to produce. The source of his success in describing the life that lay nearest to him, and describing it without any of those artistic perversions that come, as we have said, from a powerful imagination, from a cynical humor or from a desire to look, as George Eliot expresses it, for the suppressed transitions that unite all contrasts, the essence of this love of reality was his extreme interest in character. This is the fine and admirable quality in Trollope, this is what will preserve his best works in spite of those flatnesses which keep him from standing on quite the same level as the masters. Indeed this quality is so much one of the finest (to my mind at least), that it makes me wonder the more that the writer who had it so abundantly and so naturally should not have just that distinction which Trollope lacks, and which we find in his three brilliant contemporaries. If he was in any degree a man of genius (and I hold that he was), it was in virtue of this happy, instinctive perception of human varieties. His knowledge of the stuff we are made of, his observation of the common behavior of men and women, was not reasoned nor acquired, not even particularly studied. All human doings deeply interested him, human life, to his mind, was a perpetual story; but he never attempted to take the so-called scientific view, the view which has lately found ingenious advocates among the countrymen and successors of Balzac. He had no airs of being able to tell you *why* people in a given situation would conduct themselves in a particular way; it was enough for him that he felt their feelings and struck the right note, because he had, as it were, a good ear. If he was a knowing psychologist he was so by grace; he was just and true without apparatus and without effort. He must have had a great taste for the moral question; he evidently believed that this is the basis of the interest of fiction. We must be careful, of course, in attributing convictions and opinions to Trollope, who, as I have said, had as little as possible of the pedantry of his art, and whose occasional chance utterances in regard to the object of the novelist and his means of achieving it are of an almost startling simplicity. But we certainly do not go too far in saying that he gave his practical testimony in favor of the idea that the interest of a work of fiction is great in proportion as the people stand on their feet. His great effort was evidently to make them stand so; if he achieved this result with as little as possible of a flourish of the hand it was nevertheless the measure of his success. If he had taken sides on the droll, bemuddled opposition between novels of character and novels of plot, I can imagine him to have said (except that he never expressed himself in epigrams), that he preferred the former class, inasmuch as character in itself is plot, while plot is by no means character. It is more safe indeed to believe that his great good sense would have prevented him from taking an idle controversy seriously. Character, in any sense in which we can get at it, is action, and action is plot, and any plot which hangs together, even if it pretend to interest us only in the fashion of a Chinese puzzle, plays upon our emotion, our suspense, by means of personal references. We care what happens to people only in proportion as we know what people are. Trollope's great apprehension of the real, which was what made him so interesting, came to him through his desire to satisfy us on this point—to tell us what certain people were and what they did in consequence of being so. That is the purpose of each of his tales; and if these things produce an illusion it comes from the gradual abundance of his testimony as to the temper, the tone, the passions, the habits, the moral nature, of a certain number of contemporary Britons.

His stories, in spite of their great length, deal very little in the surprising, the exceptional, the complicated; as a general thing he has no great story to tell. The thing is not so much a story as a picture; if we hesitate to call it a picture it is because the idea of composition is not the controlling one and we feel that the author would regard the artistic, in general, as a kind of affectation. There is not even much description, in the sense which the present votaries of realism in France attach to that word. The painter lays his scene in a few deliberate, not especially pictorial strokes, and never dreams of finishing the piece for the sake of enabling the reader to hang it up. The finish, such as it is, comes later, from the slow and somewhat clumsy accumulation of small illustrations. These illustrations are sometimes of the commonest; Trollope turns them out inexhaustibly, repeats them

freely, unfolds them without haste and without rest.
But they are all of the most obvious sort, and they are
none the worse for that. The point to be made is that
they have no great spectacular interest (we beg pardon
of the innumerable love affairs that Trollope has described), like many of the incidents, say, of Walter Scott
and of Alexandre Dumas: if we care to know about them
(as repetitions of a usual case), it is because the writer
has managed, in his candid, literal, somewhat lumbering
way, to tell us that about the men and women concerned which has already excited on their behalf the
impression of life. It is a marvel by what homely arts,
by what imperturbable button-holing persistence, he
contrives to excite this impression. Take, for example,
such a work as *The Vicar of Bullhampton*. It would be
difficult to state the idea of this slow but excellent story,
which is a capital example of interest produced by the
quietest conceivable means. The principal persons in it
are a lively, jovial, high-tempered country clergyman, a
young woman who is in love with her cousin, and a small,
rather dull squire who is in love with the young woman.
There is no connection between the affairs of the clergyman and those of the two other persons, save that these
two are the Vicar's friends. The Vicar gives countenance,
for Christian charity's sake, to a young countryman who
is suspected (falsely, as it appears) of murder, and also to
the lad's sister, who is more than suspected of leading an
immoral life. Various people are shocked at his indiscre-
tion, but in the end he is shown to have been no worse
a clergyman because he is a good fellow. A cantankerous
nobleman, who has a spite against him, causes a Methodist
conventicle to be erected at the gates of the vicarage;
but afterward, finding that he has no title to the land
used for this obnoxious purpose, causes the conventicle
to be pulled down, and is reconciled with the parson,
who accepts an invitation to stay at the castle. Mary
Lowther, the heroine of *The Vicar of Bullhampton*, is
sought in marriage by Mr. Harry Gilmore, to whose

passion she is unable to respond; she accepts him, however, making him understand that she does not love him,
and that her affections are fixed upon her kinsman, Captain Marrable, whom she would marry (and who would
marry her), if he were not too poor to support a wife.
If Mr. Gilmore will take her on these terms she will
become his spouse; but she gives him all sorts of warnings.
They are not superfluous; for, as Captain Marrable presently inherits a fortune, she throws over Mr. Gilmore,
who retires to foreign lands, heartbroken, inconsolable.
This is the substance of *The Vicar of Bullhampton;* the
reader will see that it is not a very tangled skein. But
if the interest is gradual it is extreme and constant, and it
comes altogether from excellent portraiture. It is essentially a moral, a social interest. There is something
masterly in the large-fisted grip with which, in work
of this kind, Trollope handles his brush. The Vicar's
nature is thoroughly analyzed and rendered, and his
monotonous friend the Squire, a man with limitations,
but possessed and consumed by a genuine passion, is
equally near the truth.

Trollope has described again and again the ravages of
love, and it is wonderful to see how well, in these delicate
matters, his plain good sense and good taste serve him.
His story is always primarily a love story, and a love
story constructed on an inveterate system. There is a
young lady who has two lovers, or a young man who
has two sweethearts; we are treated to the innumerable
forms in which this predicament may present itself and
the consequences, sometimes pathetic, sometimes grotesque, which spring from such false situations. Trollope
is not what is called a colorist; still less is he a poet: he
is seated on the back of heavy-footed prose. But his account of those sentiments which the poets are supposed
to have made their own is apt to be as touching as dem-
onstrations more lyrical. There is something wonderfully
vivid in the state of mind of the unfortunate Harry Gilmore, of whom I have just spoken; and his history,

which has no more pretensions to style than if it were cut out of yesterday's newspaper, lodges itself in the imagination in all sorts of classic company. He is not handsome, nor clever, nor rich, nor romantic, nor distinguished in any way; he is simply rather a dense, narrow-minded, stiff, obstinate, commonplace, conscientious modern Englishman, exceedingly in love and, from his own point of view, exceedingly ill-used. He is interesting because he suffers and because we are curious to see the form that suffering will take in that particular nature. Our good fortune, with Trollope, is that the person put before us will have, in spite of opportunities not to have it, a certain particular nature. The author has cared enough about the character of such a person to find out exactly what it is. Another particular nature in *The Vicar of Bullhampton* is the surly, sturdy, skeptical old farmer Jacob Brattle, who doesn't want to be patronized by the parson, and in his dumb, dusky, half-brutal, half-spiritual melancholy, surrounded by domestic troubles, financial embarrassments and a puzzling world, declines altogether to be won over to clerical optimism. Such a figure as Jacob Brattle, purely episodical though it be, is an excellent English portrait. As thoroughly English, and the most striking thing in the book, is the combination, in the nature of Frank Fenwick—the delightful Vicar—of the patronizing, conventional, clerical element with all sorts of manliness and spontaneity; the union, or to a certain extent the contradiction, of official and personal geniality. Trollope touches these points in a way that shows that he knows his man. Delicacy is not his great sign, but when it is necessary he can be as delicate as any one else.

I alighted, just now, at a venture, upon the history of Frank Fenwick; it is far from being a conspicuous work in the immense list of Trollope's novels. But to choose an example one must choose arbitrarily, for examples of almost anything that one may wish to say are numerous to embarrassment. In speaking of a writer who produced so much and produced always in the same way, there is perhaps a certain unfairness in choosing at all. As no work has higher pretensions than any other, there may be a certain unkindness in holding an individual production up to the light. "Judge me in the lump," we can imagine the author saying; "I have only undertaken to entertain the British public. I don't pretend that each of my novels is an organic whole." Trollope had no time to give his tales a classic roundness; yet there is (in spite of an extraordinary defect) something of that quality in the thing that first revealed him. *The Warden* was published in 1855. It made a great impression; and when, in 1857, *Barchester Towers* followed it, every one saw that English literature had a novelist the more. These were not the works of a young man, for Anthony Trollope had been born in 1815. It is remarkable to reflect, by the way, that his prodigious fecundity (he had published before *The Warden* three or four novels which attracted little attention) was enclosed between his fortieth and his sixty-seventh years. Trollope had lived long enough in the world to learn a good deal about it; and his maturity of feeling and evidently large knowledge of English life were for much in the effect produced by the two clerical tales. It was easy to see that he would take up room. What he had picked up, to begin with, was a comprehensive, various impression of the clergy of the Church of England and the manners and feelings that prevail in cathedral towns. This, for a while, was his specialty, and, as always happens in such cases, the public was disposed to prescribe to him that path. He knew about bishops, archdeacons, prebendaries, precentors, and about their wives and daughters; he knew what these dignitaries say to each other when they are collected together, aloof from secular ears. He even knew what sort of talk goes on between a bishop and a bishop's lady when the august couple are enshrouded in the privacy of the episcopal bedroom. This knowledge, somehow, was rare and precious. No one, as yet, had been bold enough to snatch the illuminating torch from the very summit of the altar.

Trollope enlarged his field very speedily—there is, as I remember that work, as little as possible of the ecclesiastical in the tale of *The Three Clerks*, which came after *Barchester Towers*. But he always retained traces of his early divination of the clergy; he introduced them frequently, and he always did them easily and well. There is no ecclesiastical figure, however, so good as the first—no creation of this sort so happy as the admirable Mr. Harding. *The Warden* is a delightful tale, and a signal instance of Trollope's habit of offering us the spectacle of a character. A motive more delicate, more slender, as well as more charming, could scarcely be conceived. It is simply the history of an old man's conscience.

The good and gentle Mr. Harding, precentor of Barchester Cathedral, also holds the post of warden of Hiram's Hospital, an ancient charity where twelve old paupers are maintained in comfort. The office is in the gift of the bishop, and its emoluments are as handsome as the duties of the place are small. Mr. Harding has for years drawn his salary in quiet gratitude; but his moral repose is broken by hearing it at last begun to be said that the wardenship is a sinecure, that the salary is a scandal, and that a large part, at least, of his easy income ought to go to the pensioners of the hospital. He is sadly troubled and perplexed, and when the great London newspapers take up the affair he is overwhelmed with confusion and shame. He thinks the newspapers are right—he perceives that the warden is an overpaid and rather a useless functionary. The only thing he can do is to resign the place. He has no means of his own—he is only a quiet, modest, innocent old man, with a taste, a passion, for old church-music and the violoncello. But he determines to resign, and he does resign in spite of the sharp opposition of his friends. He does what he thinks right, and goes to live in lodgings over a shop in the Barchester High Street. That is all the story, and it has exceeding beauty. The question of Mr. Harding's resignation becomes a drama, and we anxiously wait for the catastrophe. Trollope never did anything happier than the picture of this sweet and serious little old gentleman, who on most of the occasions of life has shown a lamblike softness and compliance, but in this particular matter opposes a silent, impenetrable obstinacy to the arguments of the friends who insist on his keeping his sinecure—fixing his mild, detached gaze on the distance, and making imaginary passes with his fiddle-bow while they demonstrate his pusillanimity. The subject of *The Warden*, exactly viewed, is the opposition of the two natures of Archdeacon Grantley and Mr. Harding, and there is nothing finer in all Trollope than the vividness with which this opposition is presented. The archdeacon is as happy a portrait as the precentor—an image of the full-fed, worldly churchman, taking his stand squarely upon his rich temporalities, and regarding the church frankly as a fat social pasturage. It required the greatest tact and temperance to make the picture of Arch-deacon Grantley stop just where it does. The type, im-partially considered, is detestable, but the individual may be full of amenity. Trollope allows his archdeacon all the virtues he was likely to possess, but he makes his spiritual grossness wonderfully natural. No charge of exaggeration is possible, for we are made to feel that he is conscientious as well as arrogant, and expansive as well as hard. He is one of those figures that spring into being all at once, solidifying in the author's grasp. These two capital por-traits are what we carray away from *The Warden*, which some persons profess to regard as our writer's masterpiece. We remember, while it was still something of a novelty, to have heard a judicious critic say that it had much of the charm of *The Vicar of Wakefield*. Anthony Trollope would not have accepted the compliment, and would not have wished this little tale to pass before several of its successors. He would have said, very justly, that it gives too small a measure of his knowledge of life. It has, how-ever, a certain classic roundness, though, as we said a moment since, there is a blemish on its fair face. The chapter on Dr. Pessimist Anticant and Mr. Sentiment

would be a mistake almost inconceivable if Trollope had
not in other places taken pains to show us that for certain
forms of satire (the more violent, doubtless), he had absolutely no gift. Dr. Anticant is a parody of Carlyle, and
Mr. Sentiment is an exposure of Dickens: and both these
little *jeux d'esprit* are as infelicitous as they are misplaced.
It was no less luckless an inspiration to convert Archdeacon Grantley's three sons, denominated respectively
Charles James, Henry and Samuel, into little effigies of
three distinguished English bishops of that period, whose
well-known peculiarities are reproduced in the description
of these unnatural urchins. The whole passage, as we meet
it, is a sudden disillusionment; we are transported from the
mellow atmosphere of an assimilated Barchester to the air
of ponderous allegory.

I may take occasion to remark here upon a very curious
fact—the fact that there are certain precautions in the
way of producing that illusion dear to the intending
novelist which Trollope not only habitually scorned to
take, but really, as we may say, asking pardon for the
heat of the thing, delighted wantonly to violate. He took
a suicidal satisfaction in reminding the reader that the
story he was telling was only, after all, a make-believe.
He habitually referred to the work in hand (in the course
of that work) as a novel, and to himself as a novelist, and
was fond of letting the reader know that this novelist
could direct the course of events according to his pleasure.
Already, in *Barchester Towers*, he falls into this pernicious
trick. In describing the wooing of Eleanor Bold by Mr.
Arabin he has occasion to say that the lady might have
acted in a much more direct and natural way than the
way he attributes to her. But if she had, he adds, "where
would have been my novel?" The last chapter of the
same story begins with the remark, "The end of a novel,
like the end of a children's dinner party, must be made
up of sweetmeats and sugar-plums." These little slaps at
credulity (we might give many more specimens) are very
discouraging, but they are even more inexplicable; for they

are deliberately inartistic, even judged from the point of view of that rather vague consideration of form which is the only canon we have a right to impose upon Trollope. It is impossible to imagine what a novelist takes himself to be unless he regard himself as an historian and his narrative as a history. It is only as an historian that he has the smallest *locus standi*. As a narrator of fictitious events he is nowhere; to insert into his attempt a backbone of logic, he must relate events that are assumed to be real. This assumption permeates, animates all the work of the most solid storytellers; we need only mention (to select a single instance) the magnificent historical tone of Balzac, who would as soon have thought of admitting to the reader that he was deceiving him, as Garrick or John Kemble would have thought of pulling off his disguise in front of the footlights. Therefore, when Trollope suddenly winks at us and reminds us that he is telling us an arbitrary thing, we are startled and shocked in quite the same way as if Macaulay or Motley were to drop the historic mask and intimate that William of Orange was a myth or the Duke of Alva an invention.

It is a part of this same ambiguity of mind as to what constitutes evidence that Trollope should sometimes endow his people with such fantastic names. Dr. Pessimist Anticant and Mr. Sentiment make, as we have seen, an awkward appearance in a modern novel; and Mr. Neversay Die, Mr. Stickatit, Mr. Rerechild and Mr. Fillgrave (the two last the family physicians) are scarcely more felicitous. It would be better to go back to Bunyan at once. There is a person mentioned in *The Warden* under the name of Mr. Quiverful—a poor clergyman, with a dozen children, who holds the living of Puddingdale. This name is a humorous allusion to his overflowing nursery, and it matters little so long as he is not brought to the front. But in *Barchester Towers*, which carries on the history of Hiram's Hospital, Mr. Quiverful becomes, as a candidate for Mr. Harding's vacant place, an important element, and the reader is made proportionately unhappy

by the primitive character of this satiric note. A Mr.
Quiverful with fourteen children (which is the number
attained in *Barchester Towers*) is too difficult to believe
in. We can believe in the name and we can believe in
the children; but we cannot manage the combination. It
is probably not unfair to say that if Trollope derived half
his inspiration from life, he derived the other half from
Thackeray; his earlier novels, in especial, suggest an
honorable emulation of the author of *The Newcomes*.
Thackeray's names were perfect; they always had a meaning, and (except in his absolutely jocose productions,
where they were still admirable) we can imagine, even
when they are most figurative, that they should have been
borne by real people. But in this, as in other respects,
Trollope's hand was heavier than his master's; though
when he is content not to be too comical his appellations
are sometimes fortunate enough. Mrs. Proudie is excellent,
for Mrs. Proudie, and even the Duke of Omnium and
Gatherum Castle rather minister to illusion than destroy
it. Indeed, the names of houses and places, throughout
Trollope, are full of color.

I would speak in some detail of *Barchester Towers* if
this did not seem to commit me to the prodigious task of
appreciating each of Trollope's works in succession. Such
an attempt as that is so far from being possible that I
must frankly confess to not having read everything that
proceeded from his pen. There came a moment in his
vigorous career (it was even a good many years ago)
when I renounced the effort to "keep up" with him. It
ceased to seem obligatory to have read his last story; it
ceased soon to be very possible to know which was his
last. Before that, I had been punctual, devoted; and the
memories of the earlier period are delightful. It reached,
if I remember correctly, to about the publication of *He
Knew He Was Right;* after which, to my recollection
(oddly enough, too, for that novel was good enough to
encourage a continuance of past favors, as the shop-
keepers say), the picture becomes dim and blurred. The

author of *Orley Farm* and *The Small House at Allington*
ceased to produce individual works; his activity became a
huge "serial." Here and there, in the vast fluidity, an
organic particle detached itself. *The Last Chronicle of
Barset*, for instance, is one of his most powerful things;
it contains the sequel of the terrible history of Mr.
Crawley, the starving curate—an episode full of that
literally truthful pathos of which Trollope was so often
a master, and which occasionally raised him quite to the
level of his two immediate predecessors in the vivid treatment of English life—great artists whose pathetic effects
were sometimes too visibly prepared. For the most part,
however, he should be judged by the productions of the
first half of his career; later the strong wine was rather
too copiously watered. His practice, his acquired facility,
were such that his hand went of itself, as it were, and
the thing looked superficially like a fresh inspiration. But
it was not fresh, it was rather stale; and though there was
no appearance of effort, there was a fatal dryness of texture. It was too little of a new story and too much of an
old one. Some of these ultimate compositions—*Phineas
Redux* (*Phineas Finn* is much better), *The Prime Minister*, *John Caldigate*, *The American Senator*, *The Duke's
Children*—betray the dull, impersonal rumble of the mill
wheel. What stands Trollope always in good stead (in
addition to the ripe habit of writing) is his various
knowledge of the English world—to say nothing of his
occasionally laying under contribution the American. His
American portraits, by the way (they are several in
number), are always friendly; they hit it off more happily than the attempt to depict American character from
the European point of view is accustomed to do: though,
indeed, as we ourselves have not yet learned to represent
our types very finely—are not apparently even very sure
what our types are—it is perhaps not to be wondered at
that transatlantic talent should miss the mark. The weakness of transatlantic talent in this particular is apt to be
want of knowledge; but Trollope's knowledge has all the

air of being excellent, though not intimate. Had he indeed striven to learn the way to the American heart? No less than twice, and possibly even oftener, has he rewarded the merit of a scion of the British aristocracy with the hand of an American girl. The American girl was destined sooner or later to make her entrance into British fiction, and Trollope's treatment of this complicated being is full of good humor and that of fatherly indulgence, that almost motherly sympathy, which characterizes his attitude throughout toward the youthful feminine. He has not mastered all the springs of her delicate organism nor sounded all the mysteries of her conversation. Indeed, as regards these latter phenomena, he has observed a few of which he has been the sole observer. "I got to be thinking if any one of them should ask me to marry him," words attributed to Miss Boncassen, in *The Duke's Children*, have much more the note of English American than of American English. But, on the whole, in these matters Trollope does very well. His fund of acquaintance with his own country—and indeed with the world at large—was apparently inexhaustible, and it gives his novels a spacious, geographical quality which we should not know where to look for elsewhere in the same degree, and which is the sign of an extraordinary difference between such an horizon as his and the limited world-outlook, as the Germans would say, of the brilliant writers who practice the art of realistic fiction on the other side of the Channel. Trollope was familiar with all sorts and conditions of men, with the business of life, with affairs, with the great world of sport, with every component part of the ancient fabric of English society. He had traveled more than once all over the globe, and for him, therefore, the background of the human drama was a very extensive scene. He had none of the pedantry of the cosmopolite; he remained a sturdy and sensible middle-class Englishman. But his work is full of implied reference to the whole arena of modern vagrancy. He was for many years concerned in the management of the Post Office; and we can imagine no experience more fitted to impress a man with the diversity of human relations. It is possibly from this source that he derived his fondness for transcribing the letters of his lovelorn maidens and other embarrassed persons. No contemporary storyteller deals so much in letters; the modern English epistle (very happily imitated, for the most part) is his unfailing resource.

There is perhaps little reason in it, but I find myself comparing this tone of allusion to many lands and many things, and whatever it brings us of easier respiration, with that narrow vision of humanity which accompanies the strenuous, serious work lately offered us in such abundance by the votaries of art for art who sit so long at their desks in Parisian *quatrièmes*. The contrast is complete, and it would be interesting, had we space to do so here, to see how far it goes. On one side a wide, good-humored, superficial glance at a good many things; on the other a gimletlike consideration of a few. Trollope's plan, as well as Zola's, was to describe the life that lay near him; but the two writers differ immensely as to what constitutes life and what constitutes nearness. For Trollope the emotions of a nursery governess in Australia would take precedence of the adventures of a depraved *femme du monde* in Paris or London. They both undertake to do the same thing—to depict French and English manners; but the English writer (with his unsurpassed industry) is so occasional, so accidental, so full of the echoes of voices that are not the voice of the muse. Gustave Flaubert, Emile Zola, Alphonse Daudet, on the other hand, are nothing if not concentrated and sedentary. Trollope's realism is as instinctive, as inveterate as theirs; but nothing could mark more the difference between the French and English mind than the difference in the application, on one side and the other, of this system. We say system, though on Trollope's part it is none. He has no visible, certainly no explicit care for the literary part of the business; he writes easily, comfortably, and profusely, but his style has nothing in com-

mon either with the minute stippling of Daudet or the
studied rhythms of Flaubert. He accepted all the common
restrictions, and found that even within the barriers there
was plenty of material. He attaches a preface to one of
his novels—*The Vicar of Bullhampton*, before mentioned
—for the express purpose of explaining why he has introduced a young woman who may, in truth, as he says,
be called a "castaway"; and in relation to this episode he
remarks that it is the object of the novelist's art to entertain the young people of both sexes. Writers of the
French school would, of course, protest indignantly
against such a formula as this, which is the only one of
the kind that I remember to have encountered in Trollope's pages. It is meager, assuredly; but Trollope's practice was really much larger than so poor a theory. And
indeed any theory was good which enabled him to produce the works which he put forth between 1856 and
1869, or later. In spite of his want of doctrinal richness I
think he tells us, on the whole, more about life than the
"naturalists" in our sister republic. I say this with a full
consciousness of the opportunities an artist loses in leaving
so many corners unvisited, so many topics untouched,
simply because I think his perception of character was
naturally more just and liberal than that of the naturalists.
This has been from the beginning the good fortune of our
English providers of fiction, as compared with the French.
They are inferior in audacity, in neatness, in acuteness, in
intellectual vivacity, in the arrangement of material, in the
art of characterizing visible things. But they have been
more at home in the moral world; as people say today
they know their way about the conscience. This is the
value of much of the work done by the feminine wing
of the school—work which presents itself to French taste
as deplorably thin and insipid. Much of it is exquisitely
human, and that after all is a merit. As regards Trollope,
one may perhaps characterize him best, in opposition to
what I have ventured to call the sedentary school, by
saying that he was a novelist who hunted the fox. Hunting

was for years his most valued recreation, and I remember that when I made in his company the voyage of which I have spoken, he had timed his return from the Antipodes exactly so as to be able to avail himself of the first day on which it should be possible to ride to hounds. He "worked" the hunting field largely; it constantly reappears in his novels; it was excellent material.

But it would be hard to say (within the circle in which he revolved) what material he neglected. I have allowed myself to be detained so long by general considerations that I have almost forfeited the opportunity to give examples. I have spoken of *The Warden* not only because it made his reputation, but because, taken in conjunction with *Barchester Towers*, it is thought by many people to be his highest flight. *Barchester Towers* is admirable; it has an almost Thackerayan richness. Archdeacon Grantley grows more and more into life, and Mr. Harding is as charming as ever. Mrs. Proudie is ushered into a world in which she was to make so great an impression. Mrs. Proudie has become classical; of all Trollope's characters she is the most often referred to. She is exceedingly true; but I do not think she is quite so good as her fame, and as several figures from the same hand that have not won so much honor. She is rather too violent, too vixenish, too sour. The truly awful female bully—the completely fatal episcopal spouse—would have, I think, a more insidious form, a greater amount of superficial padding. The Stanhope family, in *Barchester Towers*, are a real *trouvaille*, and the idea of transporting the Signora Vesey-Neroni into a cathedral town was an inspiration. There could not be a better example of Trollope's manner of attaching himself to character than the whole picture of Bertie Stanhope. Bertie is a delightful creation; and the scene in which, at the party given by Mrs. Proudie, he puts this majestic woman to rout is one of the most amusing in all the chronicles of Barset. It is perhaps permitted to wish, by the way, that this triumph had been effected by means intellectual rather than physical; though, indeed, if Bertie

had not despoiled her of her drapery we should have lost
the lady's admirable "Unhand it, sir!" Mr. Arabin is
charming, and the henpecked bishop has painful truth;
but Mr. Slope, I think, is a little too arrant a scamp. He is
rather too much the old game; he goes too coarsely to
work, and his clamminess and cant are somewhat overdone. He is an interesting illustration, however, of the
author's dislike (at that period at least) of the bareness
of evangelical piety. In one respect *Barchester Towers* is
(to the best of our recollection) unique, being the only
one of Trollope's novels in which the interest does not
center more or less upon a simple maiden in her flower.
The novel offers us nothing in the way of a girl; though
we know that this attractive object was to lose nothing
by waiting. Eleanor Bold is a charming and natural person, but Eleanor Bold is not in her flower. After this,
however, Trollope settled down steadily to the English
girl; he took possession of her, and turned her inside out.
He never made her a subject of heartless satire, as cynical
fabulists of other lands have been known to make the
shining daughters of those climes; he bestowed upon her
the most serious, the most patient, the most tender, the
most copious consideration. He is evidently always more
or less in love with her, and it is a wonder how under
these circumstances he should make her so objective, plant
her so well on her feet. But, as I have said, if he was a
lover, he was a paternal lover; as competent as a father
who has had fifty daughters. He has presented the British
maiden under innumerable names, in every station and
in every emergency in life, and with every combination
of moral and physical qualities. She is always definite
and natural. She plays her part most properly. She has
always health in her cheek and gratitude in her eye. She
has not a touch of the morbid, and is delightfully tender,
modest and fresh. Trollope's heroines have a strong
family likeness, but it is a wonder how finely he discrim-
inates between them. One feels, as one reads him, like a
man with "sets" of female cousins. Such a person is

inclined at first to lump each group together; but presently he finds that even in the groups there are subtle differences. Trollope's girls, for that matter, would make delightful cousins. He has scarcely drawn, that we can remember, a disagreeable damsel. Lady Alexandrina de Courcy is disagreeable, and so is Amelia Roper, and so are various provincial (and indeed metropolitan) spinsters, who set their caps at young clergymen and government clerks. Griselda Grantley was a stick; and considering that she was intended to be attractive, Alice Vavasor does not commend herself particularly to our affections. But the young women I have mentioned had ceased to belong to the blooming season; they had entered the bristling, or else the limp, period. Not that Trollope's more mature spinsters invariably fall into these extremes. Miss Thorne of Ullathorne, Miss Dunstable, Miss Mackenzie, Rachel Ray (if she may be called mature), Miss Baker and Miss Todd, in *The Bertrams*, Lady Julia Guest, who comforts poor John Eames: these and many other amiable figures rise up to contradict the idea. A gentleman who had sojourned in many lands was once asked by a lady (neither of these persons was English), in what country he had found the women most to his taste. "Well, in England," he replied. "In England?" the lady repeated. "Oh yes," said her interlocutor; "they are so affectionate!" The remark was fatuous, but it has the merit of describing Trollope's heroines. They are so affectionate. Mary Thorne, Lucy Robarts, Adela Gauntlet, Lily Dale, Nora Rowley, Grace Crawley, have a kind of clinging tenderness, a passive sweetness, which is quite in the old English tradition. Trollope's genius it not the genius of Shakespeare, but his heroines have something of the fragrance of Imogen and Desdemona. There are two little stories to which, I believe, his name has never been affixed, but which he is known to have written, that contain an extraordinarily touching representation of the passion of love in its most sensitive form. In *Linda Tressel* and *Nina Balatka* the vehicle is plodding prose, but the effect is none the less poignant. And in regard to this I may say that in a hundred places in Trollope the extremity of pathos is reached by the homeliest means. He often achieved a conspicuous intensity of the tragical. The long, slow process of the conjugal wreck of Louis Trevelyan and his wife (in *He Knew He Was Right*), with that rather lumbering movement which is often characteristic of Trollope, arrives at last at an impressive completeness of misery. It is the history of an accidental rupture between two stiff-necked and ungracious people—"the little rift within the lute"—which widens at last into a gulf of anguish. Touch is added to touch, one small, stupid, fatal aggravation to another; and as we gaze into the widening breach we wonder at the vulgar materials of which tragedy sometimes composes itself. I have always remembered the chapter called "Casalunga," toward the close of *He Knew He Was Right*, as a powerful picture of the insanity of stiff-neckedness. Louis Trevelyan, separated from his wife, alone, haggard, suspicious, unshaven, undressed, living in a desolate villa on a hilltop near Siena and returning doggedly to his fancied wrong, which he has nursed until it becomes an hallucination, is a picture worthy of Balzac. Here and in several other places Trollope has dared to be thoroughly logical; he has not sacrificed to conventional optimism; he has not been afraid of a misery which should be too much like life. He has had the same courage in the history of the wretched Mr. Crawley and in that of the much-to-be-pitied Lady Mason. In this latter episode he found an admirable subject. A quiet, charming, tender-souled English gentlewoman who (as I remember the story of *Orley Farm*) forges a codicil to a will in order to benefit her son, a young prig who doesn't appreciate immoral heroism, and who is suspected, accused, tried, and saved from conviction only by some turn of fortune that I forget; who is furthermore an object of high-bred, respectful, old-fashioned gallantry on the part of a neighboring baronet, so that she sees herself dishonored in his eyes as well as condemned in those of her boy: such a personage and such a situation would be sure to yield, under Trollope's handling, the last drop of their reality.

There are many more things to say about him than I am able to add to these very general observations, the limit of which I have already passed. It would be natural, for instance, for a critic who affirms that his principal merit is the portrayal of individual character, to enumerate several of the figures that he has produced. I have not done this, and I must ask the reader who is not acquainted with Trollope to take my assertion on trust; the reader who knows him will easily make a list for himself. No account of him is complete in which allusion is not made to his practice of carrying certain actors from one story to another—a practice which he may be said to have inherited from Thackeray, as Thackeray may be said to have borrowed it from Balzac. It is a great mistake, however, to speak of it as an artifice which would not naturally occur to a writer proposing to himself to make a general portrait of a society. He has to construct that society, and it adds to the illusion in any given case that certain other cases correspond with it. Trollope constructed a great many things—a clergy, an aristocracy, a middle-class, an administrative class, a little replica of the political world. His political novels are distinctly dull, and I confess I have not been able to read them. He evidently took a good deal of pains with his aristocracy; it makes its first appearance, if I remember right, in *Doctor Thorne*, in the person of the Lady Arabella de Courcy. It is difficult for us in America to measure the success of that picture, which is probably, however, not absolutely to the life. There is in *Doctor Thorne* and some other works a certain crudity of reference to distinctions of rank—as if people's consciousness of this matter were, on either side, rather inflated. It suggests a general state of tension. It is true that, if Trollope's consciousness had been more flaccid he would perhaps not have given us Lady Lufton and Lady Glencora Palliser. Both of these

noble persons are as living as possible, though I see Lady
Lufton, with her terror of Lucy Robarts, the best. There
is a touch of poetry in the figure of Lady Glencora, but
I think there is a weak spot in her history. The actual
woman would have made a fool of herself to the end
with Burgo Fitzgerald; she would not have discovered
the merits of Plantagenet Palliser—or if she had, she would
not have cared about them. It is an illustration of the
businesslike way in which Trollope laid out his work
that he always provided a sort of underplot to alternate
with his main story—a strain of narrative of which the
scene is usually laid in a humbler walk of life. It is to his
underplot that he generally relegates his vulgar people, his
disagreeable young women; and I have often admired the
perseverance with which he recounts these less edifying
items. Now and then, it may be said, as in *Ralph the
Heir*, the story appears to be all underplot and all vulgar
people. These, however, are details. As I have already
intimated, it is difficult to specify in Trollope's work, on
account of the immense quantity of it; and there is sadness in the thought that this enormous mass does not present itself in a very portable form to posterity.

Trollope did not write for posterity; he wrote for the
day, the moment; but these are just the writers whom
posterity is apt to put into its pocket. So much of the life
of his time is reflected in his novels that we must believe
a part of the record will be saved; and the best parts of
them are so sound and true and genial, that readers with
an eye to that sort of entertainment will always be sure,
in a certain proportion, to turn to them. Trollope will
remain one of the most trustworthy, though not one of
the most eloquent, of the writers who have helped the
heart of man to know itself. The heart of man does not
always desire this knowledge; it prefers sometimes to look
at history in another way—to look at the manifestations,
without troubling about the motives. There are two kinds
of taste in the appreciation of imaginative literature: the
taste for emotions of surprise, and the taste for emotions

sufficiently related to the still newer generation in a
quasi-parental way to make our whole enumeration as
illustrational as we need it. Mr. Wells and Mr. Arnold
Bennett have their strongest mark, the aspect by which
we may most classify them, in common—even if their
three named contemporaries are doubtless most interesting in one of the connections we are not now seeking to
make. The author of *Tono-Bungay* and of *The New
Machiavelli,* and the author of *The Old Wives' Tale* and
of *Clayhanger,* have practically launched the boat in
which we admire the fresh play of oar of the author of
The Duchess of Wrexe, and the documented aspect
exhibited successively by *Round the Corner,* by *Carnival*
and *Sinister Street,* and even by *Sons and Lovers* (however much we may find Mr. Lawrence, we confess, hang
in the dusty rear). We shall explain in a moment what
we mean by this designation of the element that these
best of the younger men strike us as more particularly
sharing, our point being provisionally that Mr. Wells and
Mr. Arnold Bennett (speaking now only of them) began
some time back to show us, and to show sundry emulous
and generous young spirits then in the act of more or
less waking up, what the state in question might amount
to. We confound the author of *Tono-Bungay* and the
author of *Clayhanger* in this imputation for the simple
reason that with the sharpest differences of character
and range they yet come together under our so convenient
measure of value by *saturation.* This is the greatest value,
to our sense, in either of them, their other values, even
when at the highest, not being quite in proportion to it;
and as to be saturated is to be documented, to be able even
on occasion to prove quite enviably and potently so, they
are alike in the authority that creates emulation. It little signifies that Mr. Wells's documented or saturated
state in respect to a particular matter in hand is but one
of the faces of his *generally* informed condition, of his
extraordinary mass of gathered and assimilated knowledge,
a miscellaneous collection more remarkable surely than

any teller of "mere" tales, with the possible exception of Balzac, has been able to draw upon, whereas Mr. Arnold Bennett's corresponding provision affects us as, though singularly copious, special, exclusive and artfully economic. This distinction avails nothing against that happy fact of the handiest possession by Mr. Wells of immeasurably more concrete material, amenable for straight and vivid reference, convertible into apt illustration, than we should know where to look for other examples of. The author of *The New Machiavelli* knows, somehow, to our mystified and dazzled apprehension, because he writes and because that act constitutes for him the need, on occasion a most desperate, of absorbing knowledge at the pores; the chronicler of the *Five Towns* writing so much more discernibly, on the other hand, because he knows, and conscious of no need more desperate than that particular circle of civilization may satisfy.

Our argument is that each is ideally immersed in his own body of reference, and that immersion in any such degree and to the effect of any such variety, intensity and plausibility is really among us a new feature of the novelist's range of resource. We have seen him, we have even seen *her*, otherwise auspiciously endowed, seen him observant, impassioned, inspired, and in virtue of these things often very charming, very interesting, very triumphant, visibly qualified for the highest distinction before the fact and visibly crowned by the same after it— we have seen him with a great imagination and a great sense of life, we have seen him even with a great sense of expression and a considerable sense of art: so that we have only to reascend the stream of our comparatively recent literature to meet him serene and immortal, brow-bound with the bay and erect on his particular pedestal. We have only to do that, but have only also, while we do it, to recognize that meantime other things still than these various apotheoses have taken place, and that, to the increase of our recreation, and even if our limited space condemns us to put the matter a trifle

clumsily, a change has come over our general receptive
sensibility not less than over our productive tradition. In
these connections, we admit, overstatement is easy and
overemphasis tempting; we confess furthermore to a
frank desire to enrich the case, the historic, with all the
meaning we can stuff into it. So viewed accordingly it
gives us the "new," to repeat our expression, as an appetite
for a closer notation, a sharper specification of the signs
of life, of consciousness, of the human scene and the
human subject in general, than the three or four generations before us had been at all moved to insist on. They
had insisted indeed, these generations, we see as we look
back to them, on almost nothing whatever; what was to
come to them had come, in enormous affluence and freshness at its best, and to our continued appreciation as well
as to the honor of their sweet susceptibility, because
again and again the great miracle of genius took place,
while they gaped, in their social and sentimental sky.
For ourselves that miracle has not been markedly renewed, but it has none the less happened that by hook
and by crook the case for appreciation remains interesting.
The great thing that saves it, under the drawback we
have named, is, no doubt, that we have simply—always
for appreciation—learned a little to insist, and that we
thus get back on one hand something of what we have
lost on the other. We are unable of course, with whatever habit of presumption engendered, to insist upon
genius; so that who shall describe the measure of success
we still achieve as not virtually the search for freshness,
and above all for closeness, in quite a different direction?
To this nearer view of commoner things Mr. Wells, say,
and Mr. Arnold Bennett, and in their degree, under the
infection communicated, Mr. D. H. Lawrence and Mr.
Gilbert Cannan and Mr. Compton Mackenzie and Mr.
Hugh Walpole, strike us as having all gathered themselves
up with a movement never yet undertaken on our literary
scene, and, beyond anything else, with an instinctive
divination of what had most waved their predecessors off

it. What had this lion in the path been, we make them out as after a fashion asking themselves, what had it been from far back and straight down through all the Victorian time, but the fond superstition that the key of the situation, of each and every situation that could turn up for the novelist, was the sentimental key, which might fit into no door or window opening on closeness or on freshness at all? Was it not for all the world as if even the brightest practitioners of the past, those we now distinguish as saved for glory in spite of themselves, had been as sentimental as they could, or, to give the trick another name, as romantic and thereby as shamelessly "dodgy"?—just in order *not* to be close and fresh, not to be authentic, as that takes trouble, takes talent, and you can be sentimental, you can be romantic, you can be dodgy, alas, not a bit less on the footing of genius than on the footing of mediocrity or even of imbecility? Was it not as if the sentimental had been more and more noted as but another name for the romantic, if not indeed the romantic as but another name for the sentimental, and as if these things, whether separate or united, had been in the same degree recognized as unamenable, or at any rate unfavorable, to any consistent fineness of notation, once the tide of the copious as a condition of the thorough had fairly set in?

So, to express it briefly, the possibility of hugging the shore of the real as it had not, among us, been hugged, and of pushing inland, as far as a keel might float, wherever the least opening seemed to smile, dawned upon a few votaries and gathered further confidence with exercise. Who could say, of course, that Jane Austen had not been close, just as who could ask if Anthony Trollope had not been copious?—just as who could *not* say that it all depended on what was meant by these terms? The demonstration of what was meant, it presently appeared, could come but little by little, quite as if each tentative adventurer had rather anxiously to learn for himself what *might* be meant—this failing at least the leap into the arena

of some great demonstrative, some sudden athletic and
epoch-making authority. Who could pretend that Dickens
was anything but romantic, and even more romantic in
his humor, if possible, than in pathos or in queer perfunctory practice of the "plot"? Who could pretend that
Jane Austen didn't leave much more untold than told
about the aspects and manners even of the confined circle
in which her muse revolved? Why shouldn't it be argued
against her that where her testimony complacently ends
the pressure of appetite within us presumes exactly to
begin? Who could pretend that the reality of Trollope
didn't owe much of its abundance to the diluted, the
quite extravagantly watered strain, no less than to the
heavy hand, in which it continued to be ladled out? Who
of the younger persuasion would not have been ready to
cite, as one of the liveliest opportunities for the critic
eager to see representation searching, such a claim for the
close as Thackeray's sighing and protesting "look-in" at
the acquaintance between Arthur Pendennis and Fanny
Bolton, the daughter of the Temple laundress, amid the
purlieus of that settlement? The sentimental habit and the
spirit of romance, it was unmistakably chargeable, stood
out to sea as far as possible the moment the shore appeared
to offer the least difficulty to hugging, and the Victorian
age bristled with perfect occasions for our catching them
in the act of this showy retreat. All revolutions have been
prepared in spite of their often striking us as sudden, and
so it was doubtless that when scarce longer ago than the
other day Mr. Arnold Bennett had the fortune to lay his
hand on a general scene and a cluster of agents deficient to
a peculiar degree in properties that might interfere with
a desirable density of illustration—deficient, that is, in
such connections as might carry the imagination off to
some sport on its own account—we recognized at once
a set of conditions auspicious to the newer kind of appeal.
Let us confess that we were at the same time doubtless
to master no better way of describing these conditions
than by the remark that they were, for some reason

beautiful inherent in them, susceptible at once of being entirely known and of seeming delectably thick. Reduction to exploitable knowledge is apt to mean for many a case of the human complexity reduction to comparative thinness; and nothing was thereby at the first blush to interest us more than the fact that the air and the very smell of packed actuality in the subject-matter of such things as the author's two longest works was clearly but another name for his personal competence in that matter, the fullness and firmness of his embrace of it. This was a fresh and beguiling impression—that the state of inordinate possession on the chronicler's part, the mere state as such and as an energy directly displayed, *was* the interest, neither more nor less, *was* the sense and the meaning and the picture and the drama, all so sufficiently constituting them that it scarce mattered what they were in themselves. Of what they were in themselves their being in Mr. Bennett, as Mr. Bennett to such a tune harbored them, represented their one conceivable account—not to mention, as reinforcing this, our own great comfort and relief when certain high questions and wonderments about them, or about our mystified relation to them, began one after another to come up.

Because such questions did come, we must at once declare, and we are still in presence of them, for all the world as if that case of the perfect harmony, the harmony between subject and author, were just marked with a flaw and didn't meet the whole assault of restless criticism. What we make out Mr. Bennett as doing is simply recording his possession or, to put it more completely, his saturation; and to see him as virtually shut up to that process is a note of all the more moment that we see our selected cluster of his interesting juniors, and whether by his direct action on their collective impulse or not, embroiled, as we venture to call it, in the same predicament. The act of squeezing out to the utmost the plump and more or less juicy orange of a particular acquainted state and letting this affirmation of energy, however directed or undirected, constitute for them the "treatment" of a theme—*that* is what we remark them as mainly engaged in, after remarking the example so strikingly, so orginally set, even if an undue subjection to it be here and there repudiated. Nothing is further from our thought than to undervalue saturation and possession, the fact of the particular experience, the state and degree of acquaintance incurred, however such a consciousness may have been determined; for these things represent on the part of the novelist, as on the part of any painter of things seen, felt or imagined, just one half of his authority—the other half being represented of course by the application he is inspired to make of them. Therefore that fine secured half is so much gained at the start, and the fact of its brightly being there may really by itself project upon the course so much color and form as to make us on occasion, under the genial force, almost not miss the answer to the question of application. When the author of *Clayhanger* has put down upon the table, in dense unconfused array, every fact required, every fact in any way invocable, to make the life of the *Five Towns* press upon us, and to make our sense of it, so full-fed, content us, we may very well go on for the time in the captive condition, the beguiled and bemused condition, the acknowledgment of which is in general our highest tribute to the temporary master of our sensibility. Nothing at such moments—or rather at the end of them, when the end begins to threaten—may be of a more curious strain than the dawning unrest that suggests to us fairly our first critical comment: "Yes, yes—but is this *all?* These are the circumstances of the interest—we see, we see; but where is the interest itself, where and what is its center and how are we to measure it in relation to *that?*" Of course we may in the act of exhaling that plaint (which we have just expressed at its mildest) well remember how many people there are to tell us that to "measure" an interest is none of our affair; that we have but to take it on the cheapest and easiest terms and be thankful; and that if by our very confession we have been led the imaginative dance the music has done for us all it pretends to. Which words, however, have only to happen to be for us the most unintelligent conceivable not in the least to arrest our wonderment as to where our bedrenched consciousness may still not awkwardly leave us for the pleasure of appreciation. That appreciation is also a mistake and a priggishness, being reflective and thereby corrosive, is another of the fond dicta which we are here concerned but to brush aside—the more closely to embrace the welcome induction that appreciation, attentive and reflective, inquisitive and conclusive, is in this connection absolutely the golden *key* to our pleasure. The more it plays up, the more we recognize and are able to number the sources of our enjoyment, the greater the provision made for security in that attitude, which corresponds, by the same stroke, with the reduced danger of waste in the undertaking to amuse us. It all comes back to our amusement, and to the noblest surely, on the whole, we know; and it is in the very nature of clinging appreciation not to sacrifice consentingly a single shade of the art that makes for that blessing. From this solicitude spring our questions, and not least the one to which we give ourselves for the moment here—this moment of our being regaled as never yet with the fruits of the movement (if the name be not of too pompous an application where the flush and the heat of accident too seem so candidly to look forth), in favor of the "expression of life" in terms as loose as may pretend to an effect of expression at all. The relegation of terms to the limbo of delusions outlived so far as ever really cultivated becomes of necessity, it will be plain, the great mark of the faith that for the novelist to show he "knows all about" a certain congeries of aspects, the more numerous within their mixed circle the better, is thereby to set in motion, with due intensity, the pretension to interest. The state of knowing all about whatever it may be has thus only to become consistently and abundantly active to pass for

his supreme function; and to its so becoming active few
difficulties appear to be descried—so great may on occasion be the mere excitement of activity. To the fact
that the exhilaration is, as we have hinted, often infectious,
to this and to the charming young good faith and general
acclamation under which each case appears to proceed—
each case we of course mean really repaying attention—
the critical reader owes his opportunity so considerably
and so gratefully to generalize.

We should have only to remount the current with a
certain energy to come straight up against Tolstoy as the
great illustrative master-hand on all this ground of the
disconnection of method from matter—which encounter,
however, would take us much too far, so that we must
for the present but hang off from it with the remark
that of all great painters of the social picture it was given
that epic genius most to serve admirably as a rash adventurer and a "caution," and execrably, pestilentially, as a
model. In this strange union of relations he stands alone:
from no other great projector of the human image and
the human idea is so much truth to be extracted under an
equal leakage of its value. All the proportions in him
are so much the largest that the drop of attention to our
nearer cases might by its violence leave little of that
principle alive; which fact need not disguise from us, none
the less, that as Mr. H. G. Wells and Mr. Arnold Bennett,
to return to them briefly again, derive, by multiplied if
diluted transmissions, from the great Russian (from whose
all but equal companion Turgenev we recognize no de-
rivatives at all), so, observing the distances, we may
profitably detect an unexhausted influence in our minor,
our still considerably less rounded vessels. Highly attaching indeed the game, as might be, of inquiring as to the
center of the interest or the sense of the whole in *The
Passionate Friends*, or in *The Old Wives' Tale*, after
having sought those luxuries in vain not only through the

general length and breadth of *War and Peace*, but within the quite respectable confines of any one of the units of effect there clustered: this as preparing us to address a like friendly challenge to Mr. Cannan's *Round the Corner*, say, or to Mr. Lawrence's *Sons and Lovers*—should we wish to be *very* friendly to Mr. Lawrence—or to Mr. Hugh Walpole's *Duchess of Wrexe*, or even to Mr. Compton Mackenzie's *Sinister Street* and *Carnival*, discernibly, we hasten to add, though certain betrayals of a controlling idea and a pointed intention do comparatively gleam out of the two fictions last named. *The Old Wives' Tale* is the history of two sisters, daughters of a prosperous draper in a Staffordshire town, who, separating early in life, through the flight of one of them to Paris with an ill-chosen husband and the confirmed and prolonged local pitch of the career of the other, are reunited late in life by the return of the fugitive after much Parisian experience and by her pacified acceptance of the conditions of her birthplace. The divided current flows together again, and the chronicle closes with the simple drying up determined by the death of the sisters. That is all; the canvas is covered, ever so closely and vividly covered, by the exhibition of innumerable small facts and aspects, at which we assist with the most comfortable sense of their substantial truth. The sisters, and more particularly the less adventurous, are at home in their author's mind, they sit and move at their ease in the square chamber of his attention, to a degree beyond which the production of that ideal harmony between creature and creator could scarcely go, and all by an art of demonstration so familiar and so "quiet" that the truth and the poetry, to use Goethe's distinction, melt utterly together and we see no difference between the subject of the show and the showman's feeling, let alone the showman's manner, about it. This felt identity of the elements—because we at least consciously feel—becomes in the novel we refer to, and not less in *Clayhanger*, which our words equally describe, a source for us of

abject confidence, confidence truly *so* abject in the solidity
of every appearance that it may be said to represent our
whole relation to the work and completely to exhaust
our reaction upon it. *Clayhanger*, of the two fictions even
the more densely loaded with all the evidence in what
we should call the case presented did we but learn meanwhile for what case, or for a case of what, to take it,
inscribes the annals, the private more particularly, of a
provincial printer in a considerable way of business, beginning with his early boyhood and going on to the complications of his maturity—these not exhausted with our
present possession of the record, inasmuch as by the
author's announcement there is more of the catalogue
to come. This most monumental of Mr. Arnold Bennett's
recitals, taking it with its supplement of *Hilda Lessways*,
already before us, is so describable through its being a
monument exactly not to an idea, a pursued and captured
meaning, or in short *to* anything whatever, but just
simply *of* the quarried and gathered material it happens to
contain, the stones and bricks and rubble and cement and
promiscuous constituents of every sort that have been
heaped in it and thanks to which it quite massively piles
itself up. Our perusal and our enjoyment are our watching of the growth of the pile and of the capacity, industry,
energy with which the operation is directed. A huge and
in its way a varied aggregation, without traceable lines,
divinable direction, effect of composition, the mere
number of its pieces, the great dump of its material, together with the fact that here and there in the miscellany,
as with the value of bits of marble or porphyry, fine
elements shine out, it keeps us standing and waiting to
the end—and largely just because it keeps us wondering.
We surely wonder more what it may all propose to mean
than any equal appearance of preparation to relieve us
of that strain, any so founded and grounded a postpone-
ment of the disclosure of a sense in store, has for a long
time called upon us to do in a like connection. A great
thing it is assuredly that *while* we wait and wonder we

are amused—were it not for that, truly, our situation would be thankless enough; we may ask ourselves, as has already been noted, why on such ambiguous terms we should consent to be, and why the practice doesn't at a given moment break down; and our answer brings us back to that many-fingered grasp of the orange that the author squeezes. This particular orange is of the largest and most rotund, and his trust in the consequent flow is of its nature communicative. Such is the case always, and most naturally, with that air in a person who has something, who at the very least has much to tell us: we *like* so to be affected by it, we meet it half way and lend ourselves, sinking in up to the chin. Up to the chin only indeed, beyond doubt; we even then feel our head emerge, for judgment and articulate question, and it is from that position that we remind ourselves how the real reward of our patience is still to come—the reward attending not at all the immediate sense of immersion, but reserved for the aftersense, which is a very different matter, whether in the form of a glow or of a chill.

If Mr. Bennett's tight rotundity then is of the handsomest size and his manipulation of it so firm, what are we to say of Mr. Wells's, who, a novelist very much as Lord Bacon was a philosopher, affects us as taking all knowledge for his province and as inspiring in us to the very highest degree the confidence enjoyed by himself— enjoyed, we feel, with a breadth with which it has been given no one of his fellow-craftsmen to enjoy anything. If confidence alone could lead utterly captive we should all be huddled in a bunch at Mr. Wells's heels—which is indeed where we *are* abjectly gathered so far as that force does operate. It is literally Mr. Wells's own mind, and the experience of his own mind, incessant and extraordinarily various, extraordinarily reflective, even with all sorts of conditions made, of whatever he may expose it to, that forms the reservoir tapped by him, that constitutes his provision of grounds of interest. It is, by our thinking, in his power to name to us, as a preliminary, more of these

grounds than all his contemporaries put together, and
even to exceed any competitor, without exception, in the
way of suggesting that, thick as he may seem to lay them,
they remain yet only contributive, are not in themselves
full expression but are designed strictly to subserve it,
that this extraordinary writer's spell resides. When full
expression, the expression of some particular truth, seemed
to lapse in this or that of his earlier novels (we speak
not here of his shorter things, for the most part delightfully wanton and exempt), it was but by a hand's breadth,
so that if we didn't inveterately quite know what he intended we yet always felt sufficiently that *he* knew. The
particular intentions of such matters as *Kipps*, as *Tono-
Bungay*, as *Ann Veronica*, so swarmed about us, in their
blinding, bluffing vivacity, that the mere sum of them
might have been taken for a sense over and above which
it was graceless to inquire. The more this author learns
and learns, or at any rate knows and knows, however,
the greater is this impression of his holding it good enough
for us, such as we are, that he shall but turn out his
mind and its contents upon us by any free familiar gesture
and as from a high window forever open—an entertainment as copious surely as any occasion should demand, at
least till we have more intelligibly expressed our title to a
better. Such things as *The New Machiavelli*, *Marriage*,
The Passionate Friends, are so very much more attestations of the presence of material than attestations of an
interest in the use of it that we ask ourselves again and
again why so fondly neglected a state of leakage comes
not to be fatal to *any* provision of quantity, or even to
stores more specially selected for the ordeal than Mr.
Wells's always strike us as being. Is not the pang of
witnessed waste in fact great just in proportion as we are
touched by our author's fine offhandedness as to the
value of the stores, about which he can for the time
make us believe what he will? so that, to take an example
susceptible of brief statement, we wince at a certain quite
peculiarly gratuitous sacrifice to the casual in *Marriage*

very much as at seeing some fine and indispensable little part of a mechanism slip through profane fingers and lose itself. Who does not remember what ensues after a little upon the aviational descent of the hero of the fiction just named into the garden occupied, in company with her parents, by the young lady with whom he is to fall in love?—and this even though the whole opening scene so constituted, with all the comedy hares its function appears to be to start, remains with its back squarely turned, esthetically speaking, to the quarter in which the picture develops. The point for our mortification is that by one of the first steps in this development, the first impression on him having been made, the hero accidentally meets the heroine, of a summer eventide, in a leafy lane which supplies them with the happiest occasion to pursue their acquaintance—or in other words supplies the author with the liveliest consciousness (as we at least feel it should have been) that just so the relation between the pair, its seed already sown and the fact of that bringing about all that is still to come, pushes aside whatever veil and steps forth into life. To show it step forth and affirm itself as a relation, what is this but the interesting function of the whole passage, on the performance of which what follows is to hang?—and yet who can say that when the ostensible sequence *is* presented, and our young lady, encountered again by her stirred swain, under cover of night, in a favoring wood, is at once encompassed by his arms and pressed to his lips and heart (for celebration thus of their third meeting) we do not assist at a well-nigh heart-breaking miscarriage of "effect"? We see effect, invoked in vain, simply stand off unconcerned; effect not having been at all consulted in advance she is not to be secured on such terms. And her presence would so have re-dounded—perfectly punctual creature as she is on a made appointment and a clear understanding—to the advantage of all concerned. The bearing of the young man's act is all in our having begun to conceive it as possible, begun even to desire it, in the light of what has preceded; therefore if the participants have *not* been shown us as on the way to it, nor the question of it made beautifully to tremble for us in the air, its happiest connections fail and we but stare at it mystified. The instance is undoubtedly trifling, but in the infinite complex of such things resides for a work of art the shy virtue, shy at least till wooed forth, of the whole susceptibility. The case of Mr. Wells might take us much further—such remarks as there would be to make, say, on such a question as the due understanding, on the part of *The Passionate Friends* (not as associated persons but as a composed picture), of what that composition is specifically *about* and where, for treatment of this interest, it undertakes to find its center: all of which, we are willing however to grant, falls away before the large assurance and incorrigible levity with which this adventurer carries his lapses—far more of an adventurer as he is than any other of the company. The composition, as we have called it, heaven saving the mark, is simply at any and every moment "about" Mr. Wells's general adventure; which is quite enough while it preserves, as we trust it will long continue to do, its present robust pitch . . .

JOSEPH CONRAD

. . . If those remarks represent all the while, further, that the performances we have glanced at, with others besides, lead our attention on, we hear ourselves the more naturally asked what it is then that we expect or want, confessing as we do that we have been in a manner interested, even though, from case to case, in a varying degree, and that Thackeray, Turgenev, Balzac, Dickens, Anatole France, no matter who, can not do more than interest. Let us therefore concede to the last point that small mercies are better than none, that there are latent within the critic numberless liabilities to being "squared" (the extent to which he may on occasion betray his price!)

and so great a preference for being pleased over not being, that you may again and again see him assist with avidity at the attempt of the slice of life to butter itself thick. Its explanation that it *is* a slice of life and pretends to be nothing else figures for us, say, while we watch, the jam super-added to the butter. For since the jam, on this system, descends upon our desert, in its form of manna, from quite another heaven than the heaven of method, the mere demonstration of its agreeable presence is alone sufficient to hint at our more than one chance of being supernaturally fed. The happy-go-lucky fashion of it is indeed not then, we grant, an objection so long as we do take in refreshment: the meal may be of the last informality and yet produce in the event no small sense of repletion. The slice of life devoured, the butter and the jam duly appreciated, we are ready, no doubt, on another day, to trust ourselves afresh to the desert. We break camp, that is, and face toward a further stretch of it, all in the faith that we shall be once more provided for. We take the risk, we enjoy more or less the assistance—more or less, we put it, for the vision of a possible arrest of the miracle or failure of our supply never wholly leaves us. The phenomenon is too uncanny, the happy-go-lucky, as we know it in general, never *has* been trustable to the end; the absence of the last true touch in the preparation of its viands becomes with each renewal of the adventure a more sensible fact. By the last true touch we mean of course the touch of the hand of selection; the principle of selection having been involved at the worst or the least, one would suppose, in any approach whatever to the loaf of life with the *arrière-pensée* of a slice. There being no question of a slice upon which the further question of where and how to cut it does not wait, the office of method, the idea of choice and comparison, have occupied the ground from the first. This makes clear, to a moment's reflection, that there can be no such thing as an amorphous slice, and that any waving aside of inquiry as to the sense and value of a chunk of matter has to reckon with

the simple truth of its having been *born* of naught else
but measured excision. Reasons have been the fairies waiting on its cradle, the possible presence of a bad fairy in
the form of a bad reason to the contrary notwithstanding.
It has thus had connections at the very first stage of its
detachment that are at no later stage logically to be repudiated; let it lie as lumpish as it will—for adoption, we
mean, of the ideal of the lump—it has been tainted from
too far back with the hard liability to form, and thus
carries in its very breast the hapless contradiction of its
sturdy claim to have none. This claim has the inevitable
challenge at once to meet. How can a slice of life be anything but illustrational of the loaf, and how can illustration
not immediately bristle with every sign of the extracted
and related state? The relation is at once to what the
thing comes from and to what it waits upon—which last is
our act of recognition. We accordingly appreciate it in
proportion as it so accounts for itself; the quantity and
the intensity of its reference are the measure of our knowledge of it. This is exactly why illustration breaks down
when reference, otherwise application, runs short, and
why before any assemblage of figures or aspects, otherwise of samples and specimens, the question of what
there are, extensively, samples and specimens *of* declines
not to beset us—why, otherwise again, we look ever for
the supreme reference that shall avert the bankruptcy of
sense.

Let us profess all readiness to repeat that we may still
have had, on the merest "life" system, or that of the
starkest crudity of the slice, all the entertainment that
can come from watching a wayfarer engage with assurance in an alley that we know to have no issue—and
from watching for the very sake of the face that he may
show us on reappearing at its mouth. The recitals of Mr.
Arnold Bennett, Mr. Gilbert Cannan, Mr. D. H. Lawrence, fairly smell of the real, just as the *Fortitude* and
The Duchess of Mr. Hugh Walpole smell of the romantic;
we have sufficiently noted then that, once on the scent,

we are capable of pushing ahead. How far it is at the same time from being all a matter of smell the terms in which we just above glanced at the weakness of the spell of the happy-go-lucky may here serve to indicate. There faces us all the while the fact that the act of consideration as an incident of the esthetic pleasure, consideration confidently knowing us to *have* sooner or later to arrive at it, may be again and again postponed, but can never hope not some time to fall due. Consideration is susceptible of many forms, some one or other of which no conscious esthetic effort fails to cry out for; and the simplest description of the cry of the novel when sincere—for have we not heard such compositions bluff us, as it were, with false cries?—is as an appeal to us when we have read it once to read it yet again. *That* is the act of consideration; no other process of considering approaches this for directness, so that anything short of it is virtually not to consider at all. The word has sometimes another sense, that of the appeal to us *not*, for the world, to go back— this being of course consideration of a sort; the sort clearly that the truly flushed production should be the last to invoke. The effect of consideration, we need scarce remark, is to light for us in a work of art the hundred questions of how and why and whither, and the effect of these questions, once lighted, is enormously to thicken and complicate, even if toward final clarifications, what we have called the amused state produced in us by the work. The more our amusement multiplies its terms the more fond and the more rewarded consideration becomes; the fewer it leaves them, on the other hand, the less to be resisted for us is the impression of "bare ruined choirs where late the sweet birds sang." Birds that have appeared to sing, or whose silence we have not heeded, on a first perusal, prove on a second to have no note to contribute, and whether or no a second is enough to admonish us of those we miss, we mostly expect much from it in the way of emphasis of those we find. Then it is that notes of intention become more present or more absent; then it is that we take the measure of what we have already called our effective provision. The bravest providers and designers show at this point something still in store which only the second rummage was appointed to draw forth. To the variety of these ways of not letting our fondness fast is there not practically no limit?—and of the arts, the devices, the graces, the subtle secrets applicable to such an end what presumptuous critic shall pretend to draw the list? Let him for the moment content himself with saying that many of the most effective are mysteries, precisely, of method, or that even when they are not most essentially and directly so it takes method, blessed method, to extract their soul and to determine their action.

It is odd and delightful perhaps that at the very moment of our urging this truth we should happen to be regaled with a really supreme specimen of the part playable in a novel by the source of interest, the principle of provision attended to, for which we claim importance. Mr. Joseph Conrad's *Chance* is none the less a signal instance of provision the most earnest and the most copious for its leaving ever so much to be said about the particular provision effected. It is none the less an extraordinary exhibition of method by the fact that the method is, we venture to say, without a precedent in any like work. It places Mr. Conrad absolutely alone as a votary of the way to do a thing that shall make it undergo most doing. The way to do it that shall make it undergo least is the line on which we are mostly now used to see prizes carried off; so that the author of *Chance* gathers up on this showing all sorts of comparative distinction. He gathers up at least two sorts—that of bravery in absolutely reversing the process most accredited, and that, quite separate, we make out, of performing the maneuver under salvos of recognition. It is not in these days often given to a refinement of design to be recognized, but Mr. Conrad has made his achieve that miracle—save in so far indeed as the miracle has been one thing and the success another. The miracle is of the rarest, confounding all calculation and suggesting more reflections than we can begin to make place for here; but the sources of surprise surrounding it might be, were this possible, even greater and yet leave the fact itself in all independence, the fact that the whole undertaking was committed by its very first step either to be "art" exclusively or to be nothing. This is the prodigious rarity, since surely we have known for many a day no other such case of the whole clutch of eggs, and these withal of the freshest, in that one basket; to which it may be added that if we say for many a day this is not through our readiness positively to associate the sight with any very definite moment of the past. What concerns us is that the general effect of *Chance* is arrived at by a pursuance of means to the end in view contrasted with which every other current form of the chase can only affect us as cheap and futile; the carriage of the burden or amount of service required on these lines exceeding surely all other such displayed degrees of energy put together. Nothing could well interest us more than to see the exemplary value of attention, attention given by the author and asked of the reader, attested in a case in which it has had almost unspeakable difficulties to struggle with—since so we are moved to qualify the particular difficulty Mr. Conrad has "elected" to face: the claim for method in itself, method in this very sense of attention applied, would be somehow less lighted if the difficulties struck us as less consciously, or call it even less wantonly, invoked. What they consist of we should have to diverge here a little to say, and should even then probably lose ourselves in the dim question of why so special, eccentric and desperate a course, so deliberate a plunge into threatened frustration, should alone have seemed open. It has been the course, so far as three words may here serve, of his so multiplying his creators or, as we are now fond of saying, producers, as to make them almost more numerous and quite emphatically more material than the creatures and the production itself in whom and which we by the general law of fiction expect such

agents to lose themselves. We take for granted by the
general law of fiction a primary author, take him so much
for granted that we forget him in proportion as he works
upon us, and that he works upon us most in fact by
making us forget him.

Mr. Conrad's first care on the other hand is expressly to
posit or set up a reciter, a definite responsible intervening
first person singular, possessed of infinite sources of reference, who immediately proceeds to set up another, to the
end that this other may conform again to the practice, and
that even at that point the bridge over to the creature,
or in other words to the situation or the subject, the
thing "produced," shall, if the fancy takes it, once more
and yet once more glory in a gap. It is easy to see how
heroic the undertaking of an effective fusion becomes on
these terms, fusion between what we are to know and
that prodigy of our knowing which is ever half the very
beauty of the atmosphere of authenticity; from the moment the reporters are thus multiplied from pitch to pitch
the tone of each, especially as "rendered" by his precursor
in the series, becomes for the prime poet of all an immense question—these circumferential tones having not
only to be such individually separate notes, but to keep so
clear of the others, the central, the numerous and various
voices of the agents proper, those expressive of the action
itself and in whom the objectivity resides. We usually
escape the worst of this difficulty of a tone *about* the tone
of our characters, our projected performers, by keeping it
single, keeping it "down" and thereby comparatively impersonal or, as we may say, inscrutable; which is what a
creative force, in its blessed fatuity, likes to be. But the
omniscience, remaining indeed nameless, though constantly
active, which sets Marlow's omniscience in motion from
the very first page, insisting on a reciprocity with it
throughout, this original omniscience invites consideration
of itself only in a degree less than that in which Marlow's
own invites it; and Marlow's own is a prolonged hovering
flight of the subjective over the outstretched ground of the

case exposed. We make out this ground but through the shadow cast by the flight, clarify it though the real author visibly reminds himself again and again that he must—all the more that, as if by some tremendous forecast of future applied science, the upper airplane causes another, as we have said, to depend from it and that one still another; these dropping shadow after shadow, to the no small menace of intrinsic color and form and whatever, upon the passive expanse. What shall we most call Mr. Conrad's method accordingly but his attempt to clarify *quand même*—ridden as he has been, we perceive at the end of fifty pages of *Chance*, by such a danger of steeping his matter in perfect eventual obscuration as we recall no other artist's consenting to with an equal grace. This grace, which presently comes over us as the sign of the whole business, is Mr. Conrad's gallantry itself, and the shortest account of the rest of the connection for our present purpose is that his gallantry is thus his success. It literally strikes us that his volume sets in motion more than anything else a drama in which his own system and his combined eccentricities of recital represent the protagonist in face of powers leagued against it, and of which the dénouement gives us the system fighting in triumph, though with its back desperately to the wall, and laying the powers piled up at its feet. This frankly has been *our* spectacle, our suspense and our thrill; with the one flaw on the roundness of it all the fact that the predicament was not imposed rather than invoked, was not the effect of a challenge from without, but that of a mystic impulse from within.

Of an exquisite refinement at all events are the critical questions opened up in the attempt, the question in particular of by what it exactly is that the experiment is crowned. Pronouncing it crowned and the case saved by sheer gallantry, as we did above, is perhaps to fall just short of the conclusion we might reach were we to push further. *Chance is* an example of objectivity, most precious of aims, not only menaced but definitely compromised;

whereby we are in presence of something really of the strangest, a general and diffused lapse of authenticity which an inordinate number of common readers—since it always takes this and these to account encouragingly for "editions"—have not only condoned but have emphatically commended. They can have done this but through the bribe of some authenticity other in kind, no doubt, and seeming to them equally great if not greater, which gives back by the left hand what the right has, with however dissimulated a grace, taken away. What Mr. Conrad's left hand gives back then is simply Mr. Conrad himself. We asked above what would become, by such a form of practice, of indispensable "fusion" or, to call it by another name, of the fine process by which our impatient material, at a given moment, shakes off the humiliation of the handled, the fumbled state, puts its head in the air and, to its own beautiful illusory consciousness at least, simply runs its race. Such an amount of handling and fumbling and repointing has it, on the system of the multiplied "putter into marble," to shake off! And yet behold, the sense of discomfort, as the show here works out, *has* been conjured away. The fusion has taken place, or at any rate *a* fusion; only it has been transferred in wondrous fashion to an unexpected, and on the whole more limited plane of operation; it has succeeded in getting effected, so to speak, not on the ground but in the air, not between our writer's idea and his machinery, but between the different parts of his genius itself. His genius is what is left over from the other, the compromised and compromising quantities—the Marlows and their determinant inventors and interlocutors, the Powells, the Franklins, the Fynes, the tell-tale little dogs, the successive members of a cue from one to the other of which the sense and the interest of the subject have to be passed on together, in the manner of the buckets of water for the improvised extinction of a fire, before reaching our apprehension: all with whatever result, to this apprehension, of a quantity to be allowed for as spilled by the way.

The residuum has accordingly the form not of such and such a number of images discharged and ordered, but that rather of a wandering, circling, yearning imaginative *faculty*, encountered in its habit as it lives and diffusing itself as a presence or a tide, a noble sociability of vision. So we have as the force that fills the cup just the high-water mark of a beautiful and generous mind at play in conditions comparatively thankless—thoroughly, un-weariedly, yet at the same time ever so elegantly at play, and doing more for itself than it succeeds in getting done for it. Than which nothing could be of a greater reward to critical curiosity were it not still for the wonder of wonders, a new page in the record altogether—the fact that these things are apparently what the common reader has seen and understood. Great then would seem to be after all the common reader!

We must not fail of the point, however, that we have made these remarks not at all with an eye to the question of whether *Chance* has been well or ill inspired as to its particular choice of a way of really attending to itself among all the possible alternatives, but only on the ground of its having compared, selected and held on; since any alternative that might have been preferred and that should have been effectively adopted would point our moral as well—and this even if it is of profit none the less to note the most striking of Mr. Conrad's compositional consequences. There is one of these that has had most to do with making his pages differ in texture, and to our very first glance, from that straggle of ungoverned verbiage which leads us up and down those of his fellow fabulists in general on a vain hunt for some projected mass of truth, some solidity of substance, as to which the deluge of "dialogue," the flooding report of things said, or at least of words pretendedly spoken, shall have learned the art of being merely illustrational. What first springs from any form of real attention, no matter which, we on a comparison so made quickly perceive to be a practical challenge of the preposterous pretension of this most fatuous of the luxuries of looseness to acquit itself with authority of the structural and compositional office. Infinitely valid and vivid as illustration, it altogether depends for dignity and sense upon our state of possession of its historic preliminaries, its promoting conditions, its supporting ground; that is upon our waiting occupancy of the chamber it proposes to light and which, when no other source of effect is more indicated, it doubtless quite inimitably fills with life. Then its relation to what encloses and confines and, in its sovereign interest, finely compresses it, offering it constituted aspects, surfaces, presences, faces and figures of the matter we are either generally or acutely concerned with to play over and hang upon, then this relation gives it all its value: it has flowered from the soil prepared and sheds back its richness into the field of cultivation. It is interesting, in a word, only when nothing else is equally so, carrying the vessel of the interest with least of a stumble or a sacrifice; but it is of the essence that the sounds so set in motion (it being as sound above all that they undertake to convey sense) should have something to proceed from, in their course, to address themselves to and be affected by, with all the sensibility of sounds. It is of the essence that they should live in a medium, and in a medium only, since it takes a medium to give them an identity, the intenser the better, and that the medium should subserve them by enjoying in a like degree the luxury of an existence. We need of course scarce expressly note that the play, as distinguished from the novel, lives exclusively on the spoken word—not on the report of the thing said but, directly and audibly, on that very thing; that it thrives by its law on the exercise under which the novel hopelessly collapses when the attempt is made disproportionately to impose it. There is no danger for the play of the cart before the horse, no disaster involved in it; that form being *all* horse and the interest itself mounted and astride,

*

BIBLIOGRAPHICAL NOTE

*Following are the first magazine and book appearances
of the essays reprinted in this volume:*

"The Art of Fiction," *Longman's Magazine*, September 1884, reprinted in *Partial Portraits*, 1888.

"The Future of the Novel," in Vol. 28 of *The Universal Anthology*, 1899.

"Our Mutual Friend," unsigned, *The Nation*, December 21, 1865.

"Middlemarch," unsigned, *The Galaxy*, March 1873.

"Nana," *The Parisian*, February 26, 1880.

"The Lesson of Balzac," *Atlantic Monthly*, August 1905, reprinted in *The Question of Our Speech*, 1905.

"Gustave Flaubert" preface to *Madame Bovary* published by D. Appleton & Co. in 1902. Reprinted in *Notes on Novelists*, 1914.

"Émile Zola," *Atlantic Monthly*, August 1903, reprinted in *Notes on Novelists*, 1914.

"Guy de Maupassant," *Fortnightly Review*, March 1888, reprinted in *Partial Portraits*, 1888.

"Turgenev and Tolstoy," originally titled "Turgenev," in Vol. 25, *Library of World's Best Literature*, 1897.

"Anthony Trollope," *Century Magazine*, July 1883, reprinted in *Partial Portraits*, 1888.

"The New Novel," originally titled "The Younger Generation," *Times Literary Supplement*, March 19 and April 2, 1914, reprinted in *Notes on Novelists*, 1914.

INDEX

*HENRY JAMES was born in New York City in 1843
and died in England in 1916. He was graduated from
Harvard Law School in 1862 and devoted himself to writing from about 1865 on. In 1876 he became a resident of
London, and a year before his death was naturalized as a
British subject. Besides his many novels, he wrote short
stories, essays and criticism, and three autobiographical
works.*

*LEON EDEL, born in Pittsburgh, Pennsylvania, in 1907,
was educated in Canada and France. Critic, lecturer, and
Professor of English at New York University, he has
written and edited fifteen volumes during the past twenty
years. His best known works are* Henry James: The Untried Years, The Psychological Novel 1900–1950, *and his
editions of James's plays, ghostly tales, and selected letters.
He completed E. K. Brown's biography of Willa Cather.*

*THE TEXT of this book was set on the Linotype in Janson,
an excellent example of the influential and sturdy Dutch types
that prevailed in England prior to the development by William
Caslon of his own designs, which he evolved from these Dutch
faces. Of Janson himself little is known, except that he was a
practicing type-founder in Leipzig during the years 1660 to 1687.
The book was composed, printed, and bound by* THE COLONIAL
PRESS INC., *Clinton, Massachusetts.*

A free catalogue of VINTAGE BOOKS *will be sent at your request. Write to* Vintage Books, 457 Madison Avenue, New York, New York 10022.

VINTAGE BELLES-LETTRES

A free catalogue of VINTAGE BOOKS *will be sent at your request. Write to* Vintage Books, 457 Madison Avenue, New York, New York 10022.

A SELECT LIST OF
VINTAGE RUSSIAN LIBRARY